Reviews of Sonny Rollins: Meditating on a Riff

Ken McCarthy, *Jazz on the Tube*:

"You're gonna love this book … I love it when somebody takes the time to reveal and illuminate the lives of our great musicians … It's a great read. I really enjoyed it. Almost every page had something that made me go, 'Wow! I didn't know that,' and it really gave me a feel for Sonny's life."

~

Tom Clavin, *New York Times* bestselling author

"What makes this book unique is it combines straightforward biography with memoir elements, because Hugh Wyatt and Rollins have been close friends for many years."

~

Elaine Hegwood Bowen, M.S.J., *Chicago Crusader*:

"*Sonny Rollins' tell-all biography hits high notes about jazz legend*: … This is a fascinating book for both jazz lovers and those who are interested in reading about this legendary artist."

~

Steve Provizer, jazz brass player, vocalist and disc jockey:

"What Wyatt does well is fill in some lesser-known aspects of Rollins' narrative, limning an especially vivid sense of the drug and religio-spiritual lives of jazz, focusing on the late '40s to the '60s. From "certified thug" to wise elder, Wyatt gives us a sense of the epic outer and inner lives of Sonny Rollins."

~

Annette Hinkle, *The Southampton Press*:

"While much has been written about Mr. Rollins and his musical peers, Mr. Wyatt, whose sources included family members, close friends, anonymous sources and the musician himself, offers a unique angle on the jazz world by exploring an overlooked trend that he explains began in the late 1930s and early 1940s."

Illus. 1 - Siddhartha Gautama, otherwise known as the Buddha, was the founder of Buddhism. The ancient religion appealed not only to Sonny Rollins, but to thousands of his Jewish fans across the globe. They all found truth and beauty in Buddhism.

Sonny Rollins:

Meditating on a Riff

" *The soul loves to meditate, for in contact with the Spirit lies its greatest joy. If, then, you experience mental resistance during meditation, remember that reluctance to meditate comes from the ego; it doesn't belong to the soul."*

— PARAMAHANSA YOGANANDA[1]

SONNY ROLLINS:

MEDITATING ON A RIFF

A Journey Into His World of Spirituality

HUGH WYATT

KAMAMA BOOKS

Dedication

To my late sister, Nona Wyatt Hill

Meditation and wisdom are of one essence, not different. Meditation is the essence of wisdom, and wisdom is the function of meditation. At times of wisdom, meditation exists in that wisdom; at times of meditation, wisdom exists in that meditation."

— PLATFORM SUTRA OF
THE SIXTH PATRIARCH[2]

Acknowledgments and Credits

This biography, *Sonny Rollins: Meditating on a Riff*, would not be possible without the expert guidance, editing, and design efforts of Amanda Wyatt, my daughter. Although I have known Sonny Rollins for more than a half-century, Amanda, who is a quick study, frequently corrected me and provided additional details about Sonny that I had long forgotten.

I would also like to thank Edward Moran, a writer with a grand literary flair who helped to polish my tabloid newspaper approach to writing. He served as associate editor of the *World Musicians* reference book, as a contributing writer to *Current Biography* magazine, and as chief editor of *Rhythm* magazine.

Edward escorted 95-year-old Eubie Blake to the piano at one of the ragtime artist's last Brooklyn concerts. He was also an editor of publications in Japan and gave me invaluable advice about one of the world's great jazz capitals.

Thanks also go out to my wife, Linda Edkins Wyatt, who gave me additional crucial guidance and direction. A special nod should be given to Joanna Infeld for her input and expertise regarding spiritual matters.

Finally, I want to thank Sonny; Lucille, his late wife; Clifton Anderson, his nephew; and Gloria Anderson, his late sister, as well as scores of his friends and colleagues who helped me prepare a book that took over three decades to finish.

Hugh Wyatt

The Self is the essence of this universe, the essence of all souls...You are one with this universe. He who says he is different from others, even by a hair's breadth, immediately becomes miserable. Happiness belongs to him who knows this oneness, who knows he is one with this universe."

— SWAMI VIVEKANANDA[3]

Table of Contents

Table of Contents

Author's Note

I first met the jazz legend Sonny Rollins backstage after a concert in Munich, Germany when I was a teenager. He had returned a few years earlier in 1961 from a two-year sabbatical during which time the eccentric and reclusive Sonny had virtually lived on New York City's Williamsburg Bridge—relentlessly practicing his tenor saxophone and studying foreign religions, cultures, and cults to improve his playing, as well as change his turbulent lifestyle.

My obsession with Sonny's music began when I was eight years old in my native Atlanta, Georgia. I spent much of my childhood during the 1950s and 1960s listening ad nauseam to recordings he made with fellow jazz stars, like trumpeter Clifford Brown and drummer Max Roach.

My favorites included Duke Ellington, Mary Lou Williams, Coleman Hawkins, Charlie Parker, Dizzy Gillespie, Bud Powell, Fats Navarro, Thelonious Monk, Billie Holiday, Hank Mobley, Bill Evans, Paul Chambers, Philly Joe Jones, Miles Davis, Pepper Adams, and John

Coltrane. Many of the old jazz cats said that Mary Lou, who was a friend and mentor, was one of the key founders of bebop. She never got any real credit for her pioneering work.

Originally, I started out as a teenager playing bass with Lloyd Terry's band in Atlanta, Mary Lou's hometown. Her brother taught me in the third grade. Terry's featured vocalist was Gladys Knight. I also worked regularly with singer and drummer Hamilton Bohannon. Although they performed terrific rhythm and blues, I remained a diehard bebop jazz fanatic.

In 1965, I moved to New York City's Lower East Side (the East Village), which was the jazz mecca for young hip musicians, singers, painters, actors, writers, and other artists. The neighborhood was also home to many Eastern European Jewish, Polish, Latino, and other immigrants, as well as African Americans. Even in the 1960s, these different people got along quite well and there was little racial strife—compared to the year 2018.

I lived at 650 East 11th Street, kitty-corner from 617 East 11th Street, the apartment of tenor saxophonist John Coltrane's cousin, Mary Greenlee. Mary's apartment sometimes served as Coltrane's crash pad after late-night concerts since he lived on Long Island.

In addition, it was the gathering place for many of the young avant-garde and free jazz musicians who were becoming zealous disciples of Coltrane's so-called "spirituality" jazz movement. I had slight reservations about the avant-garde movement because it challenged the survival of bebop and hard bop, which were the styles identified most with Sonny.

Mary, who was the girlfriend of my brother, Lucius, was a big proponent of the new free-form jazz. Lucius, an actor and painter, was a close friend of Coltrane and was quite knowledgeable about the direction he was moving musically and spiritually.

I spent a lot of time with them and their friends. I also dated one of Mary's girlfriends, who had been the sweetheart of alto saxophonist Eric Dolphy. Although Coltrane was the avant-garde leader, Eric was a major pioneer of the new modal or "free thing" jazz movement developing mostly in the East Village.

Around this time, I met Sonny again. It was at a Greenwich Village club called the Village Vanguard—the "in" spot for the cats. But it was Slugs, a jazz club across town on East Third Street, that had the "free style" ambiance that young musicians preferred, even though the place was funky and dilapidated. The club also attracted young jazz players and fans because it was much cheaper than the Vanguard, which was in the high-rent district of Sheridan Square in Greenwich Village.

I felt special being part of this new, vibrant, spiritual jazz scene. Everybody hung out at Mary's apartment and also at a bar called the Annex and other nearby watering holes. They included fledgling musicians Charles Toliver, Archie Shepp, Jimmy Lott, Marion Brown, and Noah Howard, the latter of whom I rehearsed with on acoustic bass.

Beginning in the late 1960s, I started receiving what would be hundreds of personal and private letters and postcards from Sonny. However, it was the first letter he wrote that always stuck with me. He referred to me as "brash" and hinted that I should chill out. I followed his advice, but not totally.

How could I? At the time, I had become a staff police reporter for the *New York Daily News*, the city's irreverent and sassy tabloid newspaper. My first beat was covering criminal justice, which fueled my raucous tabloid edge. Later, I became health affairs editor, but I also wrote a music column for nearly three decades. My column appeared in more than 600 newspapers nationwide.

Sonny and I became good friends over the years, but he always kept his distance. He was on the surface transparent, yet secretive at the same time. He had a hermetic sort of way; I respected it, but somehow our friendship still developed and endured. I always gave him plenty of space, never intruding on his turf. I also became close friends with his family members.

There were late nights when Sonny and I would spend several hours yakking on the telephone—schmoozing about politics, jazz, women, yoga, and clothes. We even went shopping for French fashions together, as Sonny was a clotheshorse. He believed in the concept of dressing for success, which made the unconventional saxophonist at times seem like a "regular guy."

As the years passed, Sonny became more far-out and otherworldly. He had entered a world of esoteric spirituality, which he rarely shared with his wife, family, and friends. He also maintained a subtle image of the rough and tumble mean-streets connected to his young days living in Harlem. As a teenager, he had outboxed and outfought the best of them in his neighborhood.

My biggest kick came one day when "regular guy" Sonny helped me pick up some old, funky, worn-out furniture off the streets of the East Village. Sonny, the jazz superstar who was bigger than life, actually helped me pick up and haul some old, broken, and dirty furniture up to my fourth-floor walkup railroad apartment, which had a bathroom in the middle of the living room.

Young, struggling, and broke, musicians and other artists, like myself, made a regular practice of picking up junk and converting it into beautiful pieces to be used as their household furniture. My relatives, friends, and others were astonished and reluctant to believe the great Sonny Rollins had physically helped me pick up and deliver junk furniture.

When my daughter, Amanda, was born in 1988, Sonny became her godfather. It was one of the greatest moments I ever experienced. I was happy because she was the joy of my life and Sonny was my hero. He wrote a song dedicated to her called "Amanda," which appeared on the CD *Falling in Love with Jazz*.

Around this time, I decided to write a biography of Sonny. I must have written several versions over the past three decades, but I was not happy with them. They didn't focus on Sonny's spirituality and personal life. The drafts were also too effusive and made me feel like a "groupie" rather than a serious biographer. I wanted to tell the truth about a legend that I got to know intimately.

Introduction

Sonny Rollins travelled many bumpy roads during a seven-decade musical career, but it may have been his secret journey into otherworldly realms, including those of Egyptian, East Asian, and Indian spirituality, that helped to transform the former Harlem heroin addict and troubled youth into one of the most respected and beloved jazz musicians in the world.

Nonbelievers may argue that Sonny was able to kick his habit, end a petty-crime spree, and become a jazz legend through sheer force of character. They attribute his conversion to his natural talents, sharp intellect, and the strong will of a man capable of successfully fighting off his demons.

But, were these traits sufficient to satisfy a demanding man who wanted more out of life?

For the spiritually minded—be they Christian, Jewish, Buddhist, Hindu, Jain, Muslim, Rosicrucian, Taoist, or of any other belief system— the right spiritual journey can be much more than satisfactory. It may lead one to Heaven, Nirvana, Enlightenment, or a similar destination. They assert that following such paths bestows powerful, mystical experiences, such as direct contact with God, immortality, or skills beyond the natural scope of human abilities.

Sonny's quest, akin to that of an Indian swami or a Buddhist monk, was to acquire, through a life of meditation and spirituality, the knowledge and supremacy required to fight off his demons, as well as to unlock the secrets of the universe.

But would he be forced to embrace the unknown, perhaps darker, side of life in order to enter this realm? Would he be a practitioner of the occult, someone who has hidden knowledge of the paranormal?

There are many indications that he trekked along those paths, but being so secretive, he has reluctantly revealed little, such as his ability to levitate to the ceiling. Could the great Sonny Rollins be putting us on?

In his book *New Age Religion and Western Culture,* Dutch scholar Wouter Hanegraaff said of occultism that it is "a category in the study of religions, which comprises all attempts by esotericists to come to terms with a disenchanted world, or alternatively, by people in general to make sense of esotericism from the perspective of a disenchanted secular world."

Hanegraaff quoted Danish scholar Marcello Truzzi, who posited that the very term "occult" is problematic: "In many ways, the occult is a residual category, a wastebasket, for knowledge claims that are deviant in some way, that do not fit the established claims of science or religion." The occult is then a vague term for beliefs and practices ranging from astrology, alchemy, and magic to mysticism, spirit channeling, and even UFO abductions.

And many of Sonny's beliefs fall into the category of "the occult," and millions of his fans worldwide—including spiritual practitioners, diehard jazz aficionados, New Agers, and everyday people—accept him at face value for his varied and eccentric spiritual explorations. Most of them only sense his spirituality, but a few friends and family members claim to have witnessed validation of Sonny's other world.

But it is in the world of jazz where his credentials are unchallenged.

In the realm of jazz, Sonny has towered over widely-known giants of the tenor saxophone, with the exception perhaps of John Coltrane. Many fans argue that although he is technically a superior player, Coltrane's spiritual achievements may have surpassed those of Sonny's. However, these long-standing disputes among jazz aficionados and spiritualists may never be resolved.

Coltrane essentially cemented his title as leader of this new, experimental, Eastern-style jazz sound with the historic recording *A Love Supreme* in 1965, which became a benchmark for music lovers of all ages and genres seeking to pursue a more spiritual approach in life.

During his much-discussed hiatus from the music industry between 1959 and 1961, Sonny virtually lived on the Williamsburg Bridge, joining Manhattan and Brooklyn, while practicing on the pedestrian walkway. He was studying yoga, Rosicrucianism, and other ancient Egyptian and Eastern religions, as well as secretive cults in his Grand Street apartment.

It should be noted that Coltrane claimed he had experienced a "spiritual awakening" earlier in 1957, prior to Sonny's sabbatical. Afterwards, Coltrane acknowledged his involvement in Kriya yoga, a little-known but nonetheless powerful form of yoga that emphasizes God-realization.

It was during this time that the emerging "spiritual sounds" of both Sonny and Coltrane started to appeal widely to mostly young, white, avant-garde listeners and New Agers—seekers drawn to the more esoteric principles of Buddhism, Hinduism, yoga, Jainism, Taoism, Islam, and astrology. As far back as the 1920s, many young black intellectuals and artistic types had begun to explore ancient and Eastern religions when some chose to embrace the Ahmadiyya Muslim faith.

Regardless of Sonny's spiritual influence on his fans, trumpeter Miles Davis, pianist Thelonious Monk, and other stalwart jazz figures maintained that Sonny was the number-one tenor saxophonist on the planet. They argued that he outperformed other highly regarded tenor saxophonists, such as Coleman Hawkins (his idol), Lester Young, Chu Berry, Don Byas, Dexter Gordon, Ben Webster, Gene Ammons, and

Stan Getz.

Although a comparison should not be made between Sonny and Charlie "Yardbird" Parker, who was unquestionably the supreme alto saxophonist, Sonny reached similar heights on the tenor saxophone. Parker's influence, which was phenomenal, extended beyond alto saxophonists to include other instrumentalists all over the world— many of whom tried to emulate his style and sound. Both Parker and Sonny are undeniable geniuses.

Like Parker, Sonny also changed the direction of jazz. Bird, as Parker was called, introduced bebop to wider audiences, effectively ending the reign of the big band style of jazz known as swing in the early 1940s. Sonny's reign on the tenor began in the early 1950s, and his style became the gold standard.

Although the twelve-bar blues format was Sonny's initial musical foundation, due to the infusion of exotic religious sounds and stylings into his music, the blues influence was less apparent by the early 1960s. Still, Sonny continued to be as bluesy as ever, reflecting his personality. He had paid his dues and lived a life of deep suffering.

Unlike Coltrane, who incorporated Hindustani *ragas* (scales), Sonny adopted a subtler approach to integrating spiritual influence into his compositions. And his music radically changed after his 1959 sabbatical from the jazz scene.

Many older fans and purists voiced concern over his relatively new avant-garde style. Sonny, on the other hand, believed the changes were necessary for the continued improvement of his music.

This biography will not simply regurgitate previously published books, articles, and accounts of the life of Sonny Rollins. This story will depart from the conventional retrospective fare and explore the results of an intensive decades-long probe into Sonny's jazz and secretive (and not so secretive) life, both on and off stage, vis-à-vis an analysis of his lifelong journey into the world of spirituality and its practices.

It will attempt to uncover many of his hidden secrets, such as his ability to achieve a deathlike state through respiratory control and meditation, and his ability to reach deep levels of trance that helped him to develop his talent as the world's "greatest living jazz musician."

These are bold claims, but many fans have not taken issue with them.

Sonny has the extraordinary gift of being able to play continuously for more than sixty minutes nonstop while engaging in a form of deft, unparalleled improvised thematic development—an accomplishment that has been the envy of other tenor saxophonists worldwide. Many players average only about five to ten minutes per solo.

Sonny honed his skills during his time on New York City's Williamsburg Bridge. His abrupt departure caused concern throughout the jazz world and the world at large at the time, such attention being paid to a jazz musician was unique.

Today, New York City politicians are considering changing the bridge's name to the "Sonny Rollins Bridge" in homage to the legendary saxophonist. The rededication of the bridge, which could take place sometime in 2019, would represent a tribute to Sonny himself, and how he inspired others to improve the quality of their lives through the intense study of global religions and cultures—which dramatically altered his life.

Politicians are also honoring Sonny for his intensely haunting, mesmerizing, and captivating jazz sound, derived from his integration of exotic elements into both his compositions as well as his performances. His sound is a result of his study and practice of African, Asian, and Eastern religions—and even occultism—to which he was dedicated during the time he spent on the bridge.

On the bridge, Sonny would playfully honk his horn back at passing tug boats in the East River, which led in part to the incorporation of sardonic, caustic wit into his music. As part of his humor, he would frequently change the tone of a serious song and infuse a commercial, funny melody, like "There's No Business Like Show Business." He would even incorporate nursery rhymes into songs.

Sonny's other gifts include his incredible speed on his instrument, his smooth and mellow tone, and his adroit ability to improvise so well that he is seemingly composing several "new" songs within one song—ranging from five minutes to upwards of an hour. But it is his mastery of breath control that stands out, similar to that of a seasoned yogi.

Sonny's spiritual journey started with his birth. His family members appeared to be visionaries themselves when they called his arrival an "omen." His family rightly characterized his birth as that of a "special child"—someone who would make a major difference in life. Few fans would argue with their assessment.

Sonny's spiritual trek in jazz began in the mid-1940s when he was surrounded and influenced by many fellow bebop jazz musicians— men and women who had abandoned Christianity in favor of foreign faiths. During this time, he became an even stronger believer in God, though he had abandoned Christianity.

In 1967, not satisfied with his ability to properly meditate and achieve other powerful spiritual feats, Sonny went to India, where he lived in an ashram for several months learning the secrets of yoga and Hinduism. Some of them will be presented in this book.

As the world's greatest living jazz musician, Sonny follows a tradition of jazz pioneers, such as Louis Armstrong, Duke Ellington, Coleman Hawkins, Mary Lou Williams, Thelonious Monk, Dizzy Gillespie, Art Tatum, Bud Powell, Max Roach, Miles Davis, Clifford Brown, J.J. Johnson, Pepper Adams, Bill Evans, and Gil Evans, among others.

Although he retired in 2012 due to pulmonary and other medical issues, he will be remembered for his vast contributions to both jazz and spirituality, not only in America but also in Tokyo, London, Paris, Copenhagen, Stockholm, Helsinki, Lagos, Mumbai, Tel Aviv, Rome, Berlin, Madrid, Buenos Aires, São Paulo, and other big and small cities throughout the world.

In fact, audiences abroad are more responsible for Sonny's success than those inside the United States. In Japan, for instance, fans treat him with special reverence, as if he were a saint. The fans there are extremely supportive and vastly knowledgeable about his personal history, as well as jazz overall and its important relationship to spirituality.

Though on the surface it seems to be inward-looking and insular, Japan embraced and adapted many Western cultural styles and artifacts over the past two centuries. Japan has been the greatest supporter of jazz and saved the music from virtual extinction.

Since the end of World War II, American music, especially jazz and modern dance, has been exported to many countries on all continents. It is in some of these global capitals that Sonny is viewed as a rock star; a musician who can earn an estimated $100,000 for a single night's performance, ten times what most other jazz musicians earn. He filled stadiums and arenas while his peers struggled to fill up small nightclubs.

Meditating on a Riff hopes to reveal how Sonny has always had an aura of secrecy and mysticism, especially during his unconventional childhood. As an adult, he is highly regarded as a sort of sage or guru by many fans and fellow musicians—offering up images of a man possibly endowed with psychic powers, one to whom the many secrets of the universe have been revealed.

Sonny's honor extends to his business dealings. His closest friends and fellow jazz artists say that his spirituality is what prevents him from being a stereotypically greedy bandleader intent on exploiting his fellow musicians. Many former band members said he often doubled or tripled their pay compared to that of most musicians.

"Sonny was not only an incredible musician to work with, but I have to admit that I liked playing with him because he paid me and other band members quite well," recalled Bob Cranshaw, his longtime bassist of nearly a half century.

Yet, at the same time, Sonny could be "mean-spirited and demanding," according to one former band member who spoke with anonymity: "He was prone to berating some of his sidemen when they failed to live up to their musical potential or when they would show up late for gigs. He was a stickler for being on time and being correct about business affairs."

Sonny was also strongly influenced by the cultural scene in Harlem, which attracted droves of black artists, writers, and intellectuals. Many of them were also followers of Asian and African religions, including strange sects that helped define the community.

The life of Sonny Rollins has always been shrouded in mystery. There is an unknown side to the reclusive musician, who legally changed his name from "Walter Theodore Rollins" to "Theodore

Walter Rollins" in the 1950s. Some said he wanted to hide a criminal past that resulted in an almost two-year stint in New York's infamous Rikers Island jail.

The overarching issue here begs the question—was the jazz saxophonist successful in pursuing lofty spiritual goals or was he just posing as many people do? This biography attempts to answer that question and many more as it takes readers on a spiritual journey into the vast unknown with Sonny Rollins.

Meditating on a Riff also reveals a day in France during which Sonny reportedly reached the pinnacle of his spiritual journey, a time when he saw a vision of what appeared to be another world—perhaps Heaven or a similar destination.

This biography struggles against being a mere "puff piece," an expression some journalists use to describe a story that is highly complimentary and often bordering on being untrue. My noble intention is to present readers with a serious, uncompromising look at Sonny Rollins, warts and all.

Criticism aside, Sonny may go down in history as perhaps the only African American since the key founders of jazz—Louis Armstrong, Duke Ellington, and Charlie Parker—to be considered the preeminent living jazz pioneer.

Fans accept Sonny not just because of his musical genius, but because of his universal views on spirituality and religion. He firmly believes that there is "only one truth" when referring to these diverse belief systems.

Given the worldwide strife among religions and spirituality, it is important to note that there are millions of different faiths around the world whose many followers have long embraced cooperation and a peaceful coexistence.

Sonny Rollins is one of those followers.

CHAPTER 1

Prophecy of the Bells

The birth of the baby boy appeared to be an omen to family members who stood in awe and silence after hearing two bells ring out at the same time from two different churches in Harlem.

Their sonorous chiming wove a jazz-like ostinato, a gladsome riff of pure sound that swaddled the newborn in its penumbra, drowning out his piercing screams emanating from the kitchen of a sixth-floor tenement on West 137th Street where Walter Theodore Rollins was making his rollicking debut on September 7, 1930.

Two of the nation's largest and most celebrated churches flanked that block: Mother AME Zion, between Seventh and Lenox Avenues, and Adam Clayton Powell's Abyssinian Baptist, a block away on West 138th Street.

It was from the storied pulpit at Abyssinian that Adam Clayton Powell and his son, the Congressman, preached militant sermons that called down divine judgment on racism and oppression. But on this particular sabbath, alarmed neighbors likely wondered what was happening inside the Rollins flat. Was someone being beaten or killed?

The noise was coming from Valborg Rollins, a recent émigrée from the Virgin Islands, who was about to give birth to a new child.

On that Sunday, her contractions became more painful as they drew closer together. They had begun five minutes apart, but then it was only 80 seconds between each of the spasms that ran throughout her body.

As the contractions intensified, she could not so much as catch her breath, but she pushed as if her life, and that of her infant son, depended on it. The pains subsided as his head emerged, then a cute, tiny face. As the midwife lifted his shivering form from the kitchen table, young Walter Theodore cried for the first time. Valborg smiled and became silent. She had done her duty.

Years later, the man who became known to the world as Sonny Rollins recounted family lore about his birth amidst the cacophony of Harlem sounds that morning.

"My sister said that when I was born on Sunday morning, the church bells were ringing. Not that that means anything," Sonny said with a laugh.

But others would disagree. For some superstitious friends and members of the family, a birth heralded by church bells was clearly seen as a premonition, even an omen. While Africans have long prized the drumbeat as a repository of ancestral wisdom, those in the diaspora, particularly in the Christian tradition, are attuned to the significance of bells.

Bells have been used across the globe for spiritual purposes, and some faiths use them to communicate with spirits or to communicate with a deity directly. Some in the Buddhist tradition use Tibetan bells to communicate with the dead and sound them during prayer or yoga sessions.

Some believe that ringing bells can be used to drive away demons or evil spirits. For others, hearing bells can mean that one is in the presence of a holy figure. Remember the scene in the Christmas classic, *It's a Wonderful Life,* when guardian angel Joseph reminds George Bailey that a bell rings every time an angel gets his wings.

Could the ringing of the bells that September morning suggest that the little tot would one day become a special gift from God? A seer? A swami? A saint? A healer? A clairvoyant? A spiritualist? Or even a jazz great? Who knew?

Although linguists do not know the exact origin of the word "omen," some speculate that it is related to the Latin verb *audire*, which means "to hear." Some cosmologists believe that the universe is essentially made up of sound patterns, noting that creation was called into being when God spoke the words "Let there be light."

And although many people today think of the word "omen" as being foreboding and negative (hence, the term "ominous"), omens can also be positive, suggesting good fortune, prosperity, or the birth of a singular human being.

Many of Sonny Rollins' family members that September morning felt that something out of the ordinary had just taken place because of the robust pealing of Harlem's church bells during his nativity. It can be said that his birth evoked a kind of supernatural stillness that saturated all their thoughts.

They whispered and stared as if they were humbled by some newfound awe. They sensed that this child was special—whatever his actions were to be, wherever his journey would lead him. The bells suggested that Sonny would one day be extraordinary.

For one, the birth of her new grandson left Miriam Solomon ecstatic. When Sonny finally entered the world that Sabbath, she rushed out of the kitchen to find her two other grandchildren—Valdemar, 5, and Gloria, 3. Like an angel announcing the birth of a divine child, she proclaimed: "You have a new little brother!"

Family members would have easily seen the analogy. The Rollinses were devout Moravian Christians who, like many other immigrants in that era, maintained some of the strong mystical folk beliefs of the Caribbean and Africa.

"Anyone born while two church bells are ringing together must be special," Valborg Rollins finally declared that evening. Valborg—whose name was a vestige of the Danish settlers who had once colonized the Virgin Islands—was a dignified, reserved woman who spoke with a

West Indian lilt.

Valborg's mother, Miriam, agreed with her. As special as she found her other grandchildren, she couldn't help but sense that Sonny was destined to be extraordinary. "There is something about him that is truly unusual," she said. "I just know it; I can feel it."

Sonny's father, Walter William Rollins, nodded in silent agreement. A St. Croix native, he had gone to sea as a young man, hoping to see the world. Now he was a chef (and, later, a chief petty officer) in the Navy who had brought his family to New York from the West Indies in search of a better life.

"My father became a man of the world because he joined the Merchant Marines when he was very young," Sonny's sister, Gloria, later recalled. "He joined the Marines when he was still in St. Thomas, and he and my mother were married there.

"Then he took off and he went all over the world. He used to speak eloquently about the places he had visited. He lost his accent, but my mother maintained that St. Thomas accent to some degree."

In the late 1920s, Walter Rollins moved his wife and two young children to Harlem, eventually into the sixth-floor tenement walk-up apartment on West 137th Street, between Lenox and Seventh Avenues, where Sonny was born.

Also living with them was Grandma Miriam and Uncle Reuben, Valborg's mother and brother. Grandma Miriam's husband had been a physician who studied at the Sorbonne in Paris. He went on to become a general practitioner in Haiti. They eventually separated, and she moved to New York to live with her daughter.

The extended family that lived together in the 137th Street apartment was far from unusual—members of many clans with limited financial resources all sleeping under the same roof.

Unfortunately, the Rollins family arrived just in time for the Great Depression, heralded by the 1929 Wall Street crash just a year before Sonny's birth. But it is undeniable that, as the Roaring Twenties drew to a disastrous close, there was definitely a racial divide in the response. While throughout the country mostly white businessmen stared at the ticker-tape with shock and dismay, many black residents of Harlem

Illus. 2 - Abyssinian Baptist Church has served as a place for African American spirituality, politics and community. The Abyssinian Baptist Church congregation traces its history to 1809.

Illus. 3 - Mother AME Zion Church is the oldest African-American church in New York City, and the "mother church" of the African Methodist Episcopal Zion conference.

found themselves leaping from the skillet into the fire.

Members of the Rollins family were part of the massive migration of Europeans, southern African Americans, and Caribbean people to the Northeast in the 1920s. Blacks flooded New York City mostly because of the huge number of jobs and educational opportunities that were not available to them in the segregated Jim Crow south or in the nearby offshore British possessions.

All these different groups brought with them their own folk cures and superstitions, but these were more pronounced among people of color who often could not afford doctors and hospitals.

As compensation, both the American black and Caribbean immigrants relied on voodoo, hoodoo, and other beliefs branded as "superstitious" by their white counterparts. Many of these immigrants used potions and herbal draughts derived from African magical traditions, as well as other ancient remedies distinctly absent from any manual of the American Medical Association.

Although Valborg's father had been a well-educated physician, some members of the family nonetheless believed in the power of the "spirit world" and that God sent mystical beings to Earth for specific purposes.

In the Virgin Islands, there are a variety of beliefs about magical powers and superstitions, some of which stem from the African folk religions. For example, one common phrase in the Virgin Islands is "Don't let the Jumbies get ya!" Jumbies are spirits that live around households. Some say that they're the spirits of a deceased person, while others say they're the souls of living people who live in dead bodies.

Though the Rollins clan subscribed in one form or another to some of these traditional beliefs, they also subscribed to the beliefs of the Moravian Church, which offered a more "modern" approach to spirituality.

The Moravian Church is one of the oldest Protestant denominations in the world. It traces its roots back to the 15th century, when a priest named Jan Hus in Bohemia (the modern day Czech Republic) sought to reform some of the practices in the Roman Catholic Church. In the

18th century, Protestant religious refugees from the Bohemian region of Moravia fled to what is now Germany, and the church grew rapidly from there.

"The Moravian religion is similar to the Lutheran religion, except that it is more musical," said Gloria Anderson (née Rollins). "The Moravian service is laced through and through with music. They sing practically everything, and they have beautiful hymns. That's the one thing that is just great about it."

In addition to music, Moravians place particular emphasis on personal piety, ecumenism, and, notably, doing missionary work. In fact, Moravians constituted the first major Protestant missionary movement. They sent missionaries to all four corners of the world, especially the Caribbean. Today, there are roughly 1.1 million Moravians worldwide, over 200,000 of whom live in the Caribbean or Latin America. About 15,000 live in the Virgin Islands, including St. Thomas.

"My mother said that she had us christened Moravian because when there were slaves on the islands, the Moravians were the only missionaries who would marry the slaves to one another," Gloria added. "The others said they could live together and procreate and all the rest, but they would not marry slaves. Only the Moravians would do that."

Although Sonny recalled his father "wasn't too religious," it appears that Valborg was much more spiritually inclined. In addition to the Moravian Church, Valborg also took her brood to the nearby African Methodist Episcopal (AME) church.

What is significant here is that young Sonny Rollins got his start in the bosom of the church, and that made a great deal of difference in his life.

Illus. 4 - Paul Robeson was not only one of the greatest actors and singers, but one of the foremost leaders of the early Civil Rights Movement. He was one of Sonny Rollins' childhood idols.

CHAPTER 2

Politics of the Street

In the smoldering Harlem of the 1930s, civil rights activists and residents were angry, vocal. By leaving the Caribbean and the Deep South to avoid lynching, they thought New York City would provide them with some relief.

In the generation before Dr. Martin Luther King, Jr., Jesse Jackson, and Malcolm X, Harlem residents were able to hear a wide number of partisans angrily and loudly preaching black nationalism on street corners, in churches, or wherever else they could find a platform.

All points on the ideological spectrum were represented, from Marcus Garvey's Back to Africa movement to Paul Robeson's pan-Africanism with its communist undertones, to the Social Gospel protests of the Reverends Adam Clayton Powell, both father and son.

Like other protest movements during the unsettled 1930s, Harlem's black activism drove the police, the government, and the moderate and conservative establishment into a state of frenzy. These firebrands of change and revolution were mostly young, impatient, bold, and dead tired of preserving the status quo, one that urged American blacks to be patient with their subjugation. They demanded equality and they wanted it immediately.

Such was the political theater that thrilled the blood of impressionable youngsters, like Sonny Rollins. While he didn't fully understand the radical messages from the speakers, he knew something was wrong with respect to race relations.

"I was impressed by the intense look of the people who attended the rallies," Sonny said. "I could tell that they were serious about what they heard. Some of the people looked angry, and some looked mute. The main thing is I could tell they were all there for a reason."

Along with other family members, he was a regular attendee at the many rallies and meetings around Harlem's main thoroughfare of 125th Street during the mid-1930s, loudly cheering on the different speakers. As a child, he seemed to have an uncanny awareness and understanding of the cultural wars being waged during those turbulent years.

"These leaders were my heroes, they gave us a sense of independence," said Sonny, recalling his early childhood. "They stood up to the evil forces that wanted to keep us down and made progress that many of us now take for granted."

This period of enlightenment for Sonny occurred between 1935 and 1938, when he was between the ages of five and eight. Like the Chicago ghettos of Richard Wright's *Black Boy* and *Native Son*, or the Harlem cityscape of 1943 that proved an epiphany for James Baldwin, it was the vibrant and intense Harlem of the 1930s that provided Sonny Rollins with a young, curious boy's first taste of politicization.

Politicized Harlem was a highly volatile and rebellious community. It was so combustible that it sparked massive public attention that spread throughout the United States and the world. Harlem's intense political turbulence attracted a new wave of immigration—not only the "tired and poor" seeking economic gain, but a sophisticated cadre that included intellectuals, artists, and political leaders from within America as well as the Caribbean.

These newer immigrants readily joined the different civil rights movements popular in Harlem during the 1930s, such as the NAACP,

Illus. 5 - As a child, Sonny Rollins was a regular attendee at Harlem street rallies held by black nationalist leader Marcus Garvey (pictured), who urged blacks to return to "Mother Africa."

the Universal Negro Improvement Association, and the African Communities League. They also threw themselves into the thriving artistic mindscape in Harlem, which had one of the most creative communities in the world.

The earliest of these new arrivals, those who came in the 1920s, were responsible for creating the Harlem Renaissance, a colossal cultural, social, and artistic movement originally known as the "New Negro Movement," after the 1925 anthology by Alain LeRoy Locke, one of its most prominent advocates and chroniclers.

The Rollins clan jumped into this ferment, and proved exceptions to the rule that many immigrants to Harlem during this period had a politically conservative bent. Miriam Solomon, Sonny's grandmother, was a hardcore black nationalist who tried to encourage her grandson to embrace Garveyism. This was Marcus Garvey's influential Back to Africa initiative that decades later played a role in the establishment of the Nation of Islam, the Rastafarians, and other militant movements.

The Rastafarians proclaimed Garvey to be in the noble lineage of the ancient prophets. Garvey called for blacks in the diaspora to accept Africa as their homeland. In "African Fundamentalism," an editorial in *Negro World*, Garvey wrote: "Our union must know no clime, boundary or nationality … let us hold together under all climes and in every country."

Although there had been earlier powerful black leaders—such as Prince Hall, Martin Delany, Edward Wilmot Blyden, and Henry Highland Garnet—Garvey was unique in promulgating what was called a pan-African ideology, the aim of which was to create a worldwide mass return of blacks to Africa and to uplift the continent economically.

The question before the young Sonny Rollins was crucial to his identity as a young black man in the Harlem of the 1930s: Would he reject the often separatist messages of these pro-black leaders, or would he "keep on keeping on" with the politics of assimilation in which blacks would continue to accept the status quo as defined by the white political power structure, one that kept blacks at the bottom of the social, political, economic, and cultural ladder?

"I didn't fully understand all the heavy-duty talk from the speakers," Sonny admitted, years later. "But I understood enough of it to know that the black man in America suffered greatly from racism and that something should be done about it."

During this time, the Rollinses were still living at West 137th Street and Lenox Avenue, but Sonny and Miriam would often venture down to 125th Street and Lenox to take in the polemics. "Some cats would get up on the soapbox and would start rapping, you dig? A crowd of people would gather around them and they would talk about black politics, about black history."

Thus, both on the streets and at home, Sonny had been exposed to Garveyism and other Black Nationalist philosophies, which were highly influential among West Indians and others living in Harlem at the time. Sonny remembered his family even had an "African national flag" (also known as the pan-African flag) in their home.

"My grandmother was very militant," remembered Sonny. "She was into Marcus Garvey and Paul Robeson. We used to go to all the Paul Robeson rallies. He used to have big rallies in places like the Golden Gate Ballroom. I remember marching in parades down Lenox Avenue. I was just a little kid, but I was for black liberation, if you want to call it that."

Robeson was a legendary figure for Sonny, as well as other black children in Harlem and across the country. An All-American football player at Rutgers, and a Columbia Law School graduate, Robeson also played the sensational roles of the Emperor Jones and Joe in *Show Boat*. His booming rendition of "Ol' Man River" made him world famous.

Paul Robeson was also a political orator and activist. A socialist and anti-imperialist, he was involved in the Civil Rights Movement at home and participated in many international movements. His activism eventually caused him to be blacklisted and harassed during the McCarthy era.

The Rollins clan were among millions of immigrants from all over the world who had come to America in search of the so-called American Dream. To them and other people of color, it was more of a nightmare. While there was poverty in the Caribbean, there was black rule in the government, and discrimination was somewhat less pronounced in certain Caribbean countries.

This was the message that resonated on the streets of Harlem from the Jamaican-born Garvey, who preached self-reliance and urged blacks to resist discriminatory treatment at the hands of whites. Garvey's oratorical style and social activism set the tone for many of the radical black leaders who would follow him.

And this was a message that Sonny constantly heard, especially from his grandmother Miriam. As a proud member of Garvey's Universal Negro Improvement Association, she brought the impressionable Sonny to marches protesting a variety of causes: employment discrimination in Harlem stores, Italy's 1935 invasion of Ethiopia, and the unjust legal treatment of the Scottsboro Boys, a group of African-American teenagers accused of raping two white women in Alabama.

Sonny also accompanied his grandmother to the famed Abyssinian Baptist Church, where he heard firebrand preacher Rev. Adam Clayton Powell and his son Rev. Adam Clayton Powell, Jr. proclaim a gospel of civil rights and racial justice.

At home, Miriam lectured the entire family about what she referred to as "the farce of America." Instead of finding Harlem streets paved with gold, the Rollins clan found them littered with trash, poor housing, police corruption and brutality, and a lack of jobs, especially well-paying jobs with a future.

Her plaints came close to home. Although Sonny's mother, Valborg, was well educated and the daughter of a prominent Haitian physician, Paul Solomon, she could not find a job that put her true professional talents to work. She ended up becoming a maid who cleaned houses for wealthy whites.

"My mother did housework," Sonny said, recalling a painful scene. "I remember one time she took me downtown. I must have been about five years old. She was working as a maid for some white people on Park Avenue. She took me down there with her and said I should stay in one room while she cleaned the house. It was sort of demeaning. I didn't like it then, but I didn't understand. I really wasn't able to put it all together, but there was a certain hurt involved in it."

However, not all was doom and gloom in Harlem. The community was fast becoming the cultural capital of black America. Not only was Harlem bursting with famous jazz bandleaders, like Duke Ellington, Count Basie, Lionel Hampton, and great instrumentalists, such as Coleman Hawkins, Art Tatum, and Fats Waller, the community was justifiably proud of its accomplishments in literature and the fine arts.

Black writers, artists, entertainers, intellectuals, activists, and others were converging on Harlem from all over the world. Many had come to New York to escape the brutal racism of the South, as well as to be a part of the new wellspring of culture. Langston Hughes, Countee Cullen, Zora Neale Hurston, and other writers penned great poems and novels, while visual artists like Romare Bearden, Jacob Lawrence, and Aaron Douglas used paintbrush and canvas to depict the sufferings, as well as the triumphs, of their comrades.

Much of the art and literature of the period was recorded in the NAACP's highly influential magazine, *The Crisis*, whose editor, W. E. B. Du Bois, encouraged artists to leave the South and cast their fortunes in the Harlem of the day. At the heart of the Harlem Renaissance was the idea of "the New Negro," one who was proud, dignified, and demanding of respect.

All this was happening in the midst of a new climate of political militancy, partially fueled by such activists as Garvey, as well as by black World War I veterans, who had experienced greater freedom while touring Europe and were disturbed to find the racism that greeted them on their return home, just as their sons and grandsons would find at the end of World War II.

"I think that the Harlem Renaissance figures were very artistic people that were trying to assert black pride and black accomplishment, just as we have always been doing in this country," Sonny recalled.

"It was such a low period in this country for black people, from the late 1800s up to around 1930s. I mean, just everything bad that could happen to black people happened from Reconstruction up until the 1920s and 1930s. So the Renaissance probably came in around that time with the assertion of a great people fighting back: Countee Cullen, Langston Hughes, you know, all these people. I guess you could say

Paul Robeson, too.'"

As Sonny matured, he experienced a personal renaissance of sorts by attending the political rallies and absorbing the heady rhetoric of Harlem's orators and writers. "Sonny was always mischievous, but he was also quite advanced for his young age of eight years old," according to Gloria, his sister.

"He was also bright and a very cute and a loving boy," she added. "He was the baby of the family, but he also had his moments. I called him that [the baby] once when my friends came over after school. He didn't say anything while they were here but after they left, boy, was he mad! That was the only time he's ever gotten mad at me. He said, 'Don't call me a little brother!'"

At the same time, "Sonny was very affectionate. My mother was reserved, partly because of her personality and accent, and Sonny was the only one of us who kissed her goodbye and kissed her hello. It was just his way.

"Sonny was the closest to my father. My brother and I were older, more set in our ways, and it was a more difficult adjustment for us. But, Sonny had that aura and he just really admired his father."

Walter William Rollins was a large, outgoing man with a booming voice like Paul Robeson's; in fact, he resembled Robeson so much he was once mistaken for him on a street in Seattle. Although his father was away at sea much of the time during Sonny's childhood, his youngest son loved the times when his father came home.

In her husband's absence at sea, Valborg handled the business of the house and the children, also working to supplement their father's pay. "We weren't doing too well in those days," Sonny said, recalling the worst days of the Great Depression, a time some historians have dubbed "the cruelest years."

Despite the despair and poverty, the Rollins clan was determined to improve things and make a better life for themselves, embracing the noblest ideals of the Harlem Renaissance.

CHAPTER 3

Movin' on Up

During the Depression, blacks and immigrants, just having arrived from the Caribbean and the South in hopes of finding a better life, were in an economic hell.

Many of the residents of Harlem were broke and living in substandard housing, with their children attending mediocre schools. Moreover, they were subjected to racism. In Harlem, they saw themselves being pushed into a corner, and with no visible light at the end of any figurative tunnel. The hollow sound of Herbert Hoover's mantra that prosperity was "just around the corner" was no consolation to many in Harlem, even during the later Roosevelt years.

While members of the Rollins clan were poor, it didn't mean they were uninformed. They knew they needed to step up their game and become more financially savvy if they wanted to get out of the hood in Central Harlem, which was becoming more frightening and crime infested as the 1930s progressed.

They were determined to "move on up," to escape the misery

and poverty of life in Central Harlem, where they were surrounded by crime and the struggle to stay alive. From living in the bowels of Harlem, for the first time, it appeared their dreams were coming true.

Their new horizon: Sugar Hill. This was an affluent section in upper Manhattan, situated on a bluff overlooking Harlem that was famous for its majestic row houses and elegant apartment buildings. The area was also one of the most popular black communities in the world during the 1930s and 1940s.

Sugar Hill is a historic district located in the northern part of the Hamilton Heights section of Harlem, bordered by West 155th Street to the north, West 145th Street to the south, Edgecombe Avenue to the east, and Amsterdam Avenue to the west.

Both of Sonny's parents and other relatives increased their workloads, pinched pennies, and saved their money during those lean years. Soon, they discovered they had accumulated enough money to move from the skids of "downtown Harlem" to Sugar Hill.

The Hill was replete with wealthy black entertainers, physicians, bankers, civil rights leaders, lawyers, and other well-heeled people. It boasted such notables as Coleman Hawkins, Duke Ellington, Roy Wilkins, Thurgood Marshall, Paul Robeson, Cab Calloway, and W. E. B. Du Bois, all of whom were internationally known.

The Rollins clan moved to Edgecombe Avenue and lived on the same street as these luminaries, many of whom were beginning to shape not only the direction of the black literary movement and jazz, but the Civil Rights Movement itself. These men and others, such as Marcus Garvey, helped create the Civil Rights Movement long before Martin Luther King, Jr. and Malcolm X.

The new Rollins family apartment sat in a modest building at 377 Edgecombe Avenue, across the street from Colonial Park. From their living room, they looked straight across to Yankee Stadium.

The Rollins clan had arrived—just in time, for they were concerned about their three children. When they made the move, Sonny was 9, his older brother Valdemar was 14, and Gloria was 11.

Gloria recalled of the old neighborhood, "The junior high school in that district had a terrible reputation and my mother said I was not going to that school. She said there was violence there and slack supervision. The catalyst for our moving was that I was going to junior high."

Sonny Rollins was not exactly a snob at the age of nine, but he recognized the elegance and the prominence of the well-heeled residents of his new home in Sugar Hill section fit his family's ideals.

"The Hill was a gas," Sonny recalled, laughing sarcastically. "All the big shots were there. I didn't know who these people were because I was too young when we moved there. But there was something different about them. They looked and acted important, but some of them were a little too bourgeois for me."

The neighborhood was also one of New York City's best-kept secrets. Many whites and even blacks thought everybody in Harlem was poor and needy. *Au contraire.* Sugar Hill residents lived in gigantic apartment buildings, with doormen and elevator operators, and sent their children to private schools such as the famous Ethical Culture School.

Prior to the Renaissance, some blacks around the world had heard of this newly emerging enclave. They began moving there in droves—many from the Deep South and others from the Caribbean. The Hill had first been developed in the 1800s as an exclusive suburb for wealthy whites, who began their exodus in the early 1920s upon the arrival of blacks.

Sugar Hill thus became a safe community for the Rollins children, amidst the bewildering universe that was New York City in the 1920s. "It was beautiful," recalled Gloria, "because there were no houses across from us, none in front of us, just the park. It was really very pretty.

"We became middle class," Gloria said, "although I don't know what our income was. It was whatever my father's job provided. And then, there was income from whatever my mother picked up doing domestic jobs."

But in that deep Depression year of 1939, when millions were out of work and before the war economy began to bring some recovery, the steady income of a navy chef was as much a rarity in Harlem as in almost any other part of America.

"In the whole span of Edgecombe Avenue, you had a variety of people, and everyone was not on the same social or economic level," noted Gloria. "The people who lived on the Hill were very conscious of their social responsibility."

Sonny soon moved on to P.S. 89, a nearby elementary school. Gloria was at P.S. 119, an all-girls school, while older brother Valdemar attended the prestigious Music and Arts High School. At school, the children were remembered as models of deportment, reflecting their mother's strict rules of proper behavior. They were conscious of their responsibility to uphold the family's reputation.

Education was serious business for the family, which Gloria said was due to their middle-class values. "Growing up, you had to excel in school, and you didn't hang out," Gloria remembered. "We were also taught never to contradict a teacher. We were always that way."

Valborg tried to instill a love of culture in her children, even taking them on the train to Montreal to be exposed to more of the world. Music was particularly important to Valborg and Walter; they had a piano at home, and Walter was also an amateur clarinetist.

"All of us had to learn to play a musical instrument. It was just one of those things that were necessary to your cultural development. I had to learn piano. Val liked the violin. He started playing violin when he was a little guy."

Sonny's first foray into music was with the piano. At age nine, he began taking piano lessons at his mother's request, but he didn't take to the instrument. He was more interested in playing ball with his friends.

One of his pals was Raymond C. Butler, who recalled meeting Sonny around this age. "At that time Sonny was little and chubby, no kidding. And he had a high-pitched voice," he added.

"He was a competitor. He loved sports. I can see him in my mind's eye playing at a handball court on the upper part of [Edgecombe] Avenue near Stitt, a junior high school on 164th and 165th streets. He played stickball, too," Butler said.

"In fact, Sonny organized a softball team called the Edgecombe Avenue Aces. We ordered jerseys, bright red and with the name, 'Aces' in black written across on the front and our numbers on the back,"

Illus. 6 - Sonny Rollins escaped the poverty and crime of Central Harlem when he moved at the age of nine to 377 Edgecombe Avenue (pictured above) in the affluent Sugar Hill section of Harlem. The area boasted such luminaries as Supreme Court Judge Thurgood Marshall, NAACP activist W. E. B. Du Bois, and famed boxer Joe Louis.

Butler recalled.

And so, Sugar Hill became for the Rollinses an island of stability in an uncertain world, while trouble loomed just beyond the invisible boundary at the bottom of the hill. Sugar Hill was a neighborhood where black conservatives lived with little or no tolerance for crime, a place where the strength of black intellectual life manifested itself each day on the sidewalk.

Eavesdropping on Sonny's conversations during this period can offer us a good portrait of what life was like in Sugar Hill. Sitting on the steps of their building between innings of the Edgecombe Avenue Aces contests, the family often watched celebrities stroll by.

"Isn't that the great tenor saxophonist Coleman Hawkins?" Sonny would ask his friend Raymond Butler.

"Yeah!" said Butler. "And that's W. E. B. Du Bois going the other way."

William Edward Burghardt Du Bois, considered by some to be America's greatest black intellectual, was an educator who campaigned for higher education for blacks. His focus rested especially on the most gifted 10 percent of them, which he referred to as the "Talented Tenth."

He had also co-founded the National Association for the Advancement of Colored People. Du Bois was trying to forge a new social awareness among blacks, restoring the dignity robbed from them. The spirit that moved W. E. B. was the one expressed in the sermons of Marcus Garvey.

Butler also remembered seeing Jay Lewis on the street. Lewis, who lived at 381 Edgecombe, was a distinguished teacher at an elementary school, until it burned down. "When Jay Lewis walked down the street, we would follow him all the way down to 145th Street," said Butler. "We'd walk behind him, and he'd just smile at us."

According to Butler, Sugar Hill was a world away from the mean streets of Central Harlem. In the rougher sections of Harlem, "there might be thugs and gangs, while on this side of Edgecombe Avenue or the Hill, there was a tranquil, settled street of softball teams. Sugar Hill shielded the kids in an enclave of respectability," said Butler.

"Most of the guys on Edgecombe were pretty straight," Sonny

agreed. "We didn't really have any guys who were thugs. There were a lot of young gangs around in New York, but on Edgecombe Avenue, there were sort of upper-middle-class people, and they were doing quite well. The thuggery was going on down the hill, which was a more depressed area."

While Sonny liked his new affluent life on the Hill, he was still drawn to the mean streets of lower Harlem. "Wealth was not everything," he remembered. "I had a lot of friends on the Hill, but I also had a lot of good friends in Central Harlem. I missed them."

Around this time, nine-year-old Sonny also took occasional trips to the naval base at Annapolis, where his father was stationed.

Gloria remembered their father was very fond of her younger brother, and she noted there was a strong resemblance between Sonny and their paternal grandfather, Cedman Rollins. "Sonny looked exactly like my father's father. Sonny was a little guy and he just really admired my father.

"He worked with [my father] when he was in charge of the officers' mess at Annapolis. He was sort of like a little right-hand man. Val went down, too; he was busing the main dining room, but Sonny was kind of helping out in the kitchen, I guess."

The bond between father and son was strong, and they were so deeply in sync that Sonny was able to sense when his father was in peril. One night in Annapolis, Sonny noticed his father seemed especially tired and worn down. The Navy chef was not the kind to complain or mention his exhaustion to anyone—in the Navy, you carried on.

Sonny, still awake under his Navy-issue bedsheets, noticed something off in his sleeping father. The man's breathing was labored, shallow, difficult. Sonny realized something was wrong. His father was sick. One can only imagine the terror of a nine-year-old boy, off in a strange place some two hundred miles from home, his sleeping father wheezing, sputtering, and gasping for breath.

What Sonny did next was an early indication of his prescience. The boy did not ignore the situation or assume it would simply turn out all right. He was alone, without his older brother to turn to, but he instinctively knew his father was in trouble, and he had to do

Illus. 7 - As a child, Sonny saved the life of his father, Walter Rollins. Walter is seen on the left, with his grandson (and future Sonny Rollins accompanist) Clifton Anderson on the right.

something. In a day when long-distance calls were rare, Sonny phoned home to Harlem.

"Momma?"

"Sonny?" Valborg whispered into the receiver, "What's the matter? Where are you?"

"I'm in Annapolis." His voiced wavered. "Momma, Daddy's sick!"

"What do you mean?"

"He can't breathe!" Sonny cried. "He's gasping! He's really sick, Momma."

"Are you sure, Sonny?"

"Momma, he's bad!"

Sonny's call to Harlem worried Valborg, and she quickly phoned back to Annapolis to alert the Navy's physicians. Walter was immediately transferred to the base hospital, and Sonny had been right. His father had double pneumonia, a life-threatening illness in the days before penicillin and other wonder drugs. Walter's illness brought his wife and daughter to his bedside at the Navy hospital in Annapolis.

"He was really quite ill, and would always work through any adversity and would never complain," Gloria said. "There was really nobody else my father was close enough to, who would notice that he was having all this trouble breathing when he would lie down to sleep at night. Sonny really saved my father's life."

Back in Sugar Hill, Sonny would come of age and come into his own as a musician. He was, after all, surrounded by some of the finest musicians around, including popular artists like Don Redman, Andy Kirk, and Nat King Cole.

However, no one caught young Sonny's attention like Coleman Hawkins. At the time, Hawkins was regarded by many as the greatest tenor saxophonist in jazz because he had changed the dynamics and approach of how the horn should be played. Sonny would watch with utter fascination, as the suave saxman drove his Cadillac through the streets of Harlem.

"Sonny admired Coleman Hawkins," Butler remembered. "We were all crazy about 'The Man I Love' and 'Sweet Lorraine.'"

Sonny was also introduced to new music by his Uncle Reuben

and his girlfriend, who played jazz, blues, and early R&B records while babysitting Sonny. The young boy spent hours listening to them, fascinated by the sounds emerging from the turntable.

"[My uncle] played me blues records by Arthur [Big Boy] Crudup and Tommy McClennan," Sonny remembered. "And I liked what Louis Jordan was doing."

In fact, it was Louis Jordan who would kindle Sonny's lifelong love affair with the saxophone. Known as "The King of the Jukebox," Jordan was a popular singer, saxophonist, and bandleader during the 1930s, 1940s, and 1950s. He used to play at a club called Barron's, which was located near Sonny's elementary school, P.S. 89, on Lenox Avenue between 134th and 135th streets.

One day, walking home from school, Sonny came across a glossy publicity photo of the dapper Jordan with his saxophone in the window of the club. "It was so beautiful and shiny," he said. "I fell in love with the instrument."

In 1942, around the age of 12, Sonny's mother bought him a used alto saxophone, and he briefly took lessons farther downtown on 48th Street, although he was mostly self-taught.

"One day, he came home with a saxophone and began playing jazz," Gloria remembered. In the Rollins home on Sugar Hill, where Gloria's piano tinkled with Mozart and Valdemar's violin sang with Beethoven, it was a startling contrast. "Let's just say that it was not classical music," she added.

It was the beginning of a lifelong difference of opinion between Sonny and his older, more traditional brother, Val, along with most of the conservative, middle-class black world that had rejected jazz.

"Jazz was not considered bad," explained Gloria, "but it just wasn't acceptable. I guess it was just too different. When Sonny played this stuff, he always had a big tone—a big sound. I would always holler at him. I'd say, 'Sonny, cut out that noise!' It seemed like he was playing all day. My mother didn't yell at him as much as I did. I guess she understood what Sonny was doing. She was really ahead of her time."

CHAPTER 4

Puppy Love

Young Sonny Rollins was a born romantic, but he was naïve and gullible when it came to women.

The first female to capture his attention was Ginger Rogers, the blonde actress, dancer, and singer, who was famous for collaborating with Fred Astaire in musical films such as *Swing Time, Carefree,* and *The Story of Vernon and Irene Castle.*

Although only nine years old when he first saw Rogers in these and other films, Sonny looked at her with dreamy-eyed passion. "We used to go to the movies, and I fell in love with Ginger Rogers. I used to see her [films] all the time," Sonny recalled. "Ginger was gorgeous; she knocked me out whenever I would see her on screen.

"I was hoping that one day I would have a girlfriend who looked like her. It was at this time that I started looking at girls in the neighborhood, hoping that I would one day find a black Ginger Rogers. Ginger was my ideal of what a woman should look like."

Hollywood had no monopoly on gorgeous women, and Harlem

Illus. 8 - Young Sonny Rollins was enamored of Hollywood starlet Ginger Rogers.

had no shortage of beauties, either. It was the hub of entertainment, and attractive black dancers, actresses, and models from all over the country trekked to the world's black capital, seeking fame and fortune.

In Sugar Hill, Sonny became enamored with his neighborhood's beautiful actresses, models, and especially the dancers, for whom he had an affinity since his early crush on Ginger Rogers. He liked the way dancers looked, the way they strutted, and, perhaps most of all, their confident attitudes.

"Ginger had it all—good looks, talent and the successful ability to entertain her fans," he recalled years later. "She was a fantastic woman, and I adored her."

Of course, Sonny didn't discriminate against his own race when it came to beautiful women. He was also fond of Katherine Dunham, the dancer and choreographer who has been described as the "matriarch and queen mother of black dance." She had some of the most beautiful black dancers in the world in her company, many of whom Sonny would see and admire walking about the streets in Harlem.

Dunham had become famous through her success in Hollywood and on Broadway. As a dancer and choreographer, she achieved even greater worldwide fame after her troupe received applause at New York's Windsor Theater, with scores of beautiful black dancers performing in such plays as *Tropics* and *Le Jazz "Hot."* She moved to Harlem from Chicago in 1939 and soon became the talk of New York City, where she was a major celebrity.

Dunham was more than an entertainer. As an anthropology student at the University of Chicago, she had done extensive fieldwork in Haiti and elsewhere in the Caribbean. As a result, she often incorporated elements of Haitian and West Indian dance, music, and religion into her work. Like many others in Harlem at the time, she was both an entertainer and an activist who looked to the Caribbean and Africa itself as a model for celebrating blackness.

Though Sonny may have been star-struck over famous women like Katherine Dunham and Ginger Rogers, he was also beginning to notice younger, much more attainable ladies in his own neighborhood.

Sonny had first started noticing girls near his earlier home, at West

137th Street and Lenox Avenue. Since he was handsome and tall for his age, the girls flirted back, affected a kittenish air, and giggled. It became a daily routine for the boy to check out the young babes who seemed to surround him at every turn. He, too, began to develop the art of flirtation.

One day, nine-year-old Sonny was immediately smitten when he spotted a cute black girl in the neighborhood, Dominique Wilkins, who was two years older.

"I approached Dominique, and we immediately became good friends, and we eventually became boyfriend and girlfriend," he said. "I was thrilled, to say the least." He bragged about her to his friends in the neighborhood, and they were impressed because she was unquestionably one of the most attractive girls in the surrounding area.

As Sonny recalled, "We would sit on the steps of buildings and parks, and we would talk for hours about everything you can imagine. Since she was a couple of years older than me, I felt special because she was mature, and she seemed knowledgeable about a lot of things. I was impressed, to say the least."

After spotting Dominique, Ginger Rogers was history. Sonny once thought of her as the most beautiful woman in the world, but she was old news now. The pretty 11-year-old wasn't a celebrity like Rogers, but she was his star.

Sonny was jubilant when Dominique agreed to be his girlfriend. He stopped flirting with other girls, thinking, even at that young age, he should be loyal to one woman. But, puppy love didn't last long for Sonny. He spotted Dominique holding hands with another boy, while walking around his neighborhood. He didn't quite understand what was happening, especially after he spotted her with even more guys a few days later.

"I didn't know what was going on," he sighed. "I thought she was my girl. But I later found out that she was also going out with other guys in the neighborhood. I was hurt and felt betrayed because she had led me to believe that I was her number-one guy."

After the failed romance, Sonny began to lose his innocence and become a cynic. "I started distrusting a lot of girls, and I became hardened. While my first relationship was a failure, it still helped me to understand women and the world a lot better."

As he grew older, Sonny soon forgot Dominique; he became quite the "ladies' man." The females of the species adored him, and he loved them right back. All the way back to his early teens, there was no shortage of gorgeous girls in his life.

One of the earliest objects of his adolescent affection was Faith Ringgold, who later became a celebrated artist. "We shared our first kiss, and I remember her nose got in the way," Sonny said. "She was my first love. In fact, she made a quilt for me. She sews these artistic quilts."

His love escapades didn't stop with Faith Ringgold. On one occasion, there was this "wild young white wife of a Chinese man who I ran with as a teenager. My friend and I had a lot of good times together, and we used to have great times dating different girls," Sonny said.

During his teenage years, he picked up plenty of girls after jazz sessions, when they smoked dope and enjoyed life. Later, as he became famous and celebrated, Sonny became a target for even more groupies, and he didn't kick them away.

I remember very strongly that I felt a personal relationship with God. God was somebody I could talk to and get a personal response."

— SONNY ROLLINS

CHAPTER 5

A Plea to God

The last thing Sonny Rollins had on his mind as a teenager was worship. The 14-year-old boy rarely went to the Moravian Christian and AME Zion churches in Harlem, the houses of worship many members of his family had attended. Of the many reasons he failed to attend church, outstanding among them was the growing opposition to Christianity in the community, many claiming that Christianity was a "slave religion" intended to keep blacks in place.

It was the summer of 1944, a year after a major racial riot in Harlem. Residents were fearful, and the violence sent chills up their spines. Some stayed in their apartments and rarely went out, except for work and food. The community was still reeling from the riot's aftermath and it strained race relations; whites stopped visiting Harlem, which they had frequented over the years.

During this time, teenagers, who were unafraid of the violent climate, ruled the streets. They committed simple, occasionally major, crimes that challenged the authority of the police, who had acquired rising powers granted by City Hall in order to keep the peace.

One of the teenagers was Sonny Rollins, who had lost his childhood innocence on the mean streets of Harlem. Although he was described by family members and friends as essentially "a good boy," he nonetheless had to fend for himself.

At the same time, Sonny had an inherent sense of spirituality that kept him stable during these tumultuous years. Sonny recalled an incident that made him a firm believer in God. He recounted standing on top of a tenement rooftop in Harlem, grinning as he peered down at the passersby below. He was intent on causing a bit of mischief, not recognizing the seriousness of what he was about to do. He had just spotted his prey—a mailman taking a shortcut through an alley below.

At home and among friends, Sonny was somewhat subdued and cool, but on the streets of Harlem, it was a case of Dr. Jekyll and Mr. Hyde. At age 14, Sonny was a certified thug. He was tall, athletic and had a menacing look in his eyes. He could box like a professional, and he had a reputation of usually winning.

For Sonny and other youngsters in Harlem, it was a matter of survival. Harlem was no rose garden: it was a place where tough teenagers would congregate on the stoops of the tenements before heading off to cause general havoc or steal anything in sight. It was a way of life.

The rooftop was one of his usual haunts, part of a row of apartments across Edgecombe Avenue from Colonial Park that ran for five blocks—150th to 155th street. People leaving the subway station at St. Nicholas Place could take a shortcut through the buildings' backyards to reach Edgecombe Avenue.

Sonny and his cronies often played on the roof, where they caught a bird's-eye view of the short-cutters passing through the yards below. Sonny and his friends liked to stir up a little bit of trouble, thinking it was harmless: "We used to think it was fun to drop stuff on somebody passing through," he recalled.

On that fateful day, Sonny picked up a piece of the broken stone moldings that lined the roof and dropped it off the top of the building with his typically cynical, carefree laugh.

Illus. 9 - Young Sonny Rollins was obsessed with playing his saxophone, but he had a strong love for and devotion to God. He often prayed and asked for spiritual guidance.

As soon as the stone left his hand, Sonny panicked. "While it was going down, I realized, 'Damn, this thing could hit him and kill him!'"

Terrified, Sonny burst into silent prayer. "I thought, 'Please, God, don't let it hit him! Forgive me for being so stupid!'"

God heard the boy's plea because the stone narrowly missed the mailman's head. The would-be victim spared, Sonny breathed a heavy sigh of relief, his heart still pounding from fear. He was grateful everything was fine, as the mailman continued on his route, safe and sound.

The stone-throwing incident was to be Sonny's first memory of spontaneously turning to religion—a turning point in the young man's spiritual life. Reared in a Moravian and African Methodist Episcopal Zion home, he certainly knew the meaning of God and the need to be righteous.

"When I was a little boy, I always had a conscience. I always had a voice inside of me telling me stuff," he said. "And I recognized it. I was always like that."

He recalled years later, "I remember very strongly that I felt a personal relationship with God. God was somebody I could talk to and get a personal response."

His new relationship with God inspired him to embrace music as a way to connect more to religion and eventually to spirituality. At the time, since many bebop musicians were devotees of Islam and other Asian and Eastern religions, their beliefs further inspired him. However, Sonny was not drawn to Islam as countless other jazz musicians were.

"I was quite curious at the time," he said of the different Western and Eastern faiths among the beboppers. I didn't understand how these different foreign religions could have such a major impact on these American black brothers, because, at first, I thought they were Christians, like me."

Eventually, Sonny made a distinction and understood that "it was not only the religions, it was the belief in God that really ultimately matters. I was a strong believer in God, and that is what counts."

Despite their wholesale abandonment of Christianity, the bebop musicians possessed a "deep, spiritual sound that I could relate to," he said. "The music was not religious-sounding per se, but it had a special unique quality that I could identify with.

"Even as a teenager, I felt a connection between God and music," Sonny declared. "The more I got into my music, the more I became in touch with God and spirituality, although I didn't know what was going on at the time. What I do know is that I felt something different when I played my instrument."

Art Taylor, the famed drummer, and childhood friend of Sonny, said that he did not recall the stone incident, but he did remember a dramatic change in Sonny's attitude. "At one point during his teenage years, Sonny became more solemn and spiritual. He didn't seem religious, but he had an aura of spirituality about him that was quite striking.

"I noticed the change because Sonny had been one of the toughest guys in the neighborhood. You didn't mess with him if you were in your right mind," Taylor added. "A lot of young cats learned the hard way. Sonny had the hardest fists in Harlem. He'd knock you out in a minute if you were not careful."

Taylor personally knew about the wrath of his friend Sonny. One day, Art, who was a flirt and somewhat of a ladies' man, even at the young age of 15, hit on Gloria, Sonny's older sister by two years. As Taylor recalled: "She was really a cute little thing and I wanted to date her. A lot of dudes in the neighborhood had similar feelings."

The following day, Sonny approached Taylor and asked threateningly if he hit on Gloria. "No, I was just talking to her," Taylor replied. "It wasn't really a hit. I just paid her a couple of nice compliments about how pretty she looked."

Sonny, looking visibly upset, started encircling Taylor the way a prize fighter would try to spook his opponent. "I didn't mean it," Taylor pleaded, apologetically. "You shouldn't be angry at me. It was not my intention to upset you or Gloria. I just wanted to be charming."

"Leave her alone," Sonny screamed. "I don't let people mess with Gloria, and that includes you. Find someone else to flirt with. Gloria is off limits, and the sooner you understand it, the better."

Taylor clearly understood the threat and obeyed it without hesitation. Word also got around the neighborhood that Sonny was trying to create a protective shield around his big sister. Other dudes got the message: "Don't mess with Gloria—she's Sonny's sister."

Gloria had her own opinion. "Sonny was very protective. A lot of guys didn't know I existed, and as Art Taylor once said, he had eyes for me, but he knew that Sonny would kill him if he even said a really friendly hello."

Other teenagers in the neighborhood approached Sonny with caution. "Sonny was mischievous, and he was lots of fun to be around," Gloria recalled. "He always liked to laugh and even act a little silly. At the same time, he had this tough street way about him. I wasn't afraid of him because we were so close, but I could tell when other people feared him."

Sonny and Art would develop a lasting friendship, not just because of Gloria, but because they were both interested in the new jazz sounds that were permeating Harlem. By this time, Sonny was playing the alto saxophone and Taylor was playing the drums.

The new music gave them a common bond.

As Sonny moved through adolescence, his family and friends wondered what would happen to the little boy they once thought was special, perhaps a gift from God welcomed by two bells ringing from two different churches.

"Throughout his childhood, I could feel something different, something deeper about my brother that was not so apparent to others," said Gloria. "I think that one of the problems was being around so many crazy people, who influenced him in a defensive way in order to protect himself."

The years of 1944 and 1945 were a major turning point for Sonny Rollins. What did the future hold for the ruthless street thug, the renewed believer in God, and the fledgling young alto saxophonist?

Would he follow in the same footsteps as Charlie Parker, the leader of the bebop movement who was worshipped by millions of jazz fans and musicians worldwide as the new "messiah?" Or would he go the route of so many others, into crime, addiction, and licentiousness? A little bit of both, as the next few years of his life unfolded.

CHAPTER 6

Bebop: Squares Need Not Apply

The cats were supremely cool. Some wore dark sunglasses in dimly-lit rooms. Others pretended to snub adoring women, while attracting them in droves. Many competed for musical superiority against each other as if they were participants in the Olympic games.

These contestants were playing a game that came to be known as bebop. It was not only a highly competitive new jazz style, it represented a revolutionary movement for blacks. Although Duke Ellington and a few others had introduced a level of sophistication and polish in the 1920s, many jazz artists humiliated themselves through acts of erratic behavior and clowning on stage.

For young blacks (and even some older ones, too) bebop changed all that. It became a fashionable new way of life, symbolizing a politically-driven, avant-garde culture for hip black and white intellectuals, college students, bohemians, artists, and the like. While it was fiery and defiant, the music was decidedly elite due to its strong intellectual edge.

Illus. 10 - Alto saxophonist Charlie Parker and trumpeter Miles Davis, who were key founders of bebop, served as two of the main sources of inspiration for Sonny Rollins as a teenager aspiring to also become a pioneer of the music.

In the 1940s, bebop not only carried on the grand traditions of jazz, it signaled a new dramatic cultural and religious shift—igniting a new level of racial respect for African Americans and black Caribbean immigrants. According to author Norman Mailer, "many whites were so enamored of bebop at the time that they wanted to be black themselves."

Bebop was born and developed in Harlem in the late 1930s by the likes of Mary Lou Williams, Coleman Hawkins, Charlie Parker, Dizzy Gillespie, Thelonious Monk, Bud Powell, Charlie Christian, Fats Navarro, Kenny Clarke, Tommy Potter, and Al Haig.

While these innovators embraced traditional European melody, harmony, and rhythm, they distinguished themselves by creating music linked more to the religions and cultures of Ancient Egypt and Africa, in addition to the street cultures of Harlem and other African American inner cities.

Bebop, which was hip, urbane, and daring, was also differentiated by its breakneck tempos, intricate (substitute) chord progressions and changes, as well as many key shifts, extraordinary instrumental virtuosity, and deft improvisation. In addition, the music changed racial stereotypes, bringing unprecedented dignity to African Americans.

Bebop, which discouraged dancing, hand clapping, and finger popping, was not meant for nerds. The musicians—who were serious about their new culture—made "squares" feel unwanted. Beboppers often frowned, on stage and off, and rarely signed autographs requested by adoring fans. They were not entertainers; they were artists.

Most of the black musicians were well-educated, many with college degrees. They often wore elegant, up-to-the-minute European and African fashions, and could quote Nietzsche and Socrates with ease. They ran Uncle Tom out of Harlem, never to return.

Some of the cats even played with their backs to the audience, like trumpeter Miles Davis. Cocky and arrogant, he refused to announce the names of the songs his band played on stage. However, his music was original, brilliant, tender, and hauntingly beautiful. He redefined "cool."

While there were acts of arrogance on the part of the angry

musicians, they were largely justified given the racist treatment from many whites on and off stage. Prior to the bebop era, many black musicians were considered Uncle Toms. They often humiliated themselves on stage with their stereotypical behavior, laughing loudly and shaking their entire bodies. They acted like clowns when, in fact, the music they played was quite profound. Beboppers reversed these obsequious and embarrassing practices.

During those years, Sonny met composer and pianist Thelonious Monk and drummer Art Blakey. Close friends, Blakey hung out at Monk's apartment, during which time Monk became Sonny's mentor and introduced him to the "bebop lab" at Minton's, a club in Harlem that allowed musicians to experiment with bebop.

It was at Minton's that Sonny learned and experienced what the cats called "cutting," which was a fierce act of competition among them. Their contests were more like dog-fights, where the loser often wept and disappeared afterwards—humiliated and perhaps never to return. The game was a way for them to be crowned king—a title hundreds of young and older men desperately sought.

These sessions, many of which were held at Minton's or Clarke's Monroe House jazz clubs in Harlem, represented the beginning of a new musically and politically defiant jazz style. Created by African Americans, bebop was started in part as a backlash to swing, which had been taken over by predominately white big bands. Swing was created by black musicians in the 1920s, but by the height of the music's popularity in 1935, it was dominated by whites.

During the mid-1940s, the height of bebop's popularity, Sonny was drawn to the music not just because of the superiority of its players; he liked their tough and independent manner. A product of the streets by age 15, Sonny could box like a professional fighter, and other tough guys kept their distance from him.

"Everything knocked me out, the music, the cats, the whole thing," Sonny recalled. "The music was for me and I gave it my all to be part of this great movement."

Bebop was full of the energy of youth seeking new horizons in the world of music and the arts. The music was anything but what had been heard before: the songs were fast, the chord progressions were complex, the keys changed faster than the rat-tat-tat of an artillery fusillade.

Just as today's gymnasts are revered for their bodily dexterity, bebop virtuosos were praised for their overwhelming skill in blowing chord progressions and scales out the window with new, asymmetrical phrasings and syncopations.

Like clotheslines blown down by a hurricane, the written staffs and notes of a bebop composition—if they were written down at all— might look like a jumbled, wrung-out mass of flats and sharps on a piece of soggy paper.

How did they do this? Partly by using the rhythm sections in a combo as never before. During the swing era of the 1930s and beyond, the big band (up to 14 pieces playing as an ensemble) was the source of the music's energy, imparting a honeyed smoothness to the overall impact.

Bebop focused on a smaller combo consisting of a saxophone, trumpet, piano, double bass, and drums, playing music in which the ensemble played a supportive role for the soloists. Improvisation was key. Every musician was given a chance to exhibit his (or her, though it was mostly his) proficiency. Everyone had a place in the sun.

Among the most influential bebop artists were Coleman Hawkins, Monk, Charlie Parker, Dizzy Gillespie, Kenny Clarke, Max Roach, Charlie Christian, Bud Powell, with pianist Mary Lou Williams, who was a rare female of the species. Their names are still legendary, attesting to the power that bebop had in shaping the course of 20th-century jazz and the listening habits of its aficionados.

Where did the term come from? "Bebop" is thought to be a series of nonsense syllables used in scat singing. The first song it appeared in was "Four or Five Times," recorded in 1928 by McKinney's Cotton Pickers. But, typical for folk etymologies, it took another eleven years before its first appearance in print, in 1939, attesting to its oral roots.

The origin of the term also depends on who you listen to. Charlie Christian thought it sounded like something he hummed while he was playing. Dizzy Gillespie thought that audiences coined the phrase after hearing him scat his tunes to his players.

"People, when they'd wanna ask for those numbers and didn't know the name, would ask for bebop," Gillespie recounted years later in his memoir, *To Be, or Not to Bop*. And then, there was Lionel Hampton's mid-1940s song "Hey! Ba-Ba-Re-Bop." The possibilities are legion.

Unlike swing, bebop fans did not dance. It was not exactly chamber music, but serious listening was required to understand and appreciate it. The musicians were dead serious about their new art form; they wanted to avoid what they considered the crude, commercial approach to jazz, which had developed during the swing era.

However, traditional jazz lovers branded bebop as "noise" because of what they perceived as strange, unprecedented new harmonies and melodies, and the breakneck tempos that the musicians used. Virtuosity on each instrument was demanded by those who called themselves the "cats." Those who could not achieve virtuosity were shown the door.

Bebop musicians not only created their own music, they began to also create their own style of clothes and language. The word "cats" was routinely used to describe each other, and the word "gig" was used to describe a job. Many of these words went on to become incorporated into the American vernacular.

Bebop was a music that not only stressed musical superiority on the part of the participating players, it represented a cultural shift in which the beboppers were among the first black people to establish themselves as intellectual equals and, in many instances, superior to whites.

"I've always recognized that whites were not superior to blacks, or vice versa," explained Jewish writer Norman Mailer. "But bebop was something else. For the first time, I saw young and even some older whites not only trying to emulate the black musicians, but they were dressing and acting like them.

"They were talking the same talk. They wanted to be cool like them—I think some of them may have wanted to change the color of their skin. I never ever saw anything like this before," he added.

As one of the aspiring contestants at Minton's, it was none other than Sonny Rollins who repeatedly "cut," or out-played other tenor saxophonists—often putting them to shame with his overwhelming, highly competitive approach.

Though Sonny was still a teenager, he demonstrated to the older, established musicians, and their fans, that he was someone to be reckoned with and could easily go toe-to-toe with any of the other older, well known tenor saxophonists on the jazz scene.

One of the "unofficial judges" in these sessions at Minton's was Monk. After he heard Sonny, who played with the ferocity of a raging lion about to kill his prey, Monk declared Sonny to be "the greatest tenor saxophonist ever," according to writer Ahmed Basheer, who was once Charlie Parker's roommate.

"Sonny frightened a lot of younger and even older dudes—many of them were intimidated by him, and he seemed to enjoy it, although he would never admit it," Basheer added. "He could play his ass off. Of course, Bird was still the king, but Sonny was also at the top of his game. He scared the shit out of other saxophonists, whether they played alto or tenor."

Parker, or "Bird," as he was called, was another of the unofficial judges at Minton's, and he played regularly in the house band during the sessions. Other regulars were the leaders of the new bebop movement, including guitarist Charlie Christian, trumpeter Dizzy Gillespie, and drummer Kenny Clarke.

The young Sonny was clearly cutting his teeth with the greatest.

"This country was built by many people of many creeds, so it can never be divided. No kid is born and two days later says: 'I hate Jews or colored people.' He's got to be taught."

— FRANK SINATRA, SPEAKING ON RACISM AT SONNY ROLLINS' HIGH SCHOOL

CHAPTER 7

Harlem Rumblings

Harlem was undoubtedly Langston Hughes' muse as he penned some of his most memorable poems. Throughout the mid-twentieth century, many and varied were the ancient, dusky currents that washed across the mean streets of upper Manhattan.

For Du Bois's "Talented Tenth," the neighborhood was an intellectual nirvana. For the hopeful poor who flocked there from the South and the Caribbean, it was often a shambles of dilapidated housing, inadequate education, hostile police, and corrupt city government.

For affluent whites, it was a playground where they could indulge their exotic fantasies in the jazz clubs and speakeasies that thrived during the Prohibition era. For others, it could be a powder keg, a raisin in the sun that ultimately explodes.

Explode it did, on the first two days of August in 1943. Rioting erupted when a white police officer, James Collins, shot and wounded Robert Bandy, an African American soldier. Unconfirmed rumors

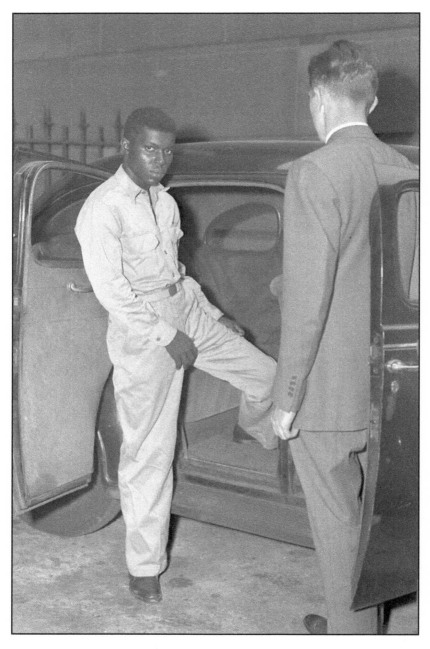

Illus. 11 - The brutal beating of soldier Robert Bandy by police sparked the Harlem riots in 1943. He is pictured outside the Braddock Hotel in Harlem. The hotel was not only where the riot started; it also served as one of the main gathering places for the creators of bebop.

spread through the streets that Bandy had been killed.

Sonny Rollins was a month short of 13 when the rioting erupted in his community. At this crucial moment in the young man's life, he witnessed the scourge of racism and racial profiling. "I don't remember all the details of the shooting," he said years later. "But I do remember that young brothers, like myself, were profiled and that a lot of them were arrested and put in jail because they were simply black."

The Harlem riots were only one of several racial insurrections throughout the country in 1943. They were connected directly to black and white tensions during World War II. Other riots exploded in Detroit, Mobile, Los Angeles, and in Beaumont, Texas.

In Harlem, riots ensued after Bandy had witnessed a black woman's arrest for "disorderly conduct" at the Braddock Hotel on 126th Street, near Eighth Avenue and the world-famous Apollo Theater. According to police accounts, Bandy hit the officer, who in turn shot the soldier as he was trying to flee from the scene. Residents disagreed, arguing that the shooting was unprovoked.

A crowd of about 3,000 residents and others gathered at police headquarters, and a smaller crowd followed Bandy and the officer to a hospital for treatment. Tensions escalated after someone in the crowd falsely stated that Bandy had been killed—sparking riots that endured for two days.

Police said there were six deaths and hundreds injured, with nearly 600 arrests, but the NAACP estimated the numbers were much higher. New York City's mayor, Fiorello LaGuardia, intervened to end the riots. He ultimately restored order in Harlem on August 2, with the recruitment of several thousand officers and volunteer forces.

As a goodwill gesture, the mayor dispatched teams of workers to clean up and repair buildings, as well as supply food and goods afterward to compensate the businesses that had been shut down.

The riots became an international embarrassment for Harlem and America itself. Writers wrote about the riots and painters drew pictures of them. They were also portrayed in the "theatrical climax" of Ralph Ellison's novel *Invisible Man*, which was a winner of the National Book Award, and in artist William Johnson's painting "Moon Over Harlem."

The young James Baldwin commented in *Notes of a Native Son* that his own father's funeral coincided with the riots in Detroit and Harlem. "On the morning of the third of August," he wrote, "we drove my father to the graveyard through a wilderness of smashed plate glass... For Harlem had needed something to smash. To smash something is the ghetto's chronic need."

A black police officer, Sergeant Andrew Stroud, echoed the views of Baldwin and Sonny Rollins: "I was a devoted officer, but the riots showed me another violent side of my police officers that really disturbed me. At the time, a lot of European cities were living in a state of occupation, but so were a lot of black people in Harlem. It was not a pretty picture. It was rather a tragic situation."

Before the riots, Harlem had been known as a playground for wealthy New York and European whites seeking black entertainment, drugs, and a fast-paced lifestyle not available in their own communities. "But it was the jazz that really turned on whites," said Ahmed Basheer, the writer. "The music was fresh, brilliant and original. I'd never seen so many great players all living in one community."

As previously mentioned, in 1939, four years prior to the riots, Sonny's family had moved about a mile from the rough and tumble West 137th Street and Lenox Avenue, north to the affluent Sugar Hill section. Although the Hill was at least a mile away from the scene of the riots, supposedly immune from the problems of downtown Harlem, its residents also felt the sting of police rage that extended all the way to City Hall.

While the Hill was considerably safer than other impoverished sections of New York City, Sonny's family soon realized they could not escape the racism so rampant throughout the Big Apple.

When Sonny turned 15, he was one of a group of black students who were sent to integrate Benjamin Franklin High School, at East 116th Street between Pleasant Avenue and the FDR Drive. Benjamin Franklin had opened its doors in 1943, and the integration move was part of a strategy to create greater diversity within the New York City school system.

Almost from the first day, Sonny found himself being chased

from East Harlem by a mob of white teenagers hell-bent on inflicting physical harm on him. Because Sonny was fast on his feet, his would-be assailants failed to catch him, as he sprinted from the east side to the safety of Harlem's predominantly black west side.

Other black youths attempting to integrate the school were not so lucky. Many of them were brutally beaten and had to seek medical attention. This level of violence foreshadowed the mayhem that occurred when blacks attempted to integrate schools during the 1950s in the South. Black youngsters were hosed, spat upon, and even killed during a period that continued through the 1970s.

In Harlem, it was a harrowing experience for Sonny, a young man in Sugar Hill. Despite his relatively comfortable home neighborhood, he confesses that "it was one of the scariest times in my life…They were calling me 'nigger' and hurling other racial epithets at me," he said. "It was horrible."

Although New York City enjoyed a reputation of being one of the most cosmopolitan and liberal communities in America, many blacks disagreed, citing police brutality as a case in point.

Sonny's sister, Gloria, believes the riots and Sonny's school chase were typical expressions of hate by whites against blacks. Benjamin Franklin High School "was a mixed school, and they singled out black kids for particular treatment," she recalled. "That was just a terrible neighborhood for black kids. It was a very, very, rough Italian neighborhood.

"Sonny had to run from the subway on Lenox Avenue all the way over to the river. All the black kids had to do that, or they would beat you up. They were just these uneducated, low socioeconomic Italians."

"It was the first busing, not that they called it that," Sonny remembered. "The black kids from Sugar Hill took the number 20 bus to Lenox Avenue." From there, they had to run to the East River, their path impeded by a rain of garbage cans, curses, and fists.

Running the gauntlet with Sonny and the other black kids was Richard Reckling, whose mother, Frances, was a concert pianist and voice teacher. She owned the first black music store on 125th Street, opposite the Apollo Theater. "It wasn't a very pleasant situation,"

Reckling, later a radio news reporter, said. "The Italians dropped trash cans down on us."

Sonny himself was hardened by dealing with these daily disturbances at—and en route to—school. He developed a rough edge on the streets of New York, "even though he was, at heart, a gentle soul," said Art Taylor, a friend and drummer who practiced and played with his band.

Happening during a crucial stage in Sonny's adolescent development, the Harlem riots and their aftermath played a major role in shaping his views of race and politics in America. Not surprisingly, he became embittered, as did many of his peers. As a young child, he had attended civil rights rallies with his grandmother, but this experience had allowed him only a superficial glimpse into the reality of racism.

"The riot and its aftermath were the real thing," said Sonny. "I remember the savagery and its impact on our community. There was also a backlash that spread not only in Harlem, but I believe it extended throughout America. It still leaves a sour taste in my mouth."

"I was surprised that many riots had not occurred previously, given the amount of abuse white cops lay on brothers," declared Andrew Stroud, a former black police sergeant who had worked in Harlem. "It was not true for all officers, but overall there was a huge amount of brutality and racism within the ranks of the police department."

Stroud, who was the husband of singer Nina Simone, said racial discrimination was widespread throughout Harlem. "It was not exactly the South where people were constantly hanged, but the Big Apple had its own version of hangings—police brutality."

Following the riots, residents demanded not only an end to police brutality, but also the creation of better housing and better-paying jobs. Walter White, then head of the National Association for the Advancement of Colored People (NAACP), went a step further and pushed for the controversial policy of integrating public schools nationwide.

Despite the intractable racial divide at Benjamin Franklin, Sonny Rollins saw firsthand the power of music to bridge cultural differences.

On September 27, 1945, tensions at the school came to a boiling point when a dispute in the locker room between African American and Italian students erupted into violence on the streets surrounding the school. To heal the wound, school officials invited superstar singers Nat King Cole and Frank Sinatra to address a school assembly.

At the time, Sinatra was considered the most popular singer in the world. White Americans, especially Italians, looked to him as their idol. He had a special mystique that had a calming effect on residents of the area. Although he was not politically liberal, he was nonetheless respected by countless African American musicians and fans for his musical prowess and tolerant political stance.

In the immediate postwar period, Sinatra made more than 30 appearances at schools around the county in support of racial harmony. The theme of his appearances, wrote *Life* magazine, was "No kid is by nature intolerant. It is one of the few forms of ignorance which has to be cultivated."

When Sinatra appeared at Benjamin Franklin on October 23, he told students to reject hate-group leaders who were trying to stir up unrest. According to *Daily News* reports, Sinatra declared, "This country was built by many people of many creeds, so it can never be divided. No kid is born and two days later says: 'I hate Jews or colored people.' He's got to be taught."

At the time, a large percentage of black jazz musicians and fans, who maintain that the origins of the music were to be found in the suffering, religion, spirituality, and culture of American blacks, respected Sinatra for what they perceived as his respect for black cultural traditions.

"Frank was cool. He could definitely sing jazz well, which was not an easy thing to do, but I believe he understood what the cats were undertaking culturally as well. Frank had hung out with the brothers and sisters a lot, so he got to understand us more than most other white singers," Sonny recalled.

"Our styles (jazz and bebop) were culturally black, so it was necessary for anyone listening to it to have an awareness and understanding of both the African and African-American cultures and experiences," he added. "Unfortunately, a lot of white cats rarely understood the culture of our music; they just made a lot of money from something we had created."

Sonny acknowledged Sinatra was not able to change the mindsets of many of the white students and teachers at the school because they were "hardcore racists," but he also noted, with optimism, Sinatra did make a difference by educating some who were on the fence.

"The school was sort of a new place, after he left; racism was still alive, but there was a slightly calmer atmosphere," Sonny recalled, noting that the riot had given him a new perspective on whites and their political feelings.

"The riot was terrible, but it was also enlightening, because of what we were able to learn about racism in America," Sonny concludes. "It ain't pretty."

CHAPTER 8

The Great Divide: East vs. West

The cats were bored stiff in the 1940s. They grumbled about the once exciting swing jazz era a decade earlier and how it was fading. They were also uptight about the Western religions' failure to keep pace with modern spirituality. They demanded change from the mundane.

These complaints came mostly from defiant, disgruntled black bebop jazz musicians who sought relief by converting to the various emerging Islamic religious sects in Harlem and black America, as well as with the new bebop musical experimentations. At the same time, many Jewish beboppers and their fans felt the same, but discovered their path lay in Buddhism.

Together, both groups went on to change the face of jazz and religion in America while simultaneously and unwittingly helping to close the centuries-old Great Divide between the East and the West—an issue that had for centuries spawned wars.

The new interest in Eastern spirituality and culture had a major impact on jazz itself. After all, African Americans were the key founders of bebop, but Jews were the secondary trailblazers. The latter group played an important role through their enormous compositions. Moreover, Jewish intellectuals and artistic types were among the majority of fans.

However, that is not to say that other ethnic groups or countries were not involved; jazz is an international music that continues to be shaped by various cultures throughout the world from such countries as Japan, France, India, Israel, Germany, the UK, Finland, Poland, Sweden, Nigeria, Denmark, Holland, Brazil, Jamaica, Cuba, Australia, and now, China.

They are among the countless worldwide contributors to jazz who support what is unquestionably an American-born and bred art form. Ironically, American support of jazz continues to decline significantly.

One of the fans influenced by bebop's shift towards the East was teenager Sonny Rollins who declined to follow the Islamic road towards religion and spirituality. The independent-minded teenager was instead drawn to yoga (Hinduism) and Buddhism, among others.

Sonny's early embrace of these foreign faiths would decades later define him, his music, and millions of his devout fans worldwide. Like-minded, his fans were also non-conformists and eventually helped set the stage for subsequent religious, music and cultural explosions in the 1950s and 1960s.

As a child, Sonny had attended Moravian and AME Zion Churches with his family, but he had grown disenchanted with Christianity by his high school years. "While I continue to have much respect for Christianity and other Western beliefs, I started back then to feel more comfortable with these other new faiths," recalled Sonny.

"It took me a long time to understand the meaning of them. Today, decades later, I am still in the learning process," he added.

During the 1940s, Sonny watched with curiosity and deep interest the trends of many older black jazz musicians, activists, and others and how they, among other things, traded in their given names for Islamic monikers. They argued that such mundane, stereotypically black names, like Willie Smith or Beulah Johnson, sounded like "slave" names and insisted they be changed to Muslim ones.

The name changes became a declaration of their allegiance to Islam. Many of these activists also wore traditional Middle Eastern attire and used certain Arabic greetings like "*As-salamu alaykum*" ("Peace be upon you").

"I thought the way that these cats talked and dressed was quite interesting and the way they changed their names was too," said Sonny, who was 16 years old and still in high school when he began to encounter these Muslim influences.

"I was totally aware of the importance of the conversions, but I can tell you that the (Muslim) brothers were also quite serious," he added. "Muslims were all over the place. When you walked down the streets, you could see them. They were everywhere in Harlem."

These conversions to Islam shocked the established religious order that proclaimed America was and would always be Christian. Among the most enraged were orthodox adherents to the different denominations of the African American church, such as the Baptists, the Methodists, the AMEs, and the Pentecostalists. They branded the converts as heretics who had fallen prey to the devil. The church rejected the new conversions and bebop, their new style of jazz.

"It was the beginning of a major rift between bebop musicians and the black church," declared Randy Weston, the bebop composer and pianist who had strong ties to African, Asian, and Eastern systems. "They see us as decadent and not worthy of acknowledgment."

There were several Islamic sects thriving in Harlem and throughout black America during the 1940s, but the Ahmadiyya Muslim Community was the most popular among musicians. Many of them were also civil rights activists who worked on behalf of African Americans and other people of color. In addition, many Ahmadis became trailblazers of the bebop movement.

Originally founded in the Punjab in British India toward the end of the 19th century, it was based on the life and teachings of Mirza Ghulam Ahmad (1835–1908).

The movement—which many orthodox Muslims consider heretical—claimed to be divinely appointed to bring about the final triumph of Islam. Today, it is estimated there are still 15,000 to 20,000 Ahmadi Muslims in the United States.

It was in the 1920s that the Ahmadiyya movement reached the United States, after the organization started to dispatch missionaries to various American cities. Some historians consider it a precursor to the postwar civil rights movement, due to the political consciousness it fostered in its followers.

Mufti Muhammad Sadiq, the first Ahmadi missionary sent to the United States, established their headquarters on Madison Avenue. A charismatic public speaker, Sadiq was soon speaking to thousands of interested people at rallies in major American cities. Among his early converts was an African American woman named Madame Rahatullah. The most active female member of the sect, she became a successful proselytizer in New York.

Sadiq soon moved the headquarters of his movement to Chicago, then to Detroit, and began advocating Muslim solidarity, regardless of ethnic or racial background. In these locations, he cultivated multiracial relations with various white, as well as black, communities.

Back in Chicago in 1923, Sadiq lectured to members of Marcus Garvey's Universal Negro Improvement Association, where he found a receptive welcome. Many of the early converts to the Ahmadi tradition were African Americans from Chicago, Detroit, St. Louis, and Gary, Indiana. One of these converts was J. H. Humpharies, a Belgian-Congolese immigrant who became disillusioned with Christianity after studying for the ministry at Tuskegee University.

The Ahmadiyya movement continued to attract African American followers through the 1930s and 1940s, as it focused its message on racial harmony and inclusiveness. The missionary Sufi Bengalee was active in this effort, proclaiming in a lecture, "Treat the colored people in a truly democratic spirit. Do not shut the doors of your churches, hotels, schools, and homes against them. Let them enjoy all the privileges which you possess. If they are poor, help them. If they are backward, uplift them, but for heaven's sake, do not despise them."[4]

After World War II, Ahmadi Muslims established communities in many American cities beyond Chicago, including Cleveland, Kansas

City, Pittsburgh, and Washington, D.C., with African American converts numbered among their members.

Black jazz musicians flocked to the Ahmadiyya movement, including bebop drummer Art Blakey, who became a vocal member of the Ahmadiyya Muslim community. He observed, "Christianity was alien to the black man in America; it did not represent his interests. If anything, it helped to preserve the slave mindset of millions of brothers who had no clue about their ancient African and Eastern ancestry."

In 1947, Blakey, or "Buhaina," as he was called, traveled to parts of Africa in search of his ancient roots. "During my three years on the African continent, I discovered that we have more in common, especially in religion, than we realize. Africa was my true education, and I will always cherish my stay in the Mother country.

"For me, going abroad to Africa and the other foreign countries after the war was one of the most fantastic experiences of my life," said Blakey, who was one of the founders of the bebop movement. "I could practice my new faith there with independence. I was psyched."

Blakey was not alone. Countless other jazz singers and instrumentalists became members of the Ahmadiyya sect. They included such stalwart figures as Yusef Lateef, Ahmad Jamal, Rudy Powell, Sahib Shihab, Dakota Staton, McCoy Tyner, Sadik Hakim, Abbey Lincoln, Talib Dawud, Ahmed Abdul-Malik and Idrees Sulieman.

While the Ahmadiyya Muslims did not directly influence Sonny's spirituality, the religion nonetheless served as inspiration for other teenagers and established leaders of the spirituality jazz movement. However, Sonny did not convert. Yet, many of these Ahmadi musicians, such as Yusef Lateef and Art Blakey, would become close friends, and some of them would work with him in the future as sidemen in his different bands.

More traditionally minded Muslims chose the Sunni branch. Sunni Islam is the largest denomination of Muslims. The differences between Sunni and Shia Muslims arose from a disagreement over who should become Muhammad's successor and first caliph after the Prophet's death in 632 CE. Another Muslim offshoot was the Nation of

Illus. 12 - Ahmadiyya convert Art Blakey was the drummer in Billy Eckstine's band, which boasted such members as Charlie Parker, Dexter Gordon, and Miles Davis.

Islam, which became popular in part due to its unique ability to cure heroin addiction.

For black bebop musicians, converting to Islam and other forms of spirituality provided a breath of fresh air. They argued that non-Western faiths supported their argument that Christianity had failed in helping them reach the higher states of spirituality that were necessary to help them fight off the demons and terminate their fast-paced lifestyles. They also asserted that organized Western religions were not supportive of civil rights.

"As a young man I was always searching and looking for something different, and I believe that my interests in yoga, Buddhism and spirituality in general represented an important phase in my life and the beginning of a learning period," recalled Sonny. "Bird, Dizzy, Monk and the other pioneers were my heroes and they were among the people who helped shape my mindset as a young man."

No matter the impact these bebop pioneers had on closing the East-West divide, they continued to be rejected by the black faith-based community, which also spread to other black sectors. Consequently, this rejection has been partially responsible for the economic hardship and emotional alienation faced by older bebop and even contemporary jazz musicians.

Weston, who spent years living abroad became an expert on African and Asian religions and cultures, said: "It was a major blow to the brothers when they discovered that the Christian church had rejected their involvement and conversions. Our church brothers and sisters do not understand that we were all in the same boat and that we [the musicians] respect and admire the Christian church, although many of us wanted to explore our early roots."

An estimated 30 percent of enslaved Africans were Muslims prior to coming to America during the 1600s. "For many of us, we were just returning to our ancient roots," said Weston.

While many Jews were sympathetic to the different foreign faiths, some were less welcoming of the black American Muslim-converts. For example, a small number of Jewish owners of record companies and clubs refused to allow Muslim-converted jazz musicians to perform and record because of their cultural and religious disagreements.

Bebop trumpeter Dizzy Gillespie, who was one of the key founders of bebop, said that not all Jewish entrepreneurs were tolerant of Muslims. In his memoir, he wrote about the pressures that American black musicians faced in their attempt to convert to Islam.

"The movement among jazz musicians towards Islam created quite a stir, especially with the surge of the Zionist movement," Dizzy said in his book entitled *To Be or Not to Bop*. "A lot of friction arose between Jews and Muslims, which took the form of a semi-boycott in New York of jazz musicians with Muslim names … Near the end of the '40s, the newspapers really got worried about whether I'd convert to Islam."

Dizzy eventually became a member of the Baháʼí faith, which is a religion teaching the basic validity of all religions—stressing the unity and equality of all people in the world. The religion was founded by Baháʼuʼlláh in 1863 and developed in Iran and other parts of the Middle East.

Jewish jazz fans gravitated more towards Buddhism, much like Sonny. American interest in Buddhism was just beginning to bud at this time, although it wouldn't really take off until the 1960s and 70s. Regardless, many of the nation's most famous converts—like Beat poet and bebop fan Allen Ginsberg—were Jewish.

But what exactly was Buddhism's appeal? Rabbi Dusty Klass attempted to answer this question in her 2014 lecture titled "Why is Buddhism so attractive to Jews?" She stated that there are three main reasons for this attraction. The first is that Buddhism, being more loosely structured, is perceived as more welcoming to Jews who are turned off by the rigidity and rituals of organized Judaism. Secondly, Buddhism, like Judaism, is a "religion" that can be practiced in a purely cultural way.

"Thus," argued Rabbi Klass, "when cultural Jews begin asking deep questions and seeking spiritual answers, they don't even think to turn to Judaism. Instead, and especially as it has been presented in white American culture, Buddhism presents itself as 'instant spirituality, just add meditation.'"

Finally, Klass maintained that Judaism (especially liberal Judaism) has become "porous" through its continual adaptation to various cultures throughout history.[5]   It is therefore not surprising that Buddhism might be embraced by Jews seeking to ally themselves with contemporary cultural practices.

Regardless, Jewish, and black beboppers alike challenged the Judeo-Christian establishment by their exploration of different faiths. In fact, it could be said that their early interest in Buddhism, Islam, Hinduism, and even astrology, helped sow the seeds for the New Age movement that would blossom in the decades to come.

It was this strong spirit of independence that played the overriding role in Sonny's unique personal and musical style as a teen and subsequently during his adult years. Through his instincts and visionary prowess, Sonny went on to become one of the bebop pioneers who narrowed the East-West divide and established jazz as an international language—one without borders and petty differences.

When we started using drugs, it wasn't just to do something which would be decadent or anything like that. We were getting it because it made us get more into ourselves, made us kind of get into our music and...get into more of our souls. Shut out all the negativity and racism around us and get with the music...I was doing it as a sacrament."

— SONNY ROLLINS

CHAPTER 9

Garment District Blues

From dusk to dawn, thousands of laborers could be seen in the streets of Manhattan, loading and pushing heavy clothes racks from the gritty garment factories to the swanky Seventh Avenue showrooms in the heart of the Big Apple. The pay was menial, and the workers lived hand-to-mouth.

Although Sonny worked only one day in the garment district, he knew he had to seek other employment because of the grueling nature of the work.

After graduating from high school in 1947, Sonny decided to join the Musicians Union; the only problem was, at age 17, he was still too young to enroll. His solution was to list his birthdate as 1929 instead of 1930.

Sonny had few work choices. Head-hunters were not exactly knocking on his door, beckoning him to enter the executive suites of elegant, well-paying jobs. Even in the prosperous years after World War II, opportunities for good-paying, upscale jobs for young black men were scarce.

But, he was a talented young man, and his choices were not as limited as they were for many of his peers. For Sonny, the options seemed simple: would he push heavy clothes racks all day in New York City's rough and tumble garment district, or would he embrace the lifestyle of a jazz musician, one that would potentially offer him big money, an elegant lifestyle, and plenty of admiring young women to feed his ego?

The decision for him was easy. The bright, talented teenager chose the profession of jazz musician. What was not easy, however, was the music industry. The music world was fiercely competitive. In fact, the style of jazz he chose—bebop—was as much of a dog-eat-dog world as any other competitive profession.

During high school, he had gotten his feet wet with a band that included pianist Kenny Drew, alto saxophonist Jackie McLean, and drummer Art Taylor, all of whom would go on to become international jazz stars famed for their prowess on their respective instruments. It was this young band that gave Sonny the confidence he would need to choose his career.

At the same time, Sonny was being mentored by bebop's elite: Bud Powell, who lived on 141st Street, was a major influence. Monk, who Sonny once referred to as his "guru," even invited the budding young tenor saxophonist to play with him. Sonny fondly remembered rehearsing with Monk's band at his home.

Sonny came from a well educated, politically savvy family. Neither he nor his kin would be content to see a family member working in a menial job. Sonny's older brother, Val, was then in medical school, following in the footsteps of their grandfather, Paul Solomon, a Haitian physician who had attended the Sorbonne in Paris.

Sonny had chosen the tenor saxophone, which meant he would be thrown into the ring against Lester Young, Gene Ammons, Chu Berry, Don Byas, Ben Webster, Dexter Gordon, Lucky Thompson, and other astonishing tenor men.

Even some of Sonny's contemporaries recognized he was a talented young man worthy to assume his place in the lineage of the jazz greats.

Illus. 13 - Pianist and composer Thelonious Monk, one of the founders of bebop, was the principal mentor of Sonny Rollins. Like Monk, who would leave his piano during his performance to dance onstage, Sonny developed a reputation for also being eccentric.

Percy Heath, the bassist who helped create bebop, recalled Sonny had almost instantly created a legacy as soon as he emerged onto the professional jazz scene in 1947.

"I can't recall the exact time, but when I first heard him play, I can say definitively that Sonny could stand up to the best of the other tenor players. He showed at such a young age that he was quite formidable and had made the right choice to play the tenor sax."

Unfortunately, Sonny didn't know paying homage to the founders had its limits. Like many other players—young and old—he started using heroin because he thought he could use the drug to play on the same level. When Bird would get high, his playing soared.

"No one was like Bird," said Ahmed Basheer, the writer who lived with Parker. "It wasn't dope that made him so miraculous. The man had a spiritual side, a charisma that people could not copy no matter how hard they tried. Consequently, a lot of cats fell by the wayside thinking that if they used skag, they would achieve the same brilliant sound as Bird. No one could do that, no matter how hard they tried."

Sonny recalled, "When I met Bird, I met him as a teenager, and he was sort of my idol, so he was always very fatherly to us. I had no experience with him as an equal person and being involved in drugs and all that. I had no kind of relationship with him on that level, so he was always fatherly to the young people who were his acolytes."

Whether Bird inspired them or not, other jazz giants became heroin addicts, like bebop trailblazers Miles Davis, Monk, Powell, Kenny Clarke, Art Blakey, and a legion of others.

For them, drugs were more than a recreational substance. "For many of the cats, it was therapeutic and they needed it to cope with all the distractions," added Basheer.

While bebop was an extraordinary new music, it was initially rejected by the public as "noise" by many people who yearned for the "good old days" of swing and ragtime. The pay was considerably less for beboppers than swing musicians. Since bebop was largely a black music style, it was mostly rejected by the public.

"Even as a teenager I fully understood what I was up against," said Sonny. "I saw all the dope, I saw all the booze, and I saw all the mental depression and all the dues the cats had to pay in order to play our music. It was not an easy profession to be in, but I decided to persevere despite all the pain and suffering."

Sonny added, "At times, it was so sad. The cats were making people happy with this great new music, but they were not the beneficiaries. Many of them couldn't pay their rent or even buy food. Certain substances became necessary for the cats to survive in this world."

It was in this environment that Sonny Rollins launched his professional jazz career as a tenor saxophonist.

At the time, Sugar Hill was the epicenter of the jazzquake sending tremors through white and black America. By 1949, bass player Percy Heath had made his way up to Harlem from Philadelphia. At that time, he considered Sonny "the greatest saxophone player on Sugar Hill." He holds that opinion to this day.

Back then, he remembered, "New York was the place, and Sugar Hill was where all the beboppers used to get together and play. We used to jam, and there were quite a few players up on St. Nicholas Avenue where I was living. Sonny was around on Edgecombe Avenue. We used to get together and play. Lowell Lewis was the only trumpet player in the group at that time."

Percy also noticed the flexibility of the young saxophonist. Sonny, he said, "could play like Coleman Hawkins. He could play like any tenor player he wanted to. At any time, he could play like any of his idols. Sonny Rollins is class. He was the greatest tenor player now and then."

"He had his own voice, but he still had the gift of deciding who he wanted to play like," said pianist Tommy Flanagan, who first heard Sonny when he was a teenager. "If he were to play like Bird, he could sound like him. It was strictly up to Sonny. He had a way of expanding on whatever he started. He would just build on that and keep on building. He was a real thinker. He still does that today. His solo is just from the ground up. He's composing on his feet."

Flanagan said that jazz of that period represented "a freeing of the spirit." It was a time when "people were trying to express themselves, especially musicians, artistically. It just so happened that Charlie Parker showed us a new way of playing music that was a departure. It wasn't accepted for years...Duke Ellington and Count Basie represented a departure for people who started to express themselves as soloists and free playing out of structure. I'm sure Sonny and myself—people of the same age group—latched onto that new form of expression," he added.

The musicians of the 1920s and 30s had been, in some cases, closet addicts. In the 40s, they were more brazen. Many shot up on skag in their dressing rooms. They came on stage, glassy-eyed and snapping their fingers. Sonny began by smoking pot, then moved on to more powerful drugs.

Could he play better when he was high?

"It was very difficult to say at that period of my development," Sonny said years later. "When I was developing, I think that everything I did was important to my getting into the music. It made my life more centered on what I was doing. When we got high, we shut everything out except the music.

"In that sense, it might have had some kind of an effect. I am not going to deny that because it is possible. But, you reach a point of diminishing returns. My life was driven by trying to reach the next high."

As for smoking pot, Sonny said, "When I smoked weed, I smoked it as more of a sacrament than as a way to have fun. When I got high, it was more like a sacrament. It was something that I was comfortable doing. I meditate. I didn't get high just to hang out and have fun. I got high just to get deeper into myself and meditate.

"Drugs made us get more into ourselves, into our souls, into spirituality," he said. "It shut out all the negativity and racism around us." The music also had the same effect, allowing musicians to fly away into a world of their own. "There was a certain spiritual aspect of getting high, of reaching a certain level of consciousness," Sonny added. The high and the music flowing together "took us away from the material world, to reaching a level of getting away from everyday life."

There are many cultures that use drugs to achieve spiritual states, such as the use of peyote in Native American traditions. Jazz also had a sense of the religious about it—it was, after all, linked to the gospel

Illus. 14 - Sonny Rollins, pictured here as a young man, had a brief stint as a worker in Manhattan's garment industry before making it big on the jazz scene.

I tried to understand them by hanging around him. He used to show me things, and I played some tunes he had written."

Brown and Sonny were both great admirers of Paul Robeson. "I loved his stance on life and everything. The man knew what was right. He was a brave and honorable man. Sonny would say the same thing. We both liked him for that."

As Brown recalled, Sonny was friendly with his fellow musicians in the late 1940s. "They loved Sonny," he said. "They loved his playing. Sonny was charismatic, and he was cool and funny and very likable. Good dude. We got very close … but I looked at him as though he was going to be an obituary. I never thought he was going to clean up."

CHAPTER 10

Oop-Pop-A-Da

Donning a turban and dressed like a regal maharaja, Ram Singh casually strolled up to the reservations desk at a ritzy Hollywood hotel of the 1940s. The receptionist smiled and greeted him as a member of Indian royalty.

With a heavily affected accent, Ram Singh exchanged pleasantries with the clerk. "How nice it is to be in your great country. This is my first time, and I am sure that I will enjoy myself," he said.

"Welcome, Mr. Singh. We will do everything in our power to make your visit pleasant and enjoyable," said the clerk, summoning an African American bellboy, who looked at Singh with suspicion.

Since the bellboy was not certain of his instincts, he remained silent and took the guest's bags to his suite. Singh did not give him a tip, noting he had to exchange his Indian currency. The bellhop glared at Singh and asked what time he should come back for the tip.

Singh replied, "You don't call me. I will call you when I make the exchange."

Alone inside the room, the distinguished guest called one of his friends. "Hey, this is Lee Brown. Waz up? I should get an Oscar for my performance here at the hotel, pretending to be an Indian maharaja," he said with a loud chuckle.

Later that day, Brown, who had taken off his regalia and makeup, passed by the hotel reservations clerk. For a moment, the clerk looked at the African American man walking by and felt as though they had met before, though he couldn't quite put his finger on it. Deception was Brown's modus operandi: dressed in the hip style of the day, he would visit jazz clubs and try to hook up with stars like Charlie Parker, Dizzy Gillespie, Thelonious Monk, Kenny Clarke, and others.

It wasn't the first or last time Lee Brown of Newark, New Jersey would use a false identity. When he was not pretending to be Ram Singh, he sometimes posed as a Mexican man by the name of Ricardo Gonzales. Brown would later re-use this Mexican alias for his stage name, by which he is better known: Babs Gonzales.

While Gonzales's theatrics might have been funny, they weren't merely done for kicks. During the 1940s (and, indeed, before and after), it was difficult for African Americans to register at upscale hotels. Even in cities like New York and Los Angeles, blacks found themselves facing de facto segregation.

Conversely, had Lee Brown pretended to be Indian and tried to register at the hotel during the 1940s, he would also have been rejected as a guest. It was thus commonplace for lighter complexioned or non-ethnic-looking blacks to "pass for white" in order to bypass discrimination.

Babs was considered a comedian, of sorts, with his wild stage antics and clothing attire. "A lot of cats saw Babs as being a comedian," Sonny said. "Babs was a survivalist. Life was hard for a brother like Babs, and he knew how to work the system." Despite Gonzales's comedic acts, musicians and others respected his talent as one of the first scat singers who clearly understood the new experimental form of jazz called bebop.

In 1944, in the middle of World War II, young Gonzales was troubled by the idea of enlisting in the American military. He had no

Illus. 15 - Bebop scat singer Lee Brown, a.k.a. Babs Gonzales, saw the potential of a young Sonny Rollins and helped him to get a recording date in 1949—launching his music career.

intention of joining the war effort. Why should he sign up to fight and possibly die for a country that was denying him basic rights? Why risk his life for a country where he couldn't even book a hotel room as an African American?

Gonzales knew he had to take a pre-induction physical before the military deemed him fit for service and part of that examination included psychiatric screening. The military at the time rejected homosexual recruits, accepting society's prevailing belief that homosexuality was a pathological illness.

Babs formulated a foolproof plan. When it came time for his physical, Gonzales asked his wife to curl his hair for him. She helped him paint his toes and fingernails red, then let him borrow a brassiere, which he stuffed with cotton. When Gonzales's mother saw him dressed up, she nearly fainted. "Why are you doing this?" she asked.

"Why should I go to the army? Why should I fight for America? It's not my war," he replied.

The military didn't even bother to give him an examination and sent him straight to the psychiatrist. Gonzales, who clearly had a penchant for drama, flirted with him.

However, there was another side to the man: he recognized true talent. That aspect of Babs Gonzales's personality led to his assistance in launching the career of Sonny Rollins. Babs was instrumental in articulating the new jazz style called bebop. The music was deadly serious, but Babs gave it an element of humor. Like Sonny, Babs' approach to jazz had a sardonic edge informed by issues of racial and social justice.

There was a musician's union recording strike between 1942 and 1944, so many early bebop pioneers were not allowed to record during this time. Babs was nonetheless active during this time and had developed a credible reputation among many fans and musicians.

Although Gonzales had enjoyed success in the 1940s, he was still struggling professionally and financially. "Every time I ate, I would leave the waiter or waitress a fifteen-cent tip. Upon leaving, I could hear them murmuring, 'le cheap ass Babs, his records are on all the jukeboxes, and he's supposed to be big, and leaving a lousy fifteen cents,'" he wrote in his memoir, *I Paid My Dues.*

In late 1948, Gonzales was approached by Capitol Records. "This was their time to cash in on the Bop movement," he wrote. "The next day, I visited their office and signed a one year's contract. Soon as I got back uptown, I told all the cats about the fresh bread at Capitol…I wanted to try something different, so I went into rehearsal with a nine-piece group…"

One of the members of the new lineup, wrote Gonzales, was "a new cat from my block uptown, Sonny Rollins, on tenor." Sonny was still in his teens, having only graduated from high school in 1947. Although he had studied with the likes of Thelonious Monk and had performed in his own band, his gig with Babs Gonzales would be his first professional recording.

They began recording in January 1949, putting out *Professor Bop, Capitolizing, Prelude to a Nightmare,* and *A Lesson in Bopology.* Under the wing of his new record company, Gonzales—and "the new cat" on the tenor sax—were on the road to success. "Babs was cool with me," remembered Sonny, who viewed him as one of his mentors. "I did my first recording with him, and looking back, we have to admire how the brothers fought to get a piece of the action back in those days."

In March of 1949, J. J. Johnson, the first jazzman to get bebop out of a trombone, hired Sonny as a sideman for his quintet. He would play at a recording date for Savoy. It was the first time Sonny was recorded and, in that session, he got off one of his earliest originals. A month later, Sonny would work again with J. J. and Babs, this time on a Capitol record. A session at Blue Note Records saw Sonny recording with Fats Navarro and Bud Powell. That year, Sonny would also travel with Babs to a number of shows in Montreal and elsewhere.

While Babs may have helped launch Sonny's career, his legacy is somewhat shaky in the jazz world. On one hand, some critics have noted he was an early pioneer of vocalese, a singing style in which words are added to musical recordings that were originally instrumental. However, some have dismissed him for his theatricality and his middling vocal talent.

Others, like the late television journalist Gil Noble, saw both Babs' merits and shortcomings. "[Babs] was a hustler, he was a wordsmith. He was clever. He wasn't much of a musician, but he was very clever," Noble said.

While Babs was considered a hustler and a mediocre singer by many jazz aficionados, he nonetheless expressed the mindset of many bebop musicians. Most of them were extremely eccentric and even outcasts in society. What distinguished them from many other people outside of the norm was that they were geniuses.

After his stint with Babs, Sonny's career continued to take off. He recorded with Bud Powell and Fats Navarro on *The Amazing Bud Powell* and with J.J. Johnson later in 1949. But, as Sonny began to make a name for himself on the jazz scene, he further delved into drugs. He soon became a full-fledged junkie.

According to trumpeter George Brown, Sonny's drug habit nearly turned fatal. "One day," he recalled, "Sonny had overdosed, and I had to revive him. He was greedy, and when he took off, he passed out. I walked him. I wouldn't let him lay. I got him up and put some cold towels on him and kept him moving. This was in 1949."

A year or two after Sonny's reported overdose, he helped Bud Powell through a similar ordeal. In the early 1950s, Powell came to Sonny in bad shape. He was strung out and needed a fix desperately.

Powell, Sonny recalled, had been arrested by the cops and beaten in jail. He had had nervous breakdowns ever since then—every now and then he would be absent from the jam sessions, his latest mental collapse having placed him in an institution.

"We went to an apartment building on 147th Street between Seventh and Eighth," Sonny later remembered. "We went up to the roof to shoot up."

Powell's tolerance for heroin had declined during his time in the institution, and the shot he'd taken was too much for his body to handle.

"He passed out on me. I thought I had killed him," Sonny recalled. As he hovered over his friend's unconscious body, he was petrified. Perhaps, deep in his subconscious, Sonny knew he needed to call upon a force greater than himself.

"I was praying and sweating bullets, and I'm telling you, man, there's a God in my life. God spoke to me and came to me and helped him to revive because I was praying, you dig? *God, please don't let this happen! Please make him all right! I am sorry! Please forgive me!*" he remembered thinking.

Reliving that harrowing time years later, Sonny reflected, "It's easy to turn to God in your life when you're in trouble, but the point is to keep God in your life when you're not in trouble. That's where it's at. But, anyway, thank God he survived."

The overdose barely slowed down his descent into addiction—skag had become his demon companion, and he was strung out much of the time.

Meanwhile, other jazz musicians were noticing Sonny's demise. Max Roach reportedly began to tell young musicians new to the New York jazz scene to avoid two people: Charlie Parker and Sonny Rollins.

You realize how many talented black peoples' lives get wasted. They have some brilliant brothers in there, man. I mean these cats, if they were white, could have been president of the United States. Once you get into that syndrome of going to jail, it is bad news.

— SONNY ROLLINS, ON PRISON

CHAPTER 11

The Pokey

H is face was gaunt. His eyes were glassy. And his voice and gun-toting hand trembled nervously as he demanded money from the smoke shop clerk. "I want it all from the cash register," the robber, a hardcore junkie, shouted repeatedly. "Give it up!"

At jazz clubs, Sonny was hailed as one of the most prodigious new tenor saxophonists on the scene. But that night, he was a 19-year-old heroin addict attempting robbery to support his drug addiction.

Sonny was not alone. Scores of other jazz musicians, especially beboppers, turned to crime to support their habits. There was a consensus, at the time, that heroin was a special substance that would help musicians perform with the same miraculous agility as their bebop founder and guru Charlie Parker.

Many musicians of the time accepted drugs as a part of the jazzman's life, quick fixes that, they said, "put the bop in bebop." Hanging out with these peers and living jazz all the way, Sonny was quickly absorbed into drug culture. He was into pot by the age of 15.

By the time he was 17 or 18, he was snorting coke and shooting heroin to emulate his idol.

Jazz's fans caught on too, and quickly jumped onto the dope train, launching an epidemic that spread across the nation. These excesses gave the jazz scene a lurid reputation, which only made it all the more fascinating for the hip, rebellious youth of the post-World War II years.

At first, it was only pot's mellow buzz that flowed sweetly with the weaving notes as the jazzmen drifted onto the stage in a cloud of musical and aromatic bliss. As Sonny remarks, that buzz soon became a constant search for a new high.

His straight, church-going sister was at first unaware of the depths of his addiction. "I was going to work, and I had my own little church-affiliated life, and it was like a different world," Gloria said. "I was sharing a room with my brother and didn't know he was on drugs until he was in jail. I felt guilty. I always feel like I should have noticed."

Sonny had graduated to coke and skag when playing gigs, backing musicians who were also users. He would shoot up before playing clubs in Harlem, as well as during his countless jam sessions with other jazzmen. Those gigs didn't mean much money—even when he was pulling down bigger gigs and making recordings, there was very little to go around. Musicians were often stiffed by club owners, booking agents, and concert managers; sometimes they were paid directly in pot or skag.

Young jazzmen, floating in their magic cocoon of sound, often didn't consider the second word in "show business." Sonny was so broke he once played a recording session using a coat hanger and rope for a neck strap. "During that year and the next year, I really got messed up," he recalled. "I was fucked up. That's when I had my experience with the penal authorities when I went to Rikers Island.

"I got into [drugs] strongly just after I got out of high school in 1947, I think," Sonny said.

A friend named Donald remembered that around this time, "There was one particular girl that I used to see Sonny with all the time, that was Holly." Holly and Sonny did drugs together, and she turned tricks to support her habit. Later, Holly's daughter, a young woman named

Suzanne, would claim that Sonny was her father.

Scarcely out of his teens, Sonny subscribed to this nefarious gospel of high living and rampant drug usage. By the time he was aged 20, he was a certified heroin addict performing under the false assumption that heroin, not his own talent, was the source of his brilliance. At the time, many musicians and music critics were saying he was the heir apparent to Parker. Other musicians who were members of the heroin club included bebop founders Bud Powell, Max Roach, Miles Davis, and Thelonious Monk, the pianist and composer who became Sonny's close friend and mentor.

Sonny was so enamored with these musicians he would, like them, take drastic steps to obtain money to support his habit. Even at home, he routinely stole money and other items from family members.

"We knew my brother was a user, but we didn't suspect he was stealing stuff from our apartment until we began to see more and more things missing," said Sonny's sister Gloria. His mother didn't suspect what Sonny had gotten into until items began disappearing from the house. Electrical appliances and Gloria's nice clothing had gone missing—easy objects to pawn, a way to pay for the next hit.

Gloria remembered, "Someone told my mother that she should count her spoons because different spoons were missing. It meant that he was probably doing drugs. "She was devastated," added Gloria. "It was so bad.

"With looks of confusion, we both asked, 'Well, what does that have to do with it?'" They didn't know then that users would place the powdered heroin on the spoon and light a match under it. The process would melt the heroin so they could shoot it directly into their veins—as dope users do to this very day.

The eternal quest for the skag high had first landed Sonny in Manhattan's Men's House of Detention. The building's grimy, monolithic stone facades had earned it the name, "the Tombs." The Tombs still squats beside the Criminal Court on Centre Street in Lower Manhattan's Foley Square.

In early 1950, Sonny was busted for attempting armed robbery with an acquaintance.

"I think there was one other cat there," Sonny said. "I remember his name, but I don't want to use it. He passed a long time ago, but he was the one who actually coerced me. He was older than I was, but I'm not blaming him. I'm not saying that. He wasn't a musician, but he hung around musicians. I ended up with the gun, so I got busted.

"We were going downtown, and there was a place he had cased where we would go, some kind of a store. We were all strung out at the time. It was in midtown in the 40's, around that time. I mean, the whole thing is so [murky]. If it had been more well-thought-out, we might have pulled it off."

Although he hadn't been the mastermind behind the plan, Sonny had been the one holding the gun when the police apprehended them, so he was sent to jail instead of his accomplice. Sonny was convicted on a charge of armed robbery and sentenced to a one-to-three-year term on Rikers Island, one of the most notorious prisons in the country.

"We were all heartbroken when we heard he had been arrested," said Gloria. "My mother was devastated. She was very close to Sonny, and he loved her, too. We also embarrassed our neighbors because we were solid members of our Sugar Hill community."

"One to three on Rikers meant one year in prison and two years' probation," Sonny said. "I did what they called a 12-10, which meant, if you didn't get in any trouble there, you get out in ten months instead of 12. I did ten months."

Upon his arrival at Rikers, Sonny was tripped up by a guard as he entered the facility. "I know who you are. You're no star in here. You're just like all the other cons in here. When you break the rules, we will break you," the guard warned.

Other officials at Rikers did not feel the same. Unlike most of the other prisoners, Sonny was well-bred, articulate, and diplomatic. He had a street edge, to be sure, but he also possessed a certain quiet, elegant charisma that distinguished him from other prisoners.

Observed Art Taylor, his childhood friend and drummer in his first band: "Sonny was always tough as nails, but he had that special thing that others didn't have. He was deep and reflective. I guess you could say he even had a spiritual quality at that young age."

The warden agreed, and assigned Sonny to work in the prison chaplaincy.

It was also in prison that Sonny began to see the value of being reclusive. "Being behind bars was no walk in the park," he said. "But it enabled me to think a lot and reflect on my past misdeeds and on my future."

Many prisoners at Rikers were staunch Christians. At the time, more than 75 percent of African Americans were Baptists, AME, Methodists or members of other Christian faiths. Some were members of the Nation of Islam, which had a dominant presence because of their sometimes rigid, strict disciplines. At the time of Sonny's incarceration, another inmate at another prison was a fellow by the name of Malcolm Little, later to be known as Malcolm X.

"Despite its reputation for being anti-white, the Nation enjoyed a certain amount of credibility among blacks," recalled Taylor, who was himself a drug user then. "The Nation was one of only a handful of organizations that could successfully take the monkey off the backs of the brothers who were addicted."

Rikers Island is located in the East River between the boroughs of Queens and the Bronx. On over 400 acres sits the infamous Rikers Island Prison, one of the biggest prisons and mental institutions in the world.

An estimated 85 percent of prisoners held on Rikers have not actually been convicted of a crime. Many are there merely because they couldn't pay bail. The other 15 percent are serving short sentences for their crimes. An overwhelming number of prisoners are people of color.

When Sonny Rollins was at Rikers, though, there was little media attention on the prison, and there were no social media or blogs by which activists and other concerned citizens could call attention to abuses in the prison. Once they passed the front gates of the prison, Sonny and other inmates of the era were on their own, and a Dante-esque "Abandon hope all ye who enter here" attitude prevailed.

Sonny soon discovered drug use was rampant at the prison. Instead of kicking the habit, he continued using heroin, marijuana, and other drugs. "Rikers didn't help my problem, it made it worse," he recalled. "I was lost. If it hadn't been for my music and my sense of spirituality, I think I would have fallen off the deep end."

Even while surrounded by hardened criminals, rapists and murderers, he said he always felt a sense of deep spirituality rooted in his childhood. Unlike many other prisoners, who came from broken homes, Sonny relied on the stability of his strong family to help him endure prison life.

Though Sonny's mother was devastated by the turns her son's life had taken, she was still a rock of support. "At the point I went to Rikers I had been so strung out that I had sort of alienated a lot of people," Sonny said.

"I had alienated my father, who was beginning to come around a lot more often. He was really down on me, so it was really my mother who stuck by me." Valborg and Gloria visited him, riding the prison bus out to the forbidding island.

His music also helped to save him. His status as a recorded musician earned him respect from other inmates. "I had gotten on the map, in a way of speaking." There were other jazzmen there too, including tenor saxophonist Dexter Gordon and pianists Elmo Hope and Randy Weston. "I was in the band over there. It was better for me than the average person."

As musicians, Sonny and the others were recruited to play hymns in the Protestant chapel, with instruments provided by the Salvation Army. "We would play for Sunday church, play religious music. It wasn't too fancy. It was Western style. It wasn't too black. I played tenor and transcribed the music. So, the musicians were able to do their thing while in the Protestant Chapel. It wasn't as bad as it could have been. The only praying I did was to get out of there."

Despite the rough atmosphere, he did a lot of reading and praying, saying, "It was the isolation at Rikers that helped me realize the power of God and spirituality."

Prison, he said, is a very enlightening experience, "because you realize how many talented black peoples' lives get wasted. They have some brilliant brothers in there, man. I mean these cats, if they were white, could have been president of the United States. Once you get into that syndrome of going to jail, it is bad news."

The time in Rikers Island passed quickly. He was released after only ten months of his sentence, and it was time for Sonny to return to jazz.

He was back on the street in 1951, and he was raring to go. The time in the pen had only served to whet his already tremendous appetite for jazz. Before his incarceration, Sonny had begun to establish a reputation as the new jazz saxophone star—someone to watch, since his playing was refreshing, dynamic, and original.

He had not only mastered the language of bebop, he demonstrated to the jazz world that it was possible, though difficult, to use it as a springboard to create other styles.

He soon hooked up with Miles Davis, a frequent partner of his at the Minton's jam sessions. It was after one of these sessions that Miles proposed a collaboration.

"After I came down from playing," Sonny recalled, "Miles came up to me and said, 'Look, man, come on and join my band.' Just like that, and that was the beginning of a beautiful friendship."

In January 1951, they recorded together for the first time, creating a lovely blend of sounds on "Whispering." Miles, who had previously recorded for Capitol Records, had joined Prestige by then.

Miles then approached the owner of the label, Bob Weinstock, and urged him to give Sonny a chance for a solo flight. The result was "I Know." Pianist John Lewis had already left the session to play with Lester Young at Birdland, so Miles Davis provided the rather spare piano accompaniment.

Miles opened many doors for Sonny, and they had another thing in common—skag. In those days, they hung out with Jackie McLean, Kenny Drew, Walter Bishop, Art Taylor, and Bud Powell, all of whom would shoot up between sessions. Despite the heroin, the jazzmen were still soaring musically. "They could all play their asses off," as Miles used to say.

The bebop that ruled the 1940s was lively and experimental. Soloists piped fast and free-wheeling, creating airy arcs of trumpet and sax. Yes, there was a defiance in bebop, but the music was just as much of an expression of individual creativity, a breaking of the rules that had held jazz together in previous decades. It was a high-spirited, rule-breaking style. Its detractors called it chaotic.

But, by the end of the decade, things were beginning to change. A new group of young musicians had entered the picture—Sonny being one of them. While Sonny had neither served in the war nor gone to college, many of his new peers had done both, returning from overseas to an education sponsored by the G.I. Bill. Where the beboppers were defiantly individualistic, these new cats were militantly so. They had seen Europe, had dated women interracially, had been given equal rights during their time in the military. To return to America was to come back to a deeply racist society—and the vets were mad as hell about it.

Influenced by this boiling sense of injustice, a new sound began to emerge in jam sessions and jazz clubs. It was smoother than bebop, more concerned with conveying emotion than with pushing the boundaries of music. The once free-wheeling solos grew tighter and fiercer, bubbling with anger, demanding attention from listeners and critics alike. The new style was called hard-bop, or post-bop, and it would continue to simmer and seethe for the rest of the 1950s.

About a month after his first recording date with Miles Davis, Sonny joined him again for a gig at Birdland. Jackie, Kenny, Art Blakey, and Percy Heath rounded out the group. Miles would later tell a story about that night—Jackie left the bandstand, went outside, puked his guts out into a garbage can, then came back in and "played his ass off." In June, Sonny played another gig at Birdland with Miles.

Sonny was still recording as a sideman. In October there was another recording session with Miles, this time accompanied by Jackie McLean, Walter Bishop on piano and Art Blakey on drums. That get-together produced "Out of the Blue" and a nice jam off of Harold Arlen's "It's Only a Paper Moon." The album was called *Miles Davis All Stars* or sometimes just *Dig*.

At twenty-one, the world of Sonny Rollins was still on a high-low trajectory. He had to borrow a sax at one session and had to again use a coat hanger for a neck strap at another. He was still shooting up skag before his sessions, and yet his music was soaring. Bob Weinstock was so impressed by the "I Know" number Sonny had recorded in January that he offered the tenor man a Prestige recording contract. In December of 1951, Sonny, no longer a sideman, led his first session.

There were no squeaks or harsh notes coming out of his horn now. Instead, the tenor sax blew with a strong, mature sound, lifting "Time on My Hands," "This Love of Mine" and "On a Slow Boat to China." That session also produced "Shadrack," as well as Sonny's own composition, entitled "Mambo Bounce," one of the first tracks on which he would bring the influence of his Caribbean ancestry to bear on his music.

The devil of drugs was still dogging Sonny, as well as Miles and most of the other jazzmen in their circle. They were musical titans at Birdland and in the studio, but on the street they were specters, broke and busted, doing anything to get their next heroin fix. In those years, the scourge of skag ran through the ranks of jazzmen like smallpox or the bubonic plague. It savaged Bird, Miles, Sonny, and countless others—and that list would soon include a rising tenor sax star named John Coltrane.

The jazzmen's dependence on dope led to a number of miserable routines. It was commonplace for soloists to hock their horns to get heroin, forcing them to borrow other players' instruments. Davis and Parker went through several periods where they had to use other horns because theirs were in pawn shops. Sometimes, musicians hocked the borrowed instruments, too. Miles once borrowed Art Farmer's horn, and Farmer waited at the bandstand after the session to get it back from him, fearing he would pawn it.

Charlie "Bird" Parker was so strung out he often stiffed his musicians, keeping the money to buy skag. Davis, who studied boxing—and later claimed that Sugar Ray Robinson's discipline helped him to finally beat drugs—physically threatened Bird on more than one occasion to get his share of the money. Davis finally quit the band, calling Bird a great musician but a terrible person.

For now, the jazzmen were sailing together on their skag cloud and their riffs.

Miles played the Audubon Ballroom that year—the venue that was made famous years later when Malcolm X was murdered there. Davis didn't use Jackie McLean for that gig, possibly because he was too strung out. Instead, he matched Sonny with another young tenor man, John Coltrane. Sonny was "awesome that night," Miles reported. He "scared the shit" out of Trane, who soon retreated to Philadelphia—but it would not be the last time the two saxophonists went head-to-head.

Though Sonny's career was reigniting, it would again be sidelined by jail time in 1952. "I went back to Rikers. I was on parole, and I was strung out again," Sonny said. "I had to go back on parole violation. [At] that point, I was like a hoodlum."

CHAPTER 12

Hard Bop: The Sequel

Sonny Rollins had his work cut out for him—literally. After being discharged from Rikers Island at the age of 23, he faced a round of formidable obstacles: the monkey of heroin addiction still on his back, transitioning into regular life as an ex-con, and simply (or not so simply) being a young black man trying to survive on the mean streets of the Big Apple.

Although he had been freed from prison a second time, he felt the need to be more spiritual since he had rejected Christianity as his faith. "It was a very confusing period in my life," he said. "I was searching for something, but I didn't know where to find it. Music became my thing."

Sonny had another obstacle that was equally difficult—cutting (or outplaying) other cats on the tenor saxophone. Competitive and street-tough, he had successfully built his reputation cutting older and younger cats in the clubs in Harlem—proving he was the new force to be reckoned with.

Illus. 16 - Bassist Percy Heath, who was one of the most respected of bebop pioneers, created controversy when he hinted that Sonny Rollins may be on par with Charlie Parker. Many musicians and fans contended that no one could compare to the genius of Parker.

Some of the older masters of the tenor saxophone included Coleman Hawkins, Chu Berry, Lester Young, Gene Ammons, Ben Webster, Yusef Lateef, Don Byas, Jimmy Heath, and Dexter Gordon. Among the talented new arrivals were Hank Mobley, Benny Golson, Frank Foster, Stan Getz, Harold Land, Joe Henderson, and John Coltrane, who would be among Sonny's greatest challengers.

Sonny's success was based largely on his technical prowess, alluring phrasing, and tone, but what distinguished his sound was its originality and his ability to go beyond merely cloning the older masters. At one point, he became so prodigious even many of the old-timers felt threatened by his dexterity.

One of the questions raised by fans and the cognoscenti in 1953 was how could Sonny and the new generation of bebop musicians create valid extensions of the music, instead of merely copying it? Would hard bop be a valid sequel to the bebop that emerged in the 1940s?

Although Sonny was one of the pivotal figures in the creation of hard bop—also known as post-bop—would his talents allow him to carry on the legacy of the trailblazers?

Bassist Percy Heath, who was one of the founders of bebop and a key figure in hard bop, believed the younger players succeeded in carrying on the legacy. He said many of the hard boppers rose to the same levels of artistry as their bebop forebears.

According to Heath: "The young cats were terrific. Their playing was superior. They understood the concept of the music that was laid out by the founders. They were great composers, too. But what was more significant was that they created a vibrant, exciting new style of jazz that would endure."

Despite being constantly plagued by his drug addiction and other personal problems, Sonny was arguably the unofficial leader of the hard boppers. To use a cliché, he was a musician's musician, and both younger and older players asserted that "he was the man."

"I'm not saying that Sonny was a better player than Bird, but when I first heard them play together, I was shocked and confused over which one was the best," recalled Heath. "Sonny actually held his own and stood up to Bird, which was rare for other acts to do. They were afraid of Bird, but Sonny wasn't at all."

During this period, Sonny recorded with Parker, Heath, who was part of the Modern Jazz Quartet, Miles Davis, Parker, and Thelonious Monk, but he did not make a name for himself until his recordings in 1954 with Horace Silver, a dynamic newcomer who successfully carried on the complex legacy of pianist Bud Powell.

Parker was not Sonny's only threat. There was another daunting and competitive tenor saxophonist lurking about—John Coltrane, who was making waves and challenging Sonny's new reign. Trane, as he was called, played with a similar ferocity and aggressiveness.

By 1954, Sonny and Trane had emerged as the two key leaders of the so-called post-bop or hard bop movement, which was led in part by Hawkins and Thelonious Monk.

Other young Turks during the early 1950s included Clifford Brown, Horace Silver, Barry Harris, Tommy Flanagan, Pepper Adams, Philly Joe Jones, Art Taylor, Kenny Drew, Kenny Dorham, and Paul Chambers. Like Sonny and Trane, they were also competitive and believed in perpetuating the practice of cutting.

These were young men who demonstrated that while they could not necessarily outplay the old masters of bebop—Parker, Dizzy Gillespie, Fats Navarro, Bud Powell, Kenny Clarke, Miles Davis, Max Roach, Art Blakey, Monk, and Hawkins—they were, at least, on a similar footing.

Horace Silver worked briefly with Getz before moving to New York in 1951. He was soon in demand as an accompanist, working with leading jazz musicians like the saxophonists Coleman Hawkins and Lester Young.

In 1953, Silver and the drummer Art Blakey formed a cooperative group, the Jazz Messengers, whose aggressive style helped define hard bop, and whose lineup of trumpet, tenor saxophone, piano, bass, and drums became the standard hard-bop instrumentation.

Paul Chambers was born in Pittsburgh in 1935 and was raised in Detroit, where he began taking lessons with a bass player in the Detroit Symphony. Chambers cut his teeth on the baritone horn and

Illus. 17 - Pianist Horace Silver and Sonny Rollins were among the heirs of the bebop movement. They were responsible for creating so-called "hard bop" during the early 1950s.

later mastered the tuba.

He came to New York at the invitation of tenor saxophonist Paul Quinichette, touring with him and other musicians before joining the Miles Davis quintet in 1955. In great demand as a session musician, Chambers was admired for his skill in playing chromatic notes in the bass lines. Heroin addiction and alcoholism led to his premature death of tuberculosis at 33, in 1969.

The hard bop genre (sometimes called funky hard bop) that Sonny dominated in the 1950s was a phrase coined by pianist John Mehegan, the jazz critic for the *New York Herald-Tribune*. It incorporated influences from a variety of sources, including blues, gospel, and rhythm and blues.

In his 1992 study *Hard Bop: Jazz and Black Music 1955-1965,* David Rosenthal argues "the mood of the music is far darker than in bebop." To make his point, Rosenthal quotes Leonard Feather's liner notes for some of Miles Davis's recordings in the mid-1950s: "Davis's solos seem to reflect the complexity of the neurotic world in which we live. The soaring spurts of lyrical exultancy are outnumbered by the somber moments of pensive gloom."

In his magisterial study, Rosenthal also quotes a long interview by A. B. Spellman about the role of Sonny Rollins in the hard bop movement. "Sonny influenced everybody uptown," Spellman recalled, "playing every instrument."

After a 1955 session, he wrote Sonny "shows a marked increase in authority, twisting the tune out of shape, reinventing it with surprising hesitations and rhythmic displacements, slowing things down to half time, returning to the theme, punctuating angular runs with gutsy cries delivered in a searing tone, fragmenting and reassembling his materials in the course of eccentrically accented up-tempo flights, and topping it all off with a throaty cadenza."

Such were the origins of the new generation's love affair with hard bop, which garnered national attention at the Newport Jazz Festival, which had its debut in 1954. As much as Davis, Sonny, and others admired the Birdland scene, they knew they needed to break new ground using music forms that had a broader appeal, such as gospel and R&B. Hence the birth of the Jazz Messengers, avatars of a new style for new audiences.

This generational shift is key to understanding the origins of hard bop in the mid-1950s, a period that saw the rapid acceptance of rock 'n' roll by white audiences. Seasoned jazz critics often did not anticipate other potential giants waiting in the wings—Miles Davis, Max Roach, Horace Silver, Clifford Brown, John Coltrane, and Barry Harris—who would replace the founding generation of jazz musicians, or at least pay tribute to them by incorporating the founders' contributions in their new creations.

"A lot of the cats didn't believe that someone could come along and challenge Bird," said Percy Heath, a bassist who had worked with Parker, Gillespie and who later became an original member of the famed Modern Jazz Quartet.

Referring to Sonny's 1959 Blue Note album, *Newk's Time*, Heath said: "I'm not saying that Newk was better than Bird. That was almost impossible for other saxophonists to achieve, but when I heard both of them play on the same set at the same time, I was pleasantly surprised that Newk stood his own against Bird."

Sonny was called Newk because of his resemblance to Don Newcombe, the nickname for the major league baseball pitcher for the Brooklyn (later Los Angeles) Dodgers.

Sonny had been privately tutored by Monk, Powell, and others in his Harlem neighborhood, but his real training came when he and other teenagers stood outside of Minton's in Harlem and other fabled jazz clubs on West 52nd Street in midtown Manhattan.

These other post-boppers included drummer Art Taylor, pianist Kenny Drew and alto-saxophonist Jackie McLean, who all lived in Sonny's neighborhood. In the 1940s, they couldn't get into the clubs because they were minors and several years younger than their bebop pioneers.

Sonny made several recordings over the next two years, including one under his own name with the Modern Jazz Quartet, as well as with Davis, Art Farmer, and Thelonious Monk. The Miles Davis recording *Bags' Groove* happened during the summer of 1954 and included three pieces that Sonny wrote: "Airegin," "Oleo," and Doxy."

In October of that year, Sonny made a sizzling studio recording with bassist Tommy Potter, his childhood chum Arthur Taylor as drummer, and Thelonious Monk as pianist. The result was a critically acclaimed rendition of several jazz standards, including "The Way You Look Tonight," "I Want to Be Happy," and "More Than You Know." It was arguably one of Sonny's best sessions to date, but he felt he had burned himself out in New York.

That winter, Sonny headed to Chicago. In a 1993 article, Bill Beuttler describes how a penniless Sonny learned the art of survival from a fellow-junkie trumpet player named Little Diz. "I was in bad shape," Beuttler quotes Sonny as saying, "sleeping in used car lots, riding the subway all night. I used to ride the CTA [Chicago Transit Authority] all the way out to the end of the line and back, this kind of stuff. In those days we called it 'carrying the stick.' That was our euphemism for not having any place to stay, and that came from the old days—they used to have the cartoons of a bum."

It was time for Sonny to make some radical changes. His next stop after Chicago would be the United States Narcotic Farm in Lexington, Kentucky.

CHAPTER 13

Narco

The monkey—quickly and without warning—latched onto Sonny Rollins' back. It wouldn't let go. It dug deep into his spine, his stomach, then his entire body. His only relief was to shoot more heroin into his veins. It eased the suffering, but only temporarily.

By 1955, Sonny had become a certified junkie, and had fallen from grace. He managed to get a few music gigs here and there after moving to Chicago, but for the most part he had acquired a new profession—janitor. He was living hand-to-mouth. It was a pathetic situation for someone many musicians had once predicted would be Charlie Parker's heir apparent.

Sonny Rollins truly hit rock-bottom in 1955. He was mentally lost and had no other recourse but to check himself into the United States Narcotic Farm in Lexington, Kentucky, to seek a cure for his heroin addiction and his emotional problems. Called "Narco," the hospital was designed to explore ways to treat drug addiction and its consequences. The 1,000-acre farm, located in the lush hills of Kentucky horse

country, was a far cry from the rough and tumble Rikers Island jail in
New York City, where Sonny had been an inmate on two occasions for
drug abuse and armed robbery.

The original mandate of Narco was to treat people who voluntarily
admitted themselves with substance abuse problems in the hope of
receiving experimental treatments. Many patients were relatively
happy to become volunteers at Lexington rather than being forced to
serve harsh sentences at rigid federal penitentiaries that offered few, if
any, rehabilitation treatments.

Lexington was a research hospital as much as a rehab center. Some
of its former patients would volunteer for re-addiction—they were
compensated for the data they provided with cash and, occasionally,
morphine to use on their own time.

For four decades, the facility, which opened its doors in 1935,
became the mecca for patients of the country's growing drug subculture.
It attracted many famous clients, including jazz musicians and actors
George Brown, Dexter Gordon, Chet Baker, Howard McGhee, Al
Haig, and Peter Lorre, as well as drug-abusing doctors and criminals.
The conditions were stern, but not as rigid as regular prisons.

"It was truly a sad day to see my brother, who was so special to me
and my family, sink to such low levels," said sister Gloria Anderson.
"Of all people, we didn't think it would happen to Sonny. He was so
special growing up. He had so much potential and then he became a
different person after he became addicted."

His personality changed from what she called "a sweet loving
boy" into what police, club owners, and others called a "monster."
Max Roach, the drummer, reportedly told people to "stay away from
Sonny—he's dangerous."

During this period, thousands of jazz musicians and fans worldwide
died from heroin addiction, but the most famous of the casualties was
bebop star Charlie Parker, who died in New York on March 12, 1955
of medical problems related to his excessive abuse of heroin, alcohol,
and other substances. Sonny suffered deeply from Parker's death, not
just because he was his idol and friend, but because he died without
witnessing Sonny's cure.

Though he was an addict, Sonny was still quite aware of the world beyond his mean surroundings. That day in March, he read headlines in newspapers and heard on the radio that his idol, Charlie Parker, had died of his addictions. A headline that appeared on page one of the *New York Daily News* echoed the cry that legions of his fans and musicians across the globe reportedly uttered as a celebration of the bebop guru.

"Bird lives!"

Outstanding among these musicians was Sonny Rollins, whom Miles Davis called the greatest tenor saxophonist. Prior to Bird's death, he had admonished the young Sonny to stop using heroin and clean up his act.

"I remember Bird giving me this advice as clearly as anything," said Sonny. "He was not only my friend and was clearly the man who revolutionized our music. He influenced me and thousands of other musicians, not just saxophonists, but pianists, trumpeters, and others."

During a record date, Sonny recalled a conversation with Bird. "He knew that, about that time, I had been fuckin' up and all that. He asked me, 'Are you cool?' And I was like, 'Yeah, man.'"

But Bird knew Sonny was lying. Drummer Philly Joe Jones had told Bird he and Sonny had just gotten high at his house.

"I don't think he meant to do it, but ... Philly must have told him, 'Yeah, well, Sonny and I were over there getting high this morning.' I'm not laying anything on him because I don't even think he thought there was anything wrong with saying that. He knew I had lied to him," Sonny said.

"I could see by his reaction how much it meant to him to see people like me, followers of him using drugs ... the way it dragged him down. I think it [tormented him]. I believe that's one of the most troubling things of his life ... all these young cats following him, using drugs, because Bird knew that drugs were a trap.

"The man wasn't a fool. He knew that drugs weren't the right way to go, but he was so hooked, so whatever the reason and whether he completely wanted to get off or he couldn't get off, I don't know. But the fact was that he was using it and he was hooked on it, but he didn't want us to get hooked on it.

"He told me that heroin was not the reason he played so well, but that his ability came from his dedication and constant practice of his horn. A lot of the cats didn't understand what Bird was all about. They just thought that he loved getting high for the fun of it."

Years later, Sonny's nephew Clifton Anderson recalled, "He wrote my mother a letter when he was incarcerated in Lexington, which I have. He was telling my mother about Charlie Parker, who had just passed away. He was saying how the world doesn't understand the magnitude of the loss of Charlie Parker, and that he was very disappointed himself that he's incarcerated at this time, locked up, and that he can't mourn him publicly, in a way. Charlie Parker told him not to go down that road, and it was very clear that he was going to change himself, he was going to restore himself."

Before Sonny checked in to Lexington, he had become a physical and mental wreck. No one who saw him shuffling through the streets of Chicago could have imagined that the wraithlike figure was one of the jazz geniuses of his generation.

Sonny looked like a typical hopeless case, just another tall young black man slowly pushing a shopping cart through the streets. His speech was slurred, his eyes were sleepy, and his skin was flush from being out on the cold and windy streets of Chicago. Despite his broken look, Sonny was still handsome, sophisticated, and articulate when he interacted with the area's residents and passersby.

In the spring of 1955, Sonny boarded a train from Chicago that took him through the forests and hills of Appalachia to (what was then called) the U.S. Public Health Service Hospital in Lexington, Kentucky.

Narco was six miles outside Lexington, a 1,000-acre tract surrounded by seven miles of fence. The campus was composed of red brick and granite buildings, isolated by the gently rolling hills that sat on all sides.

Narco, they said, was "more like a hospital than a prison and more like a prison than a hospital." For Sonny, it was more like a hospital, because he was entering voluntarily. Those who were sent there by court order had to stick around until the treatment was over. The

Illus. 18 - The Federal Medical Center, Lexington was home to famous drug addicts, including Peter Lorre, Sammy Davis Jr., William S. Burroughs, William S. Burroughs Jr., and Ray Charles, as well as Sonny Rollins, who was cured there of heroin addiction.

voluntary patients, on the other hand, "had the keys in their hands" and could leave any time they wished. Sonny remembered what had happened to Bird and to Bud Powell, and was committed to stay for the full term—four-and-a-half months.

The long days of quiet seclusion changed Sonny's spiritual thoughts into monk-like contemplation. Lexington was his monastery—but a monastery for what? Sonny had his own idea of God, a God that watched over him, who had not forsaken him on that rooftop with Bud Powell. He had to find Him again, at Narco.

Sonny was not able to precisely say what type of God this was. He remembered going into churches and seeing "a big picture of this white Jesus Christ up there." He thought, "Hey, I mean, I'm not white, so is Jesus in Heaven going to be serving white men?"

Sonny was somewhat suspicious of Christianity as it was commonly practiced, and had his own take on the stories of the Bible. For him, Jesus was a human who came to enlighten us. "There are also other people in other ages who would fit the same description as Jesus Christ. I believe in what he stands for and the fact that he was an enlightened human being, but I don't believe necessarily that this was the end-all and be-all."

The problem with Christianity was its history—whites had once used Jesus Christ to control slaves. It was a double-edged agenda. On the one hand, it would bring the slaves out of the "hedonism" of their African traditions. On the other hand, Christianity was used to justify the kind of vile, inhuman slavery practiced in America—one of the worst forms it has ever taken.

Slavery had been practiced throughout history, but in other ages and cultures slaves were often integrated into the social structure and could buy their way out of it. American slavery, on the other hand, was highly segregationist, being based upon an ideology of racism. At the same time, slave-owners wanted to make their slaves "God-like"— by teaching obedience as one facet of Christianity, the owners could control their "property" in the name of Jesus Christ.

Sonny did not throw out Christ, nor did he throw out everything taught by Christianity. Yes, it had been used as a tool for evil reasons, and blacks had a lot to resent about that, but there was a grain of truth in there as well.

He would ponder his own spirituality, looking to find some place beyond Christianity and Jesus Christ. There were other religions, other paths to serenity and control. He had heard of a practice called yoga, a vehicle for both physical and spiritual health.

Eventually, the two weeks gave way to four-and-a-half months. Each day, sensation grew clearer. There was less pain, less nausea, and more and more hope in the possibility of a clean life. Before he knew it, Sonny was saying goodbye to Lexington.

Sonny Rollins walked out of Narco cured.

Illus. 19 - Not too long after getting out of Lexington, Sonny Rollins lived at the YMCA on South Wabash Street in Chicago's historic Bronzeville district. It was here (among other places) that he successfully fought the battle to stay clean from heroin.

CHAPTER 14

Peer Pressure

Sonny Rollins had been a champion street fighter on the mean streets of Harlem, but after Lexington, he now had a new, formidable opponent—staying clean from heroin addiction. The disease was like a relentless prizefighter who would get off the floor after going down and come back again to try to knock out his opponent.

What then would a highly vulnerable Sonny do to fight off this devil in a threatening new bout with heroin addiction—one that had killed his idol Charlie Parker, and thousands of other jazz musicians and fans across the globe?

The answer would simply be for him to leave the drug rehabilitation hospital in Lexington, Kentucky and head for Chicago.

Sonny went to Chicago, in part, because he was familiar with the city. He had spent time there several years earlier, when he played with such bands as Ike Day's, and was hailed as one of the great new tenor saxophonists on the scene. He was regarded as the heir apparent to the legacy of Coleman Hawkins and other pioneers on the instrument.

This time, Sonny went to the Windy City incognito to avoid going to the Big Apple, where he feared getting involved again with the same drug nest that played a role in getting him addicted in the first place.

Upon his arrival in late 1955, he faced yet another foe. While he had beaten his drug habit, he still faced the problem of racial discrimination, which was one of the main reasons so many black musicians and fans had turned to illegal narcotics. These drugs acted as their anti-depressants, or so many of them thought.

There were jive people out there, too, and Sonny couldn't deal with deception, not just now.

He did not consider himself a religious man in any formal sense, but there was a spiritual depth to him, a yearning for understanding and the strength to fight his own devil, to stand up to the temptation of the jive and skag that lurked in the depths of the city.

Sonny had taken a room at the Central Arms Hotel, where he slept restlessly, pondering how he was going to continue his life. He could not yet face New York, Harlem, or Swing Street, and even the South Side beboppers who were too great of a risk.

The next morning, Sonny went to the newsstand on the corner and picked up a copy of the *Chicago Tribune* to check out the classifieds. He would need a job, and it couldn't be in a club just yet. He needed more time. The club scene was potentially dangerous for someone trying to escape the perils of drugs.

Walking back to is his room, he passed a record store. There in the window was his quartet album with Thelonious Monk on display. He grunted. His past life and his present life, facing each other through a glass veil. Behind that pane was a musician, a somebody on his way towards fame and fortune—and here, on the sidewalk, was a man without direction. "That was tough," he later said of that time.

The classifieds listed the usual jobs for black men in the 1950s: assembly line worker, janitor, bellhop. Well, he couldn't be choosy now, and he took a job as a janitor in a typewriter repair shop. The pay was decent, and it would be a good hiding place, too. Later, he worked at another job loading trucks. It wasn't much, but it would keep him going until he was ready.

Sonny ultimately took a room at a YMCA on South Wabash Avenue, where he could live and also practice his saxophone. Sonny still had a loose-leaf notebook he had kept all through the time at Lexington. He continued to write notes to himself, assuring himself he was strong. He needed to be strong if he was going to overcome his drug addiction for good.

He spent his time "just working on things, individual things that I wanted to work on. I was always working on something, and I was also learning songs." He would never let go of the music, no matter what, drugs be damned. He didn't have the clubs, but he still had jazz. He wasn't going to give that up without a fight.

Despite his attempts to keep a low profile, word got around Sonny was in the city, out of Narco and into Chicago. He had known he couldn't hide forever, and after the solitude of the previous months, the new attention was something of a relief. He could jam now, instead of practicing by himself. "I remember rehearsing 'There's No Business Like Show Business' in the basement of the Y with trumpeter Booker Little," he recalled.

The rumor swept through Chicago like lightning.

"Sonny's back in town."

Inevitably, he was drawn to the South Side jazz clubs, the Sutherland, the Bee Hive, and the Blue Note—and with the clubs came the jive. "I was offered a scene, and I was trying to get myself strong so I could go back to the nightclubs, where I would encounter drugs," Sonny remembered. "So I went back to the clubs, and you know, of course, it was the usual."

Sonny was in pretty good physical condition after his stay at Narco. He had filled his notebooks, practiced at the Y, kept up, kept on moving. Musically, he was as strong as ever, maybe even more so now that he was clean.

But, when it came to the jive, the constant temptation to give in and shoot up, he was on shaky ground. No matter how much you told yourself to be strong when you were alone, it was always different when the needle was right in front of you.

"There was one night I was really wrestling with the devil," Sonny remembered. "Sweat was coming out of me because I knew God had everything there for me. The temptation was enormous. It was … really, maybe I could just take a little taste. And, 'Oh, man, you'd better not do that shit, man!' I was really rumbled. We were rumbling, right?"

But, he held off the devil. "I made it that night. I didn't get high. My better sense took over, but I was sweating and praying."

His spirituality had deep roots, but he didn't wear it on his sleeve. It was just as much a deeply personal dialogue with himself as it was a prayer. "I wasn't saying, 'God, please help me.' I wasn't saying it that way because I was in the club scene," he said.

"But that was behind it. I told myself not to do it. That was what was holding it up; the prayer was holding it up. I was really too involved with the scene, the nightclub scene and all that shit, so I didn't really invoke the name of God, but God was behind my being able to finally reject this temptation, 'cause it was strong."

The skag-spirit came back to haunt him on the following nights, too. But, Sonny had already jumped the first hurdle, and he knew he could stare the demon down. "The next time, there was another temptation, but not as strong. So, then I thought, 'I got you, motherfucker! I beat you!'"

Sonny's internal struggle had been monumental, but he had triumphed. It was a turning point in his life. "That was God-based," he would say later, "and God carried me through."

During those first few months out of Lexington, dueling with the devil, Sonny held fast and fought the fight, but he was still unwilling to plunge all the way back into the club scene.

The word of Sonny's return had reached Miles Davis and he came through Chicago with a marvelous opportunity, an offer to join his new quintet. Sonny wasn't ready for the thick of it yet, and he passed on Davis's offer.

Sonny's refusal was a break for John Coltrane—he would once again be the tenor man for Miles' band. But Coltrane had his own demons to wrestle with. Sadly, he was being drawn into the same skag-pit that Sonny had barely escaped. Yet another jazzman who would become cannon fodder for the devil.

CHAPTER 15

Ups and Downs

It was a frigid night in the Windy City, but it was even colder for the forlorn janitor named Sonny Rollins. Angry and bitter, he decided to put aside his mop and broom and head for a little warmth inside the Beehive, a hip and prominent bebop jazz club in the city's Hyde Park neighborhood.

It was late November 1955, a time that for most people was the joyful Thanksgiving-Christmas holiday season. For Sonny, however, it was a depressing time because he knew he had once earned in a night what he now made working an entire week cleaning offices and warehouses.

"I should be up there playing on the bandstand myself," he sighed to himself as he watched the hard-driving Clifford Brown/Max Roach Quintet play some of the most percolating and fascinating hard bop jazz sounds ever. The club was packed with well-dressed and hip-looking people, in contrast to the janitor's inelegant attire.

Suddenly, one of the customers looked at Sonny and shouted

out: "You look just like Newk—are you Newk?" he asked. The janitor quietly and reluctantly responded, "Yes, I am." At that point, others in the audience, as well as band members, turned to acknowledge him.

The newcomer was, indeed, Newk, a.k.a. Sonny Rollins, who appeared to be incognito. He looked far less confident and imposing than the tall, statuesque figure associated with the old prodigious image of Sonny Rollins.

Sonny's four-month stint at the Lexington drug rehabilitation hospital in Kentucky and his months of work cleaning toilets and doing other janitorial work had clearly changed his image, but they had certainly not altered his virtuosity as a jazz player. He was still Sonny Rollins, perhaps even better.

That night at the Beehive was a welcome acknowledgment for Sonny, who had been hiding in the shadows and struggling to avoid becoming a junkie again by living the life of a janitor. During this time, he struggled to make ends meet, but he was able to free himself from the fast-paced life of a popular jazz musician.

The night proved to be a lucky occasion for Sonny; Roach and Brown asked him to become a member of the band, and he immediately accepted. He would replace Harold Land, the tenor saxophonist who quit the band to return to Los Angeles because of family problems.

Sonny was elated about the offer to join the quintet, but he had hidden reservations about reentering the rat race. Much to his surprise, Clifford Brown, the trumpeter, dispelled his apprehensions. Clifford appeared to have been sent from heaven to help Sonny make his new transformation from janitor to superstar.

Sonny accepted Clifford's guidance because he was on par with other jazz trumpet trailblazers like Dizzy Gillespie, Miles Davis, and Fats Navarro. He also had credibility because he was clean cut, free of drugs and possessed high levels of spirituality.

The arrival of the Max Roach-Clifford Brown Quintet brought Clifford Brown (or "Brownie," as he was called) back into Sonny's life. "Brownie was an inspiration: here was a cat who could play a heavenly trumpet, and he had never even touched skag! Brownie didn't even drink.

"He had a tremendous impact on me," Sonny said. "He was clean living. That's what amazed me, definitely, because he was so clean and he played so much, and he was still straight. I had never really seen that. Every cat I knew that played got high. So this was a revelation to me. I said, hey, this kid is an angel, man.

"Brownie had something special, something beyond the norm, that made me respect and admire him," Sonny said. "He was one of my heroes."

Brown, who briefly attended Delaware State University as a math major before he switched to Maryland State College, was an intellectual who was able to discuss things other than music, women, and drugs. Although Sonny was himself an intellectual, he had only graduated from high school.

"Clifford had a deeply profound influence on both my professional and personal life," said Sonny. "I learned from him that you don't need dope to play superior music. He was my friend and my inspiration."

"They were out of this world," said writer Ahmed Basheer. "These young guys were so brilliant and fantastic that they proved that they had their own original sound. These cats didn't need to copy the older pioneers, which is what a lot of the young guys were doing at the time."

Illus. 20 - Sonny Rollins' life was turned around when he joined the Clifford Brown and Max Roach Quintet in the mid-1950s. (Left to right: Sonny, Brown, Richie Powell, and Roach.)

With Sonny replacing Harold Land, the dazzling Max Roach Quintet was born, a group to rival the band Miles was cooking up. Sonny's tenor sax and Clifford Brown's trumpet were backed by the dynamic trio of Max Roach on drums, George Morrow on bass and Richie Powell, Bud's brother, on piano. It was a group to build a dream on, and the college kids from the University of Chicago flocked to the Sutherland Lounge to hear them play.

When the combo left Chicago in November, Sonny went with them as a full member of the group. He was back in the jazz, and soon he would take it to new and incredible heights. Musician Paul Jeffrey recalled listening to Sonny perform with the Max Roach quintet in late 1955: "I heard the band with Max and I was just completely mesmerized. George Morrow on bass and Clifford and Richie Powell." Jeffrey was carried away by Sonny's saxophone.

"Having so many creative musicians playing in one band, particularly the front line, and being so compatible," he said, "I would say that Max's band was on fire every night. Sonny and Clifford ... that set the stage. A lot of people realized that the Max Roach band was, as far as I was concerned, much more an organized affair than Miles' band, because Miles was putting his band together."

Miles had wanted Sonny for his group, but Sonny didn't feel ready to return yet, so Davis went with John Coltrane instead. "Trane was going through some stuff, getting himself together," Jeffrey said. "Miles wanted Sonny. He didn't want Trane because nobody really knew about Trane. Trane had not had really that much impact, at that time."

Sonny, who projects a somewhat deceptive personality of being modest and humble, was just the opposite. He had already built a reputation of cutting other players on stage in his early days at clubs in Harlem. He could be brutal, competitive, and rarely took any prisoners.

In his autobiography, Miles Davis notes Sonny had once given John Coltrane a humiliating lesson at the Audubon Ballroom, sending the older tenorman scurrying back to Philadelphia.

But, Paul Jeffrey, who knew them both at that time, begs to differ. "Sonny, contrary to how the media tries to pit black people against each other, was a very good friend of John Coltrane. There was mutual respect and admiration, and I remember Trane saying once, when the guys were up at a house and listening to Sonny play, 'You know, when I play a tune, a tune that I know, I can play well. Sonny can play the most obscure tunes and play it like he wrote it.'"

Sonny's next Prestige session in May of 1956 would be called *Tenor Madness*, and it would feature the top tenor saxmen of the day. "When they talk about *Tenor Madness*," Jeffrey said, "that was Sonny Rollins' gig, and he asked Coltrane to play on it."

Critics have suggested these two titans were battling it out. They claim Sonny's approach to the saxophone forced Coltrane to alter his playing and, later on, Coltrane's new style forced a similar change in Sonny. The two blazing-hot saxophonists were contemporaries—and in the minds of the critics, comparisons couldn't be avoided. Trane had gotten aboard Miles' band when Sonny dropped out to head for Lexington. Later on, Sonny would replace Trane in a Miles Davis combo at Café Bohemia, when it was Coltrane's turn to kick the gong.

At the *Tenor Madness* session, Trane came out like a fighter plane, focusing all his efforts to match those of his younger friend. While it was a cordial exchange, Sonny was always competitive, always ready to take on challengers and cut them up. It might have been a friendly rivalry, but it was still rivalry. *Down Beat*'s Nat Hentoff, who had once lacerated Sonny for his approach to the old standards, gave Sonny the nod on this album, remarking that Trane was "pressing" while Sonny was compact. After the session, Trane would remark that Sonny was "just toying" with him.

Coltrane's success also came from being a member of the Miles Davis Quintet, which featured such players as Red Garland on piano, Paul Chambers on bass, and Philly Joe Jones on drums. Beginning in late 1955, the quintet made many of historic recordings—such as *Cookin'*, *Relaxin'*, *Workin'*, and *Steamin'*. The group disbanded in part because of Coltrane's heroin addiction.

On June 22, 1956, Sonny continued his flaming comeback. He was, once again, joined by Tommy Flanagan and Max Roach, on another Prestige album—this one would be called *Saxophone Colossus*, and the session matched its name. Many aficionados maintain *Saxophone

Colossus was Sonny's best recording and stands out among the greatest jazz recordings ever. Sonny was in total command of his instrument, stronger and free of any substances that may have hindered his performances in the past.

It would go on to be his most critically lauded album. "They say it was his best recording," Tommy Flanagan remarked. "He made a whole lot of best recordings." *Colossus's* five tracks included "St. Thomas," which took its name from his island roots, and "Strode Rode," a nod to the Strode Lounge in Chicago—located in the same hotel where Freddie Webster died of an overdose. "Blue 7," "You Don't Know What Love Is," and "Moritat" rounded out the recording.

For the first half of 1956, Sonny was at the peak of his success with *Saxophone Colossus* and *Sonny Rollins, Plus 4*. These recordings were among the best in jazz history, according to critics and fans. Sonny was catapulted in music polls worldwide as the top tenor saxophonist— although Coltrane and a few others were often in contention.

Though Sonny Rollins had found himself at the top of the jazz world, Fate was not through testing him. Driving home from a gig with Richie Powell the two were involved in an auto accident that smashed Sonny's already injured jaw.

"Sonny couldn't play, and I remember Charlie Rouse took his place. I went to the Apollo to hear Max and them, and Charlie had taken Sonny's place because Sonny had messed up his teeth in the accident. There were a lot of extenuating circumstances. The accident and, of course, the use of drugs also did something to his teeth," Paul Jeffrey said.

While his teeth would never stop him from playing, they would continue to plague him for years, causing him extreme pain and forcing him to change his playing style to compensate.

And there was to be another car crash that took an even greater toll, leaving him speechless and again in a state of depression. On June 26, 1956, four days after the *Colossus* session, Clifford Brown and his pianist Richie Powell were driving to Chicago for their next appearance when Powell's wife, Nancy, who was driving so both men could sleep, crashed the car. She was driving at night, in the rain, on

Illus. 21 - Clean-living trumpeter Clifford Brown wasn't just one of Sonny's bandmates, but a dear friend and a positive influence. Sonny referred to him as "an angel." Tragically, Brown (sometimes called "Brownie") died in a car crash in 1956, which devastated Sonny.

the Pennsylvania Turnpike. All three were killed.

The death devastated Sonny not just because of Clifford; Richie was Bud Powell's brother. Bud had been part of Sonny's close group of friends in Harlem. "It was one of the most difficult periods in my life," Sonny noted. "I will never get over it."

The stellar quintet that had rocketed Sonny to greatness was gone—it had soared for only little more than six months. For Sonny, the loss of Brownie, a constant encouragement in his fight against skag, was devastating.

But even this tragic event could not halt his meteoric rise. Life went on and Sonny's legend was growing. There were more recording sessions in 1956, including one with Max Roach, pianist Kenny Drew, and bassist George Morrow that would produce *Tour de Force*. He was about as hot as you could get, a man-about-town in New York, playing gigs at Cafe Bohemia and other Village clubs.

Sonny's new prestige earned him a decent income and the privileges that came with financial independence. Finally liberated from Sugar Hill and the room he shared with his sister, he moved downtown, into an apartment at 400 Grand Street on the Lower East Side. His new digs sat in a mostly Jewish neighborhood bordering on Little Italy.

It can be said that Sonny's life soared into overdrive. He was still tangoing with whiskey and pot, perhaps an inevitability in the fast-track jazz world of the mid-1950s.

Other things about the concert scene hadn't changed either, including the white groupies.

CHAPTER 16

Ladies' Man

The tall, handsome, sculpted man who looked like an Egyptian pharaoh was juggling more than his musical notes; he was also juggling women. His face looked ancient, as though it had been carved. His muscled body was visible under his clothes. Despite his unusual look, he was an imposing hunk.

After years of being in the doldrums, Sonny Rollins had emerged as arguably the top new tenor saxophonist in jazz. He was recording top-selling and award-winning albums. But he was also rising as a playboy, charming women from coast to coast.

While he was playing a gig in Ohio with Max Roach and Clifford Brown, he met a beautiful black model named Bonnie Jean Pleasant.

"I had a pretty close thing going with her," he said. "She came to New York after that."

Sonny's sister, Gloria, described her as "very, very nice. Just a lot of fun. My mother liked her a lot."

At one point, Sonny and Bonnie Jean were engaged, but the match would not last.

"I was sort of young and wild, and there was another white chick I was messing around with at the time," he admitted. "And [Bonnie Jean] happened to come by my house when this white chick was there. It kind of dashed her hopes, you know."

For many black jazz musicians, white women held a certain mystique, which Sonny described as a sort of "indoctrination."

"You know how I am about white women . . . When you're growing up, you get to think that the white beauty is Eden. It's not that it's necessarily always true, but it is just the way we have been brought up. So you know in a way you have that white fever, which I have to admit is indoctrination," he said.

Paul Jeffrey, a fellow tenor saxophonist, longtime friend, and professor, referred to it as "the forbidden fruit syndrome. Thelonious Monk said white women were the ones who knew more than the cats about what's happening. They knew this music must be something, because their husbands and boyfriends were done in by it. So they wanted to hang too."

According to Jeffrey, many black women had a different mindset when it came to dating musicians. "The musicians were considered bums because they didn't have jobs. Black society has always considered that musicians didn't have decent jobs, and they didn't respect the endeavor," he said, adding: "Even today, most white families encourage their kids with musical talent to go into music, even if they don't think it's a lucrative profession like being a lawyer. Most black families will not do that."

Needless to say, white women who dated black musicians in the 1950s were often scorned and ostracized by white society. "The white ladies were labeled 'groupies' by white society to denigrate them," said Jeffrey. "They were mad that they were even hanging with black people."

Not too long after Bonnie Jean, Sonny fell in love again with a famous black model. While performing in California, Sonny met Dawn Finney, a stunning 19-year-old model and actress. The tall, leggy, brown-skinned beauty had recently graduated from high school in Los

Angeles and had already graced the pages of *Jet*. In the next few years, she would appear on the cover of top black magazines like *Sepia*, which dubbed her "Hollywood's busiest starlet."

By the time he met Dawn, 26-year-old Sonny had already been toying with the idea of marriage. For nearly a decade, he had been enmeshed in the chaotic, decadent jazz scene, and marriage seemed like it could be the antidote to his turbulent personal and professional life.

"I thought of getting married and finding some stability," he said. Sonny decided to propose to his new girlfriend, who gladly accepted. They were married in California and returned to New York as husband and wife.

Not only was Dawn physically beautiful, she was a kind, caring, and refreshingly innocent young woman. Gloria described Dawn as a sweet, inexperienced girl who Sonny had married "out of her mother's house."

"I met her after they were already married, and I was at my mother's house when he brought her. She's just a sweet, beautiful girl. Really nice," Gloria recalled.

Dawn became the inspiration for "Sonnymoon for Two," a 12-bar blues song that appeared in *A Night at the Village Vanguard*. But, the "Sonnymoon" was short-lived. Their marriage was rife with problems, and the two would be divorced within the year.

Dawn was perhaps too green and too mild-mannered for the wild jazz scene. According to Gloria, she was unprepared to be the wife of such a famous musician. After all, Sonny was playing clubs at all hours, living in a world saturated with drugs, liquor, and other vices. "[Dawn's] idea of marriage was a nine-to-five job," Gloria said. Dawn thought Sonny should give up music, which was an impossibility. After all, he was a jazz king, a musician who would win the *Down Beat* critics' poll for 1957.

Dawn couldn't live in the jazz world—and that was the only place for Sonny to be. Sonny Rollins was certainly not interested in becoming the Ozzie to her Harriet, or the Ward Cleaver to her June. He was hardly the type of man who would ever be content with a desk job, pushing paper and punching a time card every day.

Perhaps more importantly, Dawn was a bit too beautiful and magnetic for her own good. Wherever they went—especially in jazz clubs—men would fawn all over her. Sonny became intensely jealous and started criticizing her.

Sonny recalled, in an angry tone: "Why are you flirting back at these men? You're making me look like a fool. They are totally disrespecting me, when they hit on you in front of me."

"Sonny, you're acting crazy. These men are not flirting with me. They admire me because they've seen me in magazines, on TV, and at public forums," she would tell him.

Sonny later said he was "too quick" to judge her and should have realized, since she was so attractive, it was inevitable men would hit on her. "It wasn't all Dawn's fault. I was a little paranoid myself. I was jealous of her, and I didn't realize it. She had a right to have people admire her because she was a star. I guess my problem was that I was a star, too, and it was like two engines in a train, pulling each other, no

Illus. 22 - Long before Sonny Rollins became a man of deep spirituality, he had a fondness for beautiful Hollywood starlets, such as Dawn Finney, whom he eventually married and divorced.

end in sight, so eventually we split up."

Dawn returned to California. Though she and Sonny kept in contact and remained friendly, he was heartbroken and haunted by the divorce for years to come. As he was reeling from his failed marriage, Sonny would soon meet another woman who piqued his interest. But, this time, the object of his affection was not a glamorous fashion model, but a Plain Jane, white secretary from the Midwest.

$\sim$

Lucille Pearson had not expected to fall in love that evening.

As far as she was concerned, it was simply a night out with friends at the Blue Note, a jazz club in Chicago's Loop. She had been invited by a black girlfriend, Pat Brown, with whom she worked at the Tuberculosis Institute.

Lucille was a Kansas City girl. She was reared as a Lutheran and had attended Catholic schools during her childhood. Kansas City was conservative and totally segregated—Lucille knew no black people and little about jazz. Even though she and Bird shared the same hometown, she had never heard of him, and had certainly never been introduced to his music.

In Chicago, she had come into contact with new people and new music. She got to know Pat Brown and some of the other blacks she worked with, and Pat introduced her to South Side jazz. "Pat Brown had heard Sonny before, because her husband, Herb, had once played with him in Chicago," said Lucille.

Now, the two co-workers were in The Loop, a basement club, listening to the blasting saxophone of this hunk on the bandstand. Lucille, who was out with a date, recalled, "I dug him, but didn't think much more about it then. I thought he was okay."

Gloria told a different story. Lucille had later admitted to Gloria that the performance by Sonny moved her. "She told me she saw Sonny and that was it. She had to have him."

In any event, Lucille was soon back at the Blue Note with Pat, looking to catch an eye from the star tenor-man. Sonny had flirted with her from the bandstand, the typical hip swaying and winking that cats did to warm up the groupies.

"Come on," Pat told her, "I'll introduce you," adding, "It's okay to get involved a little, but not too much. He's a musician." Like any celebrity, a jazzman was trusted to be fickle.

Pat led Lucille to the stairs that led down to the dressing rooms, and Sonny came up to talk to them.

Lucille had never been so enamored with a black man before. In the past, she admitted, she had thought, "Gee, that's strange," when seeing interracial couples. Upon meeting the saxophone titan, such thoughts were gone. "I didn't think anything in particular about it, because nothing like it had been in my life," she recalled. "He asked me to wait for him until after the show." She waited.

On that first meeting, she recalled, they "talked for hours," though, as is typical of many early courtship rituals, she had little memory of what was said. It was the event, the reality, that stuck in her mind.

Sonny was somewhat surprised such a conservatively dressed—and politically conservative—white woman would be interested in him, but he liked her. Plain and unobtrusive, Lucille was a far cry from the likes of Dawn Finney and Bonnie Jean Pleasant, but that was part of her appeal. He was secretly relieved cats in the clubs didn't hit on her the way they did with Dawn.

"Lucille was different from the other women I'd gotten to know from the club scene," Sonny said. "I couldn't quite understand what she was all about at first, because she seemed so formal and understated. But she was a nice chick, and I liked her right away."

"I remember that I knew right away that he was going to be somebody in my life," Lucille said. "I knew that he was going to be somebody special."

But, Sonny was soon on the road again. There were some phone calls back and forth and one short visit to New York, but nothing more serious. It would be many months before the feeling in Lucille's gut instinct would come to fruition.

To be near Sonny, Lucille decided to move to New York. She took a sublet on Greenwich Avenue, and got a job as a secretary at a research corporation in the Chrysler Building.

"I just thought I'd like to see if there was anything there," she said. "I thought I should be in the vicinity."

Her persistence was not for naught. For Sonny and Lucille, it was the beginning of a lifelong relationship.

But was the notorious ladies' man ready to leave behind his womanizing ways?

Illus. 23 - Mahavatar Babaji (pictured) is a legendary Indian saint and yogi whose teachings were brought to the West by Paramahansa Yogananda. Through Yogananda, Babaji not only influenced the jazz spirituality movement, but Steve Jobs, the Beatles, Dennis Weaver, and other notables.

Chapter 17

Trane's Awakening

Was it a wild hallucination from the use of LSD or a genuine contact with a higher being?

It surely could have been either, what with talk of superhuman powers, travel through outer space, and miraculous abilities, like healing the sick or making it rain on a clear day.

But John Coltrane argued that he was not hallucinating—that he had indeed experienced a powerful spiritual conversion. In his liner notes to *A Love Supreme*, his 1965 masterpiece, he wrote: "I experienced, by the grace of God, a spiritual awakening, which was to lead me to a richer, fuller, more productive life. At that time, in gratitude, I humbly asked to be given the means and privilege to make others happy through music."

Within the history of spiritual and religious belief systems, there is a tradition that awakening, or illumination, can happen spontaneously in a moment, and from then on the person's life will be changed forever. For Sathya Sai Baba, for example, it is alleged that his life completely changed at 14, after he was stung by a scorpion. He could suddenly speak in Sanskrit, a language he had no previous knowledge of, and began to claim he was the reincarnation of a previous guru and sage, Sai Baba of Shirdi, who had died in 1918.

Coltrane's "awakening" occurred in 1957, about a year after Sonny Rollins devoured Coltrane on a recording called *Tenor Madness*, which showed his technical superiority on the horn and revealed his rival as the weaker player. The exchange between both titans was embarrassing for Coltrane. *Tenor Madness* was not the only major recording that thrust Sonny into the spotlight. He had other albums that mirrored his new, straight-ahead sound. Among them were *Way Out West* and *Newk's Time*.

One reason for Sonny's success was that he had kicked the heroin habit two years earlier. He became stronger and more resilient, easily demonstrating his natural genius on the instrument during his performances.

On the other hand, Coltrane, who was still fighting his heroin addiction, sounded almost limp as they traded solos with one another. Sonny, who had been an amateur boxer as a teenager, knew about the art of competition. Plus, he had lots of experience in "cutting" (competition contests) at Minton's and other jazz clubs in Harlem.

Sonny's crown, however, would be soon taken from him. Once Coltrane experienced his spiritual awakening and started to connect with—and win over—millions of fans worldwide who were advocates of non-Western spirituality, Sonny lost many followers who preferred Coltrane's spirituality in his music.

What was significant about Coltrane's spirituality is that it represented a mixture of both Eastern styles and American Christian influences. Jazz, it should be remembered, was often unwelcome in the black church because of its long association with sexual promiscuity, the fast life, and drug addiction.

While Coltrane was a heroin addict during his creation of *A Love Supreme* and other "sacred" recordings, his connection to the black Christian church was stronger than ever. His music was reverent and as much an acknowledgment of Christianity as it was an acknowledgment of his new foreign influences. Conversely, Sonny Rollins' refusal to accept Jesus as his Savior, as well as many other Christian teachings, may have prevented him from having the same massive appeal to both Christian and "spiritual" audiences.

Coltrane understood Sonny's spirituality, but he knew he could not reach the same technical levels. Coltrane's awakening was directly linked to several of his beliefs, some of which emanated from ancient Egyptian teachings, Buddhism, Taoism, astrology, and different forms of Islamic mysticism. His new fans—black and especially white— were devotees of some of these practices, and many of them favored Coltrane's new haunting, exotic style that was shaped by these practices.

Outstanding among them was Coltrane's practice of Kriya yoga, which had links to ancient Hinduism. Kriya is regarded as one of the most far-out branches of yoga because of its beliefs in reincarnation (and bringing people back to life after death). According to its practitioners, Kriya is an ancient form of yoga that was reintroduced in the 19th century by Mahavatar Babaji through his disciple, Lahiri Mahasaya.

Babaji is believed to be immortal and has reportedly lived in the Himalayan Mountains for over 2,000 years. He makes a practice of appearing to only a handful of disciples and other people. In 1861, Babaji met Lahiri Mahasaya and taught him the secrets of Kriya yoga.

"The Kriya Yoga that I am giving to the world through you in this nineteenth century is a revival of the same science that Krishna gave millenniums ago to Arjuna; and was later known to Patanjali, and to Christ, St. John, St. Paul, and other disciples," Babaji told Lahiri.

(There is a tradition in Christianity that Jesus went to India before he began his public ministry at the age of thirty. Syrian Christians believe that Thomas, one of the twelve apostles, brought Christianity to India in the decades following Christ's resurrection and ascension. Thomas was allegedly martyred near Chennai in 72 CE.)

Lahiri later became the guru of Yukteswar Giri, who became the teacher of perhaps the most famous yogi in history: Paramahansa Yogananda. It was Yogananda who spread the word not only about Kriya yoga but popularized the very idea of yoga in the west.

Born and raised in India, Yogananda moved to the United States in 1920 to bring Kriya yoga to new audiences. After decades of teaching and speaking across the country, Yogananda published his landmark 1946 book, *Autobiography of a Yogi*, which introduced Americans, Europeans, and others across the globe to Indian spirituality.

Yogananda wrote that a description of Kriya yoga can be found in the yoga classic *Yoga Sutras of Patanjali*, which states: "Liberation can be attained by that *pranayama* which is accomplished by disjoining the course of inspiration and expiration."

Practitioners of Kriya yoga seek spiritual liberation through breathing techniques. By controlling the breath—as well as integrating other techniques, like stretching, postures, meditation, special hand gestures (*mudras*), and chanting (*mantras*), yogis hope to deepen their sense of spirituality. Ultimately, Kriya yoga practitioners hope to enter into a state of union with God, or "pure awareness," which they believe is possible to attain while living on Earth.

Even before their incursions into spiritual practices, both Coltrane and Sonny had previously established their credentials as jazz musicians. Sonny, however, had been a giant-killer in the early 1950s who successfully seized the crown from tenor saxophone pioneers like Coleman Hawkins, Lester Young, Chu Berry, Don Byas, and Dexter Gordon. All these men were virtuosos on their instruments.

There were other reasons for the success of John Coltrane. Though he embraced Kriya, he did not jettison his belief in Jesus as Savior or other beliefs he inherited from the Moravian and AME churches of his youth. The Moravian Church is one of the oldest forms of Protestantism, predating even Martin Luther himself. Moravians trace their lineage to Jan Hus, the reformer who lived in Bohemia in the 15th century. He was burned at the stake in 1415, a full century before Luther nailed his 95 theses to the church door at Wittenberg.

Moravians fled to the American colonies in the early 1700s and also initiated large-scale missionary work in the Caribbean. Today, the church has roughly one million members across the world; it emphasizes ecumenism, personal piety, and—fittingly for Sonny—music.

Two other similarly-named churches that impacted both Sonny and Coltrane, are the African Methodist Episcopal (AME) and African Methodist Episcopal Zion (AMEZ) Churches.

Founded in 1816 by the Right Reverend Richard Allen in Philadelphia, the AME Church was the first independent Black Protestant denomination. The Rt. Rev. Allen was the leader of a group of five Black Methodist churches in the mid-Atlantic region that wanted freedom from the racism they encountered in the white Methodist church.

Unlike many churches, which split from parent organizations because of doctrinal differences, race was the driving factor in establishing the church. The church grew exponentially over the next few decades and became a pillar of the African American community. The AME Church emphasized education, and started and operated thousands of schools, and even a historically-black college in Ohio. It was also highly active in the civil rights movement. Today, there are between 2.5 and 3.5 million members of the church.

The AME Zion Church, on the other hand, was founded in New York City in 1821. As with the AME Church, the AMEZ Church grew out of frustration with the racism that black parishioners had experienced in white Methodist churches. Today, the church's headquarters are in North Carolina.

One of its most notable members was John Coltrane, the grandson of not one, but two AMEZ ministers. Coltrane's maternal grandfather, Rev. William Blair, was the pastor of an AMEZ church in High Point, North Carolina while his paternal grandfather, Rev. William H. Coltrane, was an AMEZ minister in Hamlet. Coltrane grew up practicing music in the church, and its influence on him cannot be understated.

Although the Moravian, AME, and AMEZ churches were not exactly Pentecostal, they nonetheless shared some of the vibrant worship experiences of Pentecostalism. While Coltrane may have been deeply rooted in these Christian faiths, he had begun to explore other religions by the time of his spiritual awakening. In 1955, he married a woman named Naima (née Juanita Grubbs), who was a convert to

Illus. 24 - Tenor saxophonist John Coltrane experienced his first spiritual awakening in 1957. He and his friend Sonny Rollins prevailed as the leaders of both jazz and spirituality. They went on to spark worldwide interest in Kriya yoga and other forms of spirituality.

Islam. Her deep commitment to her Muslim faith had a profound influence on him.

In 1963, Coltrane left Naima for another woman, Alice McLeod, a pianist who shared many of his spiritual beliefs, including Indian philosophy. Still, it was his Pentecostal faith that laid the foundation for Coltrane's deep spirituality, which was on full display in his seminal 1965 album, *A Love Supreme*. Often hailed as Coltrane's magnum opus, the album was recorded in a single session on December 9, 1964, and was released the following month.

A Love Supreme begins with a bang—literally. Introduced by a gong (tam-tam) and cymbal washes, the album maintains an otherworldly, haunting quality from the first note. All of its four tracks—each representing a part of the suite—point to spirituality in their very names: "Acknowledgement," "Resolution," "Pursuance," and "Psalm."

Throughout the album, Coltrane chants and repeats mantras that showcase his exploration of Eastern religions, though he remains deeply steeped in a Gospel tradition. At the end, he plays what he referred to as a "musical narration" of a devotional poem that appears in the liner notes of the album. The poem ends with the declaration: "Elation. Elegance. Exaltation. All from God. Thank you God. Amen."

Many critics lauded *A Love Supreme* as one of the greatest jazz recordings ever. Calling it a "legendary album—long hymn of praise," *Rolling Stone* declared "the indelible four-note theme of the first movement, "Acknowledgement," is the humble foundation of the suite. But Coltrane's majestic, often violent blowing (famously described as 'sheets of sound'), is never self-aggrandizing. Aloft with his classic quartet ... Coltrane soars with nothing but gratitude and joy. You can't help but go with him."

Yet, not everyone was taken with Coltrane's sound. A reviewer from *The Daily Telegraph* scoffed that *A Love Supreme* "marked the point at which jazz—for good or ill—ceased for a while to be hip and cool, becoming instead mystical and messianic ... *A Love Supreme*, Miles Davis noted in a slightly double-edged way, 'reached out and influenced those people who were into peace. Hippies and people like that.' If you're in the mood, it's majestic and compelling; if you're not, it's interminable and pretentious."

Regardless of opinion, *A Love Supreme* reached more listeners than was typical for a jazz album. Within five years, it sold 500,000 copies, compared to Coltrane's typical sales of around 30,000. Even those who weren't typically jazz fans embraced the album, such as rock musicians, like Carlos Santana, John McLaughlin, and the band U2, all of whom have paid homage to *A Love Supreme*.

For Coltrane, *A Love Supreme* was comparable to a victory bout at Minton's. By the 1960s, the Lower East Side of Manhattan had replaced Harlem as the new jazz capital. Many of the new styles performed downtown were dubbed modal, avant-garde, and the "new thing."

They challenged the prevailing popular hard bebop style, the genre originally associated with Sonny and Coltrane. It was downtown, with its densely populated arts community, that helped to fuel the notion that Sonny had lost his crown because of Coltrane's own journey into spirituality.

"We all love Sonny and believe that he was one of the greatest tenor players ever, but John is without a doubt the top new tenor," declared Mary Greenlee, Coltrane's first cousin, whom he lived with when he arrived in Philadelphia in the 1950s, where he worked as a laborer. "He is one of the most spiritual men I have ever known. His spiritual message is demanding and powerful."

Coltrane wrote a song for her titled "Cousin Mary" to express his love for and devotion to her, because she had helped him during his turbulent years as a heroin addict. In the mid-1960s, she lived at 617 East 11th Street, in the East Village, where Coltrane, Archie Shepp, Noah Howard, Marion Brown, Jimmy Lott and other avant-garde musicians often congregated to discuss the new music styles then in vogue.

"No one can compare to John; his deep level of spirituality is unquestionable," said tenor saxophonist Jimmy Lott, one of Coltrane's closest friends and followers. "It is his deep faith in God and his religion that makes him special. He is the man; it's just that simple."

On the other hand, bassist Percy Heath, one of the architects of bebop, argued Sonny was so superior to other saxophonists that he even challenged Charlie Parker's hegemony. "I cannot think of anybody, other than Bird, who has reached the same levels as Sonny," he said.

But the spiritual journeys of the two men cannot be easily compared. From a technical, academic, and improvisational perspective, Sonny is arguably far more superior to Coltrane. However, Coltrane was more deeply religious in the Christian sense than Sonny.

It was this sanctified Southern Christian influence, coupled with the ancient secretive and sacred sounds of yoga, that gave Coltrane the edge over Sonny. Since a large number of black jazz fans came from a Christian tradition, many were more responsive to Coltrane for what they perceived as his deeper, more innocent level of spirituality, one that was more haunting and intense. It is no exaggeration to say that, as a result of Coltrane's popularity bump, Sonny Rollins had many concerns during the 1960s.

Illus. 25 - Nephew Clifton Anderson, sister Gloria Anderson, and Sonny Rollins share a happy family moment at Sonny's former home in Germantown, NY.

Illus. 26 - Author Hugh Wyatt, the gifted bassist Larry Ridley, and Sonny Rollins.

Illus. 27 - Sonny Rollins and his older brother, Valdemar Rollins, a physician and violinist.

Illus. 28 - Sonny Rollins and his goddaughter, Amanda Wyatt, the author's daughter.

Illus. 29 - Actress Ruby Dee and Sonny Rollins.

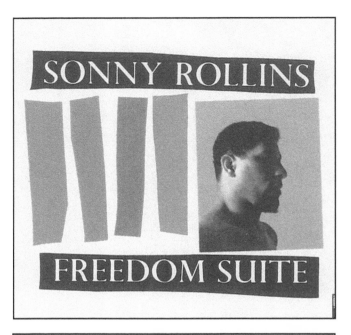

Illus. 30 - Sonny Rollins and Max Roach were on the same page when it came to jazz innovations, but differed strongly when it came to the issue of civil rights.

CHAPTER 18

The Titans

It was seething, but secretive—this rivalry between two powerful
and outspoken titans of jazz, Sonny Rollins and Max Roach. It was
a nasty and, at times, brutal battle between two men who were among
the most competitive giants in jazz.

The enmity came to a head between 1958 and 1959 when the men,
each with militant, warrior-like personalities, began to publicly feud
over the relationship between jazz and the indignities of life for African
Americans, Native peoples, and other people of color.

In early 1958, Sonny, who was so upset about the lack of justice
for blacks, made a powerful album entitled *Freedom Suite*, an epic
recording that denounced American racism. Sonny himself wrote the
liner notes, which read in part:

"America is deeply rooted in Negro culture: its colloquialisms; its
humor; its music. How ironic that the Negro, who more than any other
people can claim America's culture as his own, is being persecuted and
repressed; that the Negro, who has exemplified the humanities in his

very existence, is being rewarded with inhumanity."

Sonny's comments were sparked by America's horrendous legacy of racism, especially in the South where blacks were regularly lynched and denied basic equality. Even in so-called liberal Manhattan, Sonny— even after he had become an international jazz star—was unable to rent some desirable apartments because of racial discrimination.

"I was pretty well-known at the time. I had all these magazine and newspaper articles and pictures about me," Rollins quipped. "It didn't matter to the landlords. I was a still a nigger, which is why I didn't get the apartment I wanted. This is the reason I wrote the notes and recorded the suite."

Roach, who served as a drummer on the recording, decided that he would outdo Sonny by recording his own album to decry discrimination, *We Insist!* The album has five selections based on the Emancipation Proclamation and the growing civil rights movement in America and around the world. It contained a suite that Roach and lyricist Oscar Brown Jr. had begun to develop in 1959.

Although a variety of civil rights movements had been around for centuries, the push for equality literally exploded between 1953 and 1957. On May 17, 1954, the Supreme Court of the United States handed down two rulings that would change the course of history— *Brown v. Board of Education of Topeka, Kansas,* and *Bolling v. Sharpe.* In *Brown*, the court overturned *Plessy v. Ferguson*, an 1896 decision that sanctioned "separate but equal" facilities for blacks and whites. *Bolling* prohibited segregation in the public schools of the District of Columbia.

Just a few months after these landmark Supreme Court decisions, 23 black students were barred from attending white elementary schools in Montgomery, Alabama. In 1955, Mississippi passed a law declaring that whites who attended schools with black students could be fined or even jailed. Later that year, the Georgia Board of Education issued an order to fire all teachers advocating integration.

August of 1955 saw the brutal lynching of Emmett Till, a 14-year-old African-American boy, for whistling at a white woman in Mississippi. That December, Rosa Parks famously refused to give up her bus seat

Illus. 31 - Rivals Sonny Rollins and Max Roach had a quiet blow-up during the 1950s over the issue of the civil rights struggles that engulfed the nation and the world.

to a white woman. Although Parks had not been the first person to refuse to give up her seat, the incident sparked the Montgomery Bus Boycotts and went down in history as one of the seminal events of the civil rights movement in the 1950s.

Throughout the following decades, African Americans in the South and elsewhere protested, boycotted, staged sit-ins, and took legal action against rampant racism. Meanwhile, racist white groups—often supported by federal, state, and city governments—tried to quell the burgeoning movement.

In 1956, infamous FBI director J. Edgar Hoover instituted the Counter Intelligence Program (COINTELPRO), which began surveilling, harassing, and disrupting civil rights protests and other activities deemed "subversive" or "dissident." One of its targets would be the Rev. Dr. Martin Luther King, Jr., chairman of the Southern Christian Leadership Conference, which was formed the following year.

In 1957, Little Rock, Arkansas became the focus of national outrage when Governor Orval Faubus brought in the National Guard to prevent nine African American students from attending Central High School. In response, President Dwight D. Eisenhower ordered the U.S. Army to bring the National Guard under its control and escort the black students to the school.

Two church bombings in Birmingham during these years galvanized the movement: the bombing of the Bethel Baptist Church on June 29, 1958—it was also bombed in 1956 and 1961—and the bombing of the 16th Street Baptist Church on September 15, 1963, which killed four young girls. Ku Klux Klan members were involved in both acts of terrorism. Both incidents caused the nation and the world to ponder the atrocities being suffered by Negroes in their quest for dignity and equality in the American South.

By the time *Freedom Suite* was released in 1958, the nation was reeling. Sonny had recorded the album in February and March of that year with recent sit-ins, boycotts, and demonstrations very much on his mind.

Of course, Sonny had always been politically conscious. His grandmother (and frequent babysitter) Miriam had been a member of Marcus Garvey's Universal Negro Improvement Association. She made sure Sonny accompanied her to many marches and demonstrations in Harlem when he was a young child in the 1930s.

The jazz medium itself has long been a crucible of protest and activism, especially among the bebop and post-bop generations. Sonny feels that his generation sometimes looked disdainfully at the older, less politically involved musicians, like Louis Armstrong.

"I knew that [Armstrong] was somebody great, and I really dug him. I mean, I would see him in all these Bing Crosby movies and all that, so to me he was great. But later on, there was a period when people of my age and people I was hangin' out with thought that Louie

Armstrong was tomming.

"And then I went through that for a while without really understanding the whole scene ... He was a product of the time that he came out of, so he was not a Tom. But [he appeared that way] to young, militant black guys like us coming into the bebop era.

"After the war was over and all this shit, people wanted freedom. For a while, I would think of these people as toms, but I soon got out of that. I realized that this was a very young adolescent way of viewing him. We made judgments about people because there was a lot going on at that time, as you know. I mean, there was a lot of racial riots going on all during that time, so the lines were drawn as to who was on what side," Sonny said.

In a later article in *The Atlantic* by the esteemed writer George Goodman, Sonny echoed these comments: "You can't have jazz without protest. Protest may be too narrow a word to apply to men like Basie, Ellington, and Hawkins. But by carrying themselves with pride, just by acting like men, the older musicians influenced younger guys like me. So did the Pullman porters, fighting for their dignity. We looked up to those guys and, when we were old enough, went a step further. It was a generational thing. The world was changing."

Still, taking such an overtly political stance was daring in the late 1950s. Sonny had hinted at his politics in some of his earlier works, such as 1954's *Airegin* ("Nigeria spelled backwards"), but the liner notes to *Freedom Suite* made his dissatisfaction with American racism abundantly clear.

In Art Taylor's *Notes and Tones*, Sonny mentioned a book called *Black Nationalism and the Revolution in Music* by Frank Kofsky, which asserted that Sonny was one of the first contemporary jazz musicians to bring politics into music. "Now that I look back on it, this is true; they were some of the first things that were said about the subject, although it was on everybody's mind, of course," he was quoted as saying.

Sonny's vocal support of the Civil Rights Movement rubbed off on Max Roach, who, quite literally, recorded a *Freedom Suite* of his own. *We Insist!* was subtitled *Freedom Now Suite*—which can be interpreted as either a nod or an affront to Sonny's same-named album.

Roach's avant-garde album included tracks like "Driva' Man," which was about a white slave driver, and "Freedom Day," a response to the Emancipation Proclamation. The third track of the album, "Triptych: Prayer, Protest, Peace," included screaming vocals from Abbey Lincoln, a singer/songwriter, actress, and activist.

Roach began working with lyricist Oscar Brown, Jr. on the album with the goal of performing it at the 1963 centennial of the Emancipation Proclamation. However, the two had disagreements—not political, but artistic—and Brown ultimately backed out. Brown was reportedly upset that Roach rearranged his compositions without his knowing.

By the time *We Insist!* was released, the civil rights movement had kicked into high gear; sit-ins had been staged at lunch counters, and organizations like the Congress of Racial Equality (CORE) and the Southern Christian Leadership Conference (SCLC) had been gaining national attention for their efforts to promote racial equality.

At the same time, the public was increasingly aware of the political changes occurring in Africa, where many independent nations had been forming after years of oppression by European colonial governments. African-American students were especially cognizant of these African political movements, through media attention and also through African classmates who were studying at American schools. Roach's album reflects this awareness through the tracks "All Africa" and "Tears for Johannesburg."

Both Sonny's and Roach's *Freedom Suites* helped to serve as manifestos for civil rights activists, as well as jazz musicians, the latter of whom had been somewhat silent. There were exceptions, of course. Composer and bandleader Duke Ellington had forcibly spoken out during the 1930s, and his comments helped to integrate jazz clubs in Harlem and elsewhere in the world. However, bebop and hard bop musicians became the strongest and most militant when compared with prior generations of jazz players.

Sonny and Max had their first encounter in the late 1940s at Harlem jazz clubs, such as Monroe's and Minton's. Sonny, who was always a highly competitive player known for "cutting" musicians on stage, developed a reputation of not liking drummers, who often controlled the flow of the rhythms. Max, who was also brilliant like Sonny, had developed the reputation of overwhelming soloists out front on the stage. Although a saxophonist, Sonny took an approach to the instrument that was more percussive than others did.

"If I had to do it all over again, I would have chosen to play the drums because they tend to dominate the direction of the music," Sonny told sister Gloria Anderson. "I need my own space, and I need to set the direction, not the drummers."

Although he had performed with Clifford Brown and Max Roach during the 1950s, sources said that Sonny loved Clifford's trumpet playing because of their great compatibility, but thought that Max's drumming "often got in the way and was too overwhelming. Max wanted to control everything."

Nonetheless, Sonny had "great respect" for Max, for whom he recognized as one of the major founders of bebop and an influence on thousands of other jazz drummers over the course of several decades, said a source, who noted the problem was that "drummers did not know their place with Sonny." There was one exception, drummer Elvin Jones, Sonny's favorite, who "understood the value of [drumming as] accompaniment rather than as a soloist."

The rift between Sonny and Max reached a boiling point over the *Freedom Suites* in the late 1950s. "I don't want to criticize Max, but I should be given credit for starting it, yet Max wanted credit," said Sonny.

The tug-of-war between both Sonny and Max may seem trivial, but it was not. A source said, "Sonny is routinely abusive to drummers and is known to criticize them verbally in front of other players. His wrath also extended at times to other players, including his long-time bassist Bob Cranshaw, who was frequently berated by Sonny."

But, in Cranshaw's words, "Sonny is cool with me. Maybe it's this kind of control and strength that has made him the great artist that he is."

My mother and I have the same kind of philosophy toward Sonny. Sonny was not like the run-of-the-mill person. If [you're] driven by talent and you're driven by the need to play, the need to do what you have to do, you don't act like other people do. Because if you act like everybody else, then there's no genius there. So she really understood that he was different and you shouldn't be punished for being different, and I felt the same way."

— GLORIA ANDERSON

CHAPTER 19

A Mother's Love

There was a loud pounding on the door outside of Sonny Rollins' Grand Street apartment on the Lower East Side of Manhattan. The frantic knocking and shouting were relentless. It was neither a police raid, nor rabid fans trying to break down his door; it was his own family trying to get into his apartment.

"Please open the door, Sonny!" pleaded his older sister, Gloria.

From inside the apartment, Sonny tried to ignore his family's pleas. Consumed by grief and guilt, he had been ignoring their calls and refusing to see them.

But the banging continued, no matter how hard he tried to ignore it. The pounding grew louder, and his family's pleas grew more frantic.

At the tender age of 28, Sonny had already lived enough for a lifetime. He had overcome near-fatal dope addiction, imprisonment in merciless Rikers Island, and an intensely painful divorce. Through all this, he had nearly lost his title as the king of the tenor saxophone. But nothing had been as painful as the loss of his beloved mother, just a few months earlier. It was her death on November 8, 1958, that sent him into a tailspin, hurtling toward rock bottom.

Valborg Rollins, who Sonny described as looking like Billie Holiday, had only been 53 years old when she had an unexpected stroke at home.

"My mother died very suddenly," said Gloria. "She was fine in the morning, as my father said. He left his wife putting on her makeup and he comes home, and she's in a coma."

Although his older brother, Val, was a doctor, he was unable to help his mother. Valborg died suddenly, leaving Sonny distraught. He was so devastated that he couldn't stomach the idea of attending her funeral.

"He said, 'I can't be at mom's funeral,'" Gloria remembered. "And I said, 'don't worry, it's all right.'"

The night of Valborg's funeral, Sonny tried to distract himself from his pain by attending a gig, to little avail. He was distressed and ashamed of having missed the ceremony, even though his family understood.

"I knew that if he didn't feel that it was in himself, I don't think he could have really endured my mother's funeral. He was entirely too close to her," Gloria said. "It would have been horrible for him. He needed to feel that it was okay to do what he had to do. So I told him, go ahead and play."

Following his mother's death, Gloria said, Sonny "dropped out of sight."

"It was either the end of November into December, and we had been trying to get in touch with him. We felt bad. My father and I felt bad that he couldn't get in touch with us, or he didn't want to get in touch with us," she recalled. "Or he felt that there was going to be some big family brouhaha with everyone coming down on him. I tried to call him, and he wasn't answering the phone."

Sonny's sister, father, and brother-in-law tried to see him after a performance at the Apollo Theater, but he refused to meet. He left after the show and went home alone. Eventually, Gloria decided they'd have to take a more aggressive approach if they wanted to see Sonny.

And so, Gloria went down to Sonny's apartment on Grand Street with their father and her husband and began to knock on the door. Even though Sonny wouldn't answer, the family persisted.

"I insisted that he had to talk to us because he just had to know that we weren't holding him in any—we weren't holding any ill feeling against him. We were making this racket out in the hallway, and so he said, 'I'd better open the door and let these crazy people in.' So he opened the door and we barged in."

While guilt and shame had been eating away at Sonny, Gloria knew their mother wouldn't have faulted him going to a gig instead of the funeral. "I had told him not to worry about it, that she really understood. She was like his number-one fan in the entire world.

"My mother and I have the same kind of philosophy toward Sonny. Sonny was not like the run-of-the-mill person. If [you're] driven by talent and you're driven by the need to play, the need to do what you

Illus. 32 - Sonny's parents, Valborg and Walter William Rollins, smile for the camera.

have to do, you don't act like other people do. Because if you act like everybody else, then there's no genius there. So she really understood that he was different and you shouldn't be punished for being different, and I felt the same way."

Gloria fondly remembered their mother as "a great cook" with "a magnificent sense of humor … She just really communicated so much love and caring and she just did everything for us. Everything she felt that she could possibly do for us to advance us in this world, she did."

Valborg had been born in St. Croix to Miriam, who was from St. Thomas, and a Haitian doctor named Paul Solomon who had been educated at the prestigious Sorbonne in Paris. However, Miriam left Paul when Valborg was a baby and took her back to St. Thomas to raise her.

As a teenager, Valborg married Walter Rollins, who was eight years her senior. In 1925, they emigrated to New York City. They settled in Harlem, where they lived with their three children, as well as Valborg's mother. Walter, a seaman, was usually away, while Valborg worked mostly as a maid.

Although the family went to an AME Church at one point, Valborg raised her children mostly in the Moravian Church. Gloria remembered that Moravian services were structured and very musical, with a litany that "was sung, not read." She mentioned that her mother liked the Moravians because their missionaries had historically been the only church willing to marry slaves on St. Croix.

In fact, there is an 18th-century story about two German Moravians who wanted to minister to African slaves on the islands St. Thomas and St. Croix. When they were told they couldn't minister to slaves, the two Moravians reputedly sold themselves into slavery and boarded a ship heading towards the Caribbean.

The story might not be entirely true, although the two missionaries did claim they would become slaves themselves if it was the only way to minister to them. They and other Moravian missionaries established churches on many Caribbean islands and reportedly baptized 13,000 people. It was also the first organized religious body to create schools for slaves in the West Indies.

Valborg was also a member of the Order of the Eastern Star, a Masonic order open to both men and women. While it is based on Biblical teachings, the group allows people of all faiths to join. The order, which was established by an American Freemason in 1850, only allows men who are Masons and women who are related to Masons to join.

According to its website, the Order of the Eastern Star is not a secret society but a group of "dedicated women and men who sincerely reflect the spirit of fraternal love and the desire to work together for good. It gives them the opportunity to give a part of their time to many projects that benefit mankind. Our lessons are scriptural, our purposes are beneficent, and our teachings are moral."

Perhaps it was his mother's Masonic affiliation that led Sonny to join the more secretive and esoteric Rosicrucian Order. Whatever the reason, Valborg's spirituality certainly influenced Sonny, who would spend much of his life searching for spiritual meaning and purpose.

Sonny was the most affectionate of the three Rollins kids and, even after he reached adulthood, they remained tight-knit. While his father was somewhat "strict" and often away at sea, he bonded with his mother, a fellow music lover.

"I really loved her," Sonny recalled. "She was a very gentle, kind person."

"Sonny was the only one of her children who always kissed her hello and always kissed her good-bye, and I was always amazed at that because I always felt too shy to do that with my mother who was, like, just this special person," Gloria recalled.

It was Valborg who encouraged Sonny to play music. She had first enrolled him in piano lessons and supported him when he switched to the alto and, later, tenor saxophone. She continued to be his greatest fan, up until her last breath.

Gloria said that their mother originally had doubts about "Sonny's decision to play jazz and all the problems that would follow him. She was right." But once all the numerous accolades started flowing in about the greatness of his albums and his concert performances, Valborg determined that her son had made the right career move after all.

Despite her approval of Sonny's career choice, Valborg didn't like some of Sonny's friends. One day, trumpeter Miles Davis showed up at their apartment with Sonny. Miles was acting arrogant and cursing constantly and loudly as he was prone to do, and, within minutes, Valborg ordered him to leave and never come back.

"My mother couldn't handle his profanity. He was a very talented musician and a good friend of Sonny's, but he lacked basic manners," said Gloria. "She didn't care how famous he was. He just needed to improve his behavior and curb his tongue."

During Sonny's days of addiction and incarceration, most of the people he believed were his real friends abandoned him. Some returned after he kicked the habit and after he became a big star, but, by then, he had reached a cynical and distrustful phase and rejected them.

"He didn't trust most of them," said trombonist Clifton Anderson, Gloria's son. "I believe that my uncle only trusted my grandmother and my mother. Of course, he liked a lot of his friends, but his real trust only extended to them."

Sonny had faith in the two women because they were some of his only visitors when he was imprisoned at Rikers Island. "They were always there for Sonny when a lot of his so-called friends had disappeared," Anderson added.

"My mother and my sister stuck by me the whole time," Sonny said. "I had alienated everybody else."

Whether it was cold or hot, Valborg frequently visited Sonny. Gloria visited him once. They brought Sonny food, books, and other treats that helped him bear his imprisonment. They didn't justify his crimes as a robber and junkie, but they understood the problem, as Harlem had its share of addiction and crime.

"We both understood that men who were denied good jobs and faced terrible discrimination were prone to being locked up in jail," Gloria said. "It was hard for Sonny to escape these problems, which continued to get worse. I guess Sonny was lucky that he overcame these problems."

Sonny credited his mother's love—and some admonishment from

Charlie Parker—in helping him to finally kick the habit.

"After the incident with Charlie Parker where I told Bird, 'Well, yeah, I'm straight,' and then Bird finds out that I was still fucking around, I felt bad about that, and I went and got myself straight. So those two, I would say, had a big influence in really getting me to realize where I was at and stop fucking around," he said.

While Bird may not have lived long enough to see Sonny clean up his act, Valborg did. "She saw me begin to turn around, and it justified some of what she said I had in me," he recalled.

Indeed, before his mother died, Sonny was at the top of his game. He had beaten his heroin addiction; he had learned about being clean-cut from jazz genius Clifford Brown; he had defeated his rival, John Coltrane; and he had a few new love interests, like secretary Lucille Pearson.

Unlike his former wife, Dawn Finney, the beautiful model and actress, Sonny felt a sense of security and comfort with Lucille, who directed all her love and attention to him. Sonny and Dawn, on the other hand, had fought like cats and dogs until they divorced.

During this time of personal grief for Sonny, his genius was being acknowledged abroad, and in 1959, he went on his first European tour. He toured Sweden, the Netherlands, Germany, Italy, and France, where he was greeted with open arms.

Despite all the accolades he received both at home and abroad, Sonny continued to grieve for his mother. He was further stressed by his efforts to keep at the top of the jazz game, as well as by his failed marriage to Dawn.

All of these anxieties coalesced in the summer of 1959, when Sonny abruptly dropped out of the jazz scene, appalling fans and critics alike. The eccentric tenor saxophonist traded in the clubs and concert halls for an unexpected new venue: the Williamsburg Bridge.

It was beautiful up there. You feel suspended above the skyline, the water, and the harbor. The grandeur gives you a perspective above music, people, everything. You can blow as loud as you like without bothering anyone. New Yorkers being discreet as they are, nobody bothers you."

— SONNY ROLLINS, ON THE
WILLIAMSBURG BRIDGE

CHAPTER 20

The Bridge

The stoic-looking, imposing man stood like a specter wreathed in shadow, a looming giant framed by the imposing silhouette of the bridge's towers and cables. He held a brand new tenor saxophone and honked it in defiance of the freezing wind that wailed among the steel beams.

He started blowing his horn loudly back at the tugboats with a resounding *bonnnnk*! When one of them blew their horns, he would blow back, as if they were having a conversation. The tugboat sounds were loud and noisy. By contrast, the angry and sarcastic tones of the saxophone were mellow, haunting, and magnificent.

Passersby on New York City's Williamsburg Bridge stopped and listened to the somewhat humorous exchange of horns blaring at each other. Some thought they recognized the man, but they couldn't identify him. Others looked at him as if he were crazy and moved on in disbelief—why would a normal man be standing on the bridge in the cold, frigid weather blowing a saxophone?

The man on the bridge was jazz colossus Sonny Rollins, who had abruptly and, without announcement, dropped out of the music scene for two years, from 1959 until 1961. He did it to "woodshed" (in other words, to perfect his "ax"); to get out of the rat race of liquor and illegal drugs; to avoid groupies seeking sex, and to repudiate the decadent lifestyle that had swept through the jazz world.

Sonny could not remain anonymous for long. He was discovered accidentally by Ralph Berton, a jazz writer who regularly commuted over the bridge, which connected the Lower East Side of Manhattan to Brooklyn. "I thought I recognized him when I first looked at him, but I kept changing my mind and finally concluded it was, indeed, Sonny Rollins."

Berton asked himself: *Where had Sonny Rollins been? Was he dead? Had he gone back to Lexington for another cure?* The only thing he knew for sure was Sonny had disappeared from the jazz clubs, from the concert stage, and from the recording studios.

Now a Mohawk-styled genie blowing on a magical horn, Sonny was not easily recognizable standing on the bridge. His preferred perch was far up on the walkway. Upon his return to society in 1961, *Metronome Magazine* published an article by Berton called "The Bridge," a story about a lone saxophonist who practiced on the Brooklyn Bridge. Meanwhile, the tale of the Williamsburg specter had made its way to the clubs, leaving jazzmen and fans dumbstruck.

Sonny had reportedly gone into self-imposed isolation to work on his music. It was woodshedding time—time to shut himself in the back room and practice until he played as well as everyone expected of him. His apartment was out of the question. Sonny, ever considerate, was reluctant to bring out his powerful sound in such confined quarters— there were his neighbors to think about.

"There was this pregnant girl in a neighboring apartment," he said. "I couldn't subject her to all that sound, and I couldn't do myself any good by inhibiting my practicing."

Faced with this dilemma, he habitually strolled the streets of the Lower East Side. One fateful day, he sauntered over to the East River. "I was down on the Lower East Side one day, where I lived in an

Illus. 33 - New York's Williamsburg Bridge, between Brooklyn and Manhattan, was part-time home to Sonny Rollins. He used the Bridge to practice his horn without distractions.

apartment on Grand Street, and I looked up and saw the steps," he said. "That's how I found out about the bridge. I was just standing there and saw the steps, and I thought about it.

"At the time, I just wanted someplace to practice. I walked up there and saw this empty space. I walked across the bridge, and I said, 'Damn, I could come up here, and there's hardly anybody who would be walking across here.' So that's how the whole thing started.

"[I thought], 'Wow, this is great!' I went home and got my horn and went up there and walked to the middle of the bridge. There at a certain point, you were above the trains, and the cars, and nobody could really see you.

"It was beautiful up there. You feel suspended above the skyline, the water, and the harbor. The grandeur gives you a perspective above music, people, everything," Sonny recalled. "You can blow as loud as you like without bothering anyone. New Yorkers being discreet as they are, nobody bothers you."

On top of the span overlooking the East River, there was no one to disturb him. Here and there could be found the occasional pedestrians from Williamsburg or the Lower East Side, but they didn't seem to care—and even if they did, they didn't show it; they just quickened their pace and moved along.

Sonny wasn't there to socialize. He was in his own world, a warrior looking for new ways to wield his weapon of choice. He was searching, reevaluating, looking for the things he had missed along the way—and the paths that no one had yet considered. He was a novice climbing a mountaintop, a mystic seeking a vision. Up on the bridge, he was in the thick of his element, and the notes flowed.

Month after month, the tenor sax honked and whistled, blasting away in wild flights that sometimes caused passing motorists to wonder if the Williamsburg Bridge was haunted by the ghosts of jazzmen. The sounds that Sonny took from the city would later appear in his music, earning his sax the moniker "the honking horn of Sonny Rollins."

An eclectic woodshed it was, one destined to go down in the annals of jazz history. Weird tales wormed their way through the community. For Sonny, the bridge was freedom and release. "I took my music books up there with me; not so much spiritual and religious books because I could do that at the apartment. It was mainly that I would go up there and play my horn, which is what it was actually about."

Sonny loved his new studio and he took to it constantly, even when the weather turned against him. Jeffrey remembered the lengths to which the lone saxophonist would go: "In the center of the bridge, there was a walkway, and there he would play, even in freezing cold. It was numbing. He'd be wearing a sweater. There was a little place where we would go and get a brandy, and then go back up there."

The bridge let Sonny do battle with the elements, challenging him to perform in the most trying conditions. It allowed him to stretch his muscles and send his sound soaring across the city, uncontained by the walls of clubs or studios or concert halls. Atop the steel spars was freedom, a freedom that could break through the limits he had once placed on his music.

But the bridge was also freedom from other people. Though it was the center of a major thoroughfare, it was also a remote parapet that allowed Sonny to be alone, a hermit unseen by the eye of the public.

As his sister Gloria Anderson recalled, "A lot of mystique has grown around this blowing on the bridge, but there is a practical side to it. He was in this apartment, and if Sonny wants to blow out, the whole building would collapse. So, he would go out to practice and be able to blow out.

"He needed to play out; he needed to play loud. He needed to explore his ideas, and he couldn't do that in that apartment. So, part of it was just the necessity to be free to play loud and expand. The other part that compelled him not to play before an audience was that he was not satisfied. He felt that he was in a state of transition, and he just wanted to nail it," she added.

But, in transition to what? He was already arguably the greatest tenor man on the scene, overwhelmingly praised by jazz fans and critics. By 1959, he was playing for two grand a night. But money was never enough, and never would be. As he worked on his music, studying his books, practicing in heat or cold, there was no opposition that drove Sonny more strongly than his own measurement of himself.

The main reason he dropped out, he said, was because he wasn't satisfied with his music. He would teach himself, as he had always done and always would.

"Sonny always felt that he didn't have a formal music education," said Lucille Rollins, who was his girlfriend at the time. "He was trying to further his musical knowledge, which anybody else would say, 'Why do you have to do that?' Because when you're Sonny Rollins, you don't need to do that. But he always felt he wished he had formal training."

He was, she said, "the most intelligent person I've ever known, and the best read."

And so, for nearly two years, the dissatisfied pilgrim, who could have found a welcome reception anywhere in the jazz world, lived the life of a dropout, a recluse. He trained his mind and his body, searching for new founts of musical wisdom and inner spiritual strength, zeroing in, as always, on the music that lay at the center of his being.

Many have pondered what sparked this trip to the mountain, to the bridge: Was Sonny searching for freedom from drugs? Was this a quest for a vital religious life, a journey whose object was philosophical enlightenment and peace? Was it a time of healing, a chance to escape the grief arising from his mother's death or the pain of his messed-up teeth?

The 50s had been a time of enormous conflict for Sonny, and the fever pitch to which his career had built by the end of the decade had no doubt exacerbated the stress he felt. The birth of the 60s signaled a time for self-reflection and renewal, an opportunity to get out of the rat race and pause—a moment to put everything back in place.

But, in Sonny's mind, it was about getting the music right. Jazz was the central thread around which all his conflict and all the tension had been woven, the warp and the woof on which Sonny had built his life. Everything spiritual, philosophical, religious—mediation, yoga, vegetarianism, exercising, sobriety, and Rosicrucianism—was about the music.

It was all about competition, about cutting challengers, about becoming the best, about surpassing the titans who had brought him into the fold—it was about overcoming the legacy of Bird.

This stoic, ascetic, single-minded search for perfection—a perfection never truly achieved no matter how others praised it—this drive was what cemented the legend of Sonny Rollins. It was a drive that would take on all comers with energy to spare. It was the force that drove Sonny's life.

Those were the reported reasons, but there were other unknown issues that consumed him—a failure to attend his beloved mother's funeral, a bitter divorce that he mistakenly initiated, and the ongoing, nagging problem of how to take back the crown from John Coltrane, whose tenor saxophone sound became the new favorite among both traditional jazz fans and those in the world of spirituality.

The end of the 50s had seen Coltrane rise to prominence in his own right—and critics were quick to compare the two saxophonists. Their reviews pitted the two musicians against each other, some declaring Sonny the winner, others favoring Coltrane.

On the one hand, the music press' emphasis on competition dismayed Sonny. He and Coltrane were close friends, and each of the two men respected and admired the work of the other. The inability of the press to applaud the music of one without degrading the other must have stung at Sonny's sensitive soul.

On the other hand, many jazz fans certainly did see "Trane" as a rival. Yes, Sonny had outshone Coltrane on *Tenor Madness*, but this older man was quickly building up steam, a challenge to Sonny's position as the best of the best. Sonny, however, denied Coltrane was his rival.

Perhaps Sonny's competitive spirit helped to spur on his woodshedding—maybe he did not wish to run with Coltrane at a time when he felt unsure about the quality of his music. He would retreat to the woodshed and regroup, strengthening his technique to fight again another day.

And there was more that drove Sonny out of the spotlight— his personal disgust with the music business. He was one of the most sought-after jazz musicians of the day, but the structure of the recording industry prevented him from seeing much of the money his compositions earned—the record companies had control of publishing and recording rights to his originals.

"Sonny should have made a fortune out of 'Airegin,' 'St. Thomas,' and lots of other songs he had written," said Jeffrey. "What happened is he didn't get any money for those songs. He had to share all of the publishing and recording royalties with everybody who recorded."

Black jazz musicians were being routinely exploited, the profits of their artwork funneled into corporate pockets. Meanwhile, white artists like Stan Getz and Dave Brubeck were enjoying financial success by cloning black artists. They were wealthy and living in luxurious digs while Sonny found it difficult to make ends meet.

"A majority of musicians were being exploited as far as not getting just compensation for their talents," Jeffrey said. "The record companies gave you the figures they chose to give you, and there wasn't much you could do about it. They knew how to cover their tracks.

"Sonny was hurt by the racism, the economic exploitation and the discriminatory treatment of him and other black musicians and decided he wasn't going to do it anymore from a business standpoint," he added.

As Sonny later told Art Taylor in *Notes and Tones*: "One of the reasons I stopped then was because things had got to the point where I found that playing was getting to be a real job and a chore, which I didn't dig.

"I spend as much money as necessary to get equipment, clothes or whatever I need to make an impression and to be into the music. It's all done for the music first, regardless of what it costs me. Many people have said that I have a lot of energy, which I do, because I'm playing for the music.

"For instance, I played a three-hour set one night in a nightclub, and they were trying to get us off the stage to turn the house over. In other words, I'm playing and thinking about trying to get the music across and nothing else. Time doesn't matter.

"Maybe a lot of the younger cats might not have that same energy. I've found that a lot of musicians I played with don't have the same kind of incentive. I thought it might be because I was who I am and they were working for me, so I was supposed to have more incentive than they did."

Sonny also recalled having little money during his bridge period. "Lucille took a job as a private secretary so we could eat," he said. "Later, I retired her."

For Lucille, Sonny's sabbatical was all rather bizarre.

"I was working during the day at a regular job," she said. "He was going out and practicing on the bridge at night. I would go to sleep. Sometimes he was out all night. If you think of somebody doing that now, you'd say, 'My God!' I didn't know any better, or maybe things were not as bad then."

When not on the bridge, Sonny continued his spiritual search for truth and enlightenment. Lucille often came home from work to find Sonny immersed in contemplation and study, candles burning. Sometimes, she would discover him in states of profound meditation.

"He was hanging from a bar," she remembered, "and I was bewildered. Hanging there in an out-of-body state, like in a trance, and I didn't know where he was. It scared the heck out of me."

He was, in fact, inside himself, seeking answers. Sonny had contemplated Christianity and found it wanting. Its history had condemned it—it had once been a tool used to control and befuddle slaves, a means towards the goal of oppression. Now his gaze was spread wider, searching into the traditions that had grown outside of the world of white Christianity—including Buddhism and yoga.

Buddhism espouses a perfection of the soul through karma. If an act of bad karma might trigger a wave that ripples across many lifetimes, what is the effect of good karma? Each positive act will build upon the one before it, an upward spiral into realms of new awareness and compassion.

"A belief in reincarnation means that you live many lives," Sonny said. "You have one soul that is reincarnated into many bodies." The practice of good karma allows the soul to advance through more elevated stages of development, "until you reach a point where you are more perfect, more God-like."

Ultimately, perfection of the soul results in freedom from the cycle—*moksha*. "When you get to the point where you are cool, you don't have to be reincarnated into another body," he said. "The ultimate place is where God gives you the piano, and you can play it."

Within his lifetime, the message Sonny took from Buddhism was a simple one: "I will try not to do too much harm in this lifetime."

The subcontinent that had birthed Buddhism also provided another vehicle for Sonny's spiritual journey—yoga. A disciplined system of breathing exercises and physical fitness, yoga provides heightened levels of self-awareness and contemplation. It also stretches and tones the body, bolstering longevity and increasing energy. Sonny credited certain yogic techniques as important factors in the liberation of his mind.

"I had a chinning bar in my living room," Sonny recalled. "I had a set of weights. I was trying to get really physically healthy. As they say, you never have a healthy soul without a healthy body. I was getting a deep appreciation of the sanctity of the human body and the human soul together.

"It was all one quest. It sort of awakened within me the possibility that you could do whatever you wanted to do. I realized there was a higher power out there. When you are young you kind of forget about God and you think that you can do everything by yourself.

"You know, it is kind of hard to get close to God when you are out in the secular world, especially when you're a musician, and you're involved in lawsuits and all that stuff and you're getting all this notoriety and living the high life. It's hard to bring a spiritual element into your life. It was during this period that I was also getting into yoga and studying Eastern religions and reading a lot. So I think all of that coalesced together," he said.

He found that yoga made him feel better. "I got down on the floor and did my poses. It involves the whole mental and physical thing. It is very natural," he said. "There's nothing spooky about it. It is just a real natural thing to make you breathe better and feel better. It just keeps your eyes on the prize."

Sonny also studied Rosicrucianism during this period. "Rosicrucianism goes back to an Egyptian pharaoh that's supposed to be the spiritual father of the movement," Sonny said. "This pharaoh believed in one God. All the pharaohs before him believed in different gods. Rosicrucianism didn't really conflict with my Christian values. Most Rosicrucians are Christians."

The Rosicrucian Order, based in San Jose, California, describes itself as an international nonsectarian fraternity that studies the higher principles of life as expressed in humanity and nature. Members of the order learn about philosophy and the arts and sciences. The order came to America in 1694.

Many of its members have conducted studies dealing with music, art, and painting. Rosicrucians study the trends of history and attempt to apply their philosophy to meeting life's problems. They believe that people must understand and live in harmony with nature. The Rosicrucian Order asserts it is not a religion. Its emblem is a gold cross with a red rose in the center.

Sonny's friend Jeffrey recalled this about the saxophonist's time on the bridge: "We would just be rapping about different things. We didn't talk about Rosicrucianism all the time, but I knew that he was into it. He would tell me what he was reading, and he would show me some of the books."

Except for Jeffrey and a few others, Sonny made himself scarce during his sabbatical. "He wouldn't answer his phone or his door," Jeffrey recalled. "There was a funny story that some guys came into the building and knocked on Sonny's door. He wouldn't answer. These cats kept knocking on the door, and Sonny came out there with a cap pistol. Those guys broke the door down getting out of there."

Sonny also faithfully kept in touch with his older sister. "I talked with Sonny sometimes on the phone. He told me not to worry and that he was okay. I asked if I should bring something down for him to eat. He said not to bother because he was fine," Gloria said.

"So he didn't bare his soul to me or anything," she added. "He just reassured me that there was nothing to worry about. Sonny is very interesting because you cannot always tell what Sonny is thinking. He doesn't express his emotions, even if he's very close to you. He holds back and is very reserved."

During his time on the bridge, Sonny found a grounding force in girlfriend Lucille. The Kansas native brought stability to his life, and with it came a business acumen that would later ensure the success of Sonny's career and the financial success that resulted from it. Where the winds of Sonny's life had blown him in many different directions, she represented order from the chaos that had consumed his life.

And yet, she did not attempt to curb Sonny's often inscrutable behavior. Lucille's laissez-faire accommodation of his peculiarities was a character trait that helped ensure a lasting relationship between the two of them. She didn't nag him, didn't question him, didn't meddle in his activities. "I was just there," she said.

Lucille, a political conservative, didn't like pot smoking, she admits. Sometimes she would show her displeasure when a few of Sonny's jazz friends dropped by out of the blue. But mainly, she let Sonny be alone, allowed him to work out whatever he was working out. Her primary role was that of a companion.

"He was a different person after that," Lucille said. "He was never a bad person, but he became an exceptional person."

When he returned to the Jazz Gallery in 1961, the transformation was complete. The old druggie playboy social jazzman was no more. In his place was a mystic, a warrior ready to challenge any soloist or record executive who would dare stand in his way.

Like the New York City melting pot from which he had emerged, Sonny Rollins crafted himself a unique mixture of religious traditions from around the world—becoming a spiritual seeker, a disciple of his own personal faith. He was a mystic, a believer in enlightenment and the possibility of greater things. Such belief would set the path that Sonny followed for the rest of his life.

By the time he was ready to descend the bridge for the last time, he was chattering up a storm, fighting the subway and boats and trucks and beating them all. He even spat out a few brash honks, mimicking a passing flock of seagulls. And then, he was playing alone, his music bright against the silent canopy of the night. He was playing a jazz that was thick and rich and full of life.

Sonny Rollins walked away from the bridge and arced his horn toward Manhattan, coming down from the mountain a changed man.

CHAPTER 21

Comeback Kid

There were no ticker-tape parades with confetti flying all over the place. No marching bands blasting out patriotic songs. No politicians promising pipe dreams over megaphones before thousands of well-wishers.

While the comeback of Sonny Rollins was not greeted with the traditional solemnity of a hero-soldier or jock, the different kinds of reception for the jazz giant were equally momentous. From Tokyo to Toledo, fans demonstrated they had sorely missed the tenor saxophonist during his two years of self-imposed exile from the jazz scene.

It began with his comeback in 1961 and lasted for several years afterwards. Whether it was on the streets or nightclubs in the Big Apple or in other parts of the country and the world, fans loudly shouted out: "Welcome back, Sonny," and "Sonny, we missed you!"

Sonny's comeback to the jazz scene was heralded by an article in the jazz magazine *Metronome* in the summer of 1961. It was written by critic Ralph Berton, who was commuting over the bridge from

Manhattan to Brooklyn when he discovered Sonny sarcastically blowing his saxophone at the tugboats as they tooted their horns.

"The discovery was amazing," said Berton. "Imagine the great Sonny Rollins perched atop a bridge blowing his heart out. I had never seen anything like it, and I wanted the world to know what had transpired during those years. I was thrilled with his comeback and I'm sure millions of his fans around the world felt the same."

Sonny's comeback proved he had morphed into an intriguing worldwide figure, and it was met with massive media attention: newspapers, magazines, television, and radio stations carried the news of his return—at the time a rare event of acknowledgment for a black man, and especially for a jazz musician who had abruptly vanished without public notice two years earlier.

RCA Victor announced it had signed a several-year, multimillion dollar recording contract with Sonny, making it one of the largest contracts ever for a jazz musician, black or white. Club owners and concert promoters also upped the ante. Prior to his return, he had been able to earn an estimated $2,000 per night for a one-night concert. Now, his fee was double or triple that amount.

Sonny's style still had much of the original hard bop sound that he introduced in the late 1940s, but now he had begun to incorporate many of the avant-garde and modal jazz sounds that were sweeping the jazz world. Though he was only 31 years old in 1961, many of the new jazz fans were already much younger and some thought he wanted to appeal to them to expand his fan base.

During live performances, he began to increasingly meld some of the erratic new sounds into his music, much to the chagrin of many fans. He was losing some of the oldsters, but he was becoming more relevant to younger audiences. Many of them were white new agers, bohemians, and artists who were drawn to both his music and his spiritual image. However, he seemed to retain the same type of black fans, but more of the hip and grass-roots.

"Sonny couldn't care less about public opinion," explained his close friend Ahmed Basheer, the writer and jazz expert who had lived with Charlie Parker. "He went with the new flow, the so-called avant-garde or free jazz, because many of the cats of this music were breaking new ground, which appealed to Sonny.

Max Gordon, the owner of the Village Vanguard in Greenwich Village, a club that always maintained a level of artistic integrity with its top-notch bands, said he preferred the old Sonny. "His old sound was clearly the best. It took me a while to adjust to his new approach, but I soon became a fan. It was different, but exciting. Plus, all the fans loved him."

The Vanguard, located in the heart of the Village at Sheridan Square, featured the more esoteric players of the day—old and young— but it also served as one of their gathering spots. The musicians usually hung out in the kitchen, where they ate dinner standing up and talked about everything, including women, the new jazz, and politics.

Many of the new cats under the scrutiny of the jazz cognoscenti included Ornette Coleman, Eric Dolphy, and John Coltrane, the latter of whom had started as a bebop musician but was emerging as the leader of these new free-style players. They were severely criticized by the jazz establishment.

Downbeat magazine, a leading jazz periodical, produced several articles in 1961 lambasting Coleman, Coltrane, and Dolphy's music. They questioned the legitimacy of free jazz—suggesting that it was noise rather than music. Among other things, the issue was whether the players could in fact effectively utilize conventional harmony, rhythm and especially melody, the latter of which critics said was missing.

Due in part to the pressure of the critics, Coleman had to disband his quartet. What kept him afloat, however, was the praise heaped upon him by pianist and composer John Lewis, the leader of the Modern Jazz Quartet. "Ornette is a very fine musician who knows traditional music as much as anybody. He is moving in a musical direction that is valid for him and I just happen to like it a lot," said Lewis, who was highly respected for his formal European classical training.

Lewis himself was criticized for using what some critics and musicians said was an excessive infusion of classical music into jazz. "Sometimes, you just cannot win. The best thing a musician can do is play what he feels and knows what is right for him. That was the case for Ornette and I applaud him for his courage."

Sonny, who was a friend and ardent supporter of Coleman, asserted: "Ornette helped to change the face of our music and to hell with what the critics said about him. I won't compare him with Bird, but they said the same nasty things about him. We all know what happened and how Bird became the main man on alto."

Sonny would soon hire many of Coleman's top alumni, including Don Cherry on trumpet and Billy Higgins on drums. These and other musicians played a pivotal role in moving Sonny from hard bop to the new free-style sound. They also helped to change the direction of jazz, much to the chagrin of jazz traditionalists who rarely accepted this new approach.

Sonny's return showed he had developed a mastery of yoga, Buddhism, and other religions after intensive years of study and application. It was just the beginning of what was to become a lifelong commitment to those disciplines, both in terms of physical and mental strength, as well as self-control and a regimen of daily exercise.

At the same time, he projected a new mystique, which fans adored because it added another dimension of mystery and intrigue to a man who some believed had discovered many secrets of the universe owing to his spiritual practices.

Gloria said that Sonny had "drastically changed" during his sabbatical. "I accepted the new, mysterious Sonny, but I didn't fully understand some of these foreign religions and cultures. I had heard about them, but I didn't quite understand all of them. They were far-out, and so was Sonny. I witnessed a lot of unusual things around him, but I won't go into them."

Sonny was equally secretive, only superficially discussing his spiritual studies. When asked about details of his new life, he would laugh as loudly as he played his horn, with a sarcastic tone that suggested he didn't want to talk about it.

When fellow musicians and fans read about Sonny's studies, many of them began to explore these exotic faiths and cultures. Zen Buddhism became a fad for musicians and his new fans, which included New Agers and other followers of Eastern faiths and practices. In addition, more tenor saxophonists wanted to copy Sonny's "new" style, and some even abandoned his hard bop trademark sound.

"Sonny always seemed a little different after his comeback," recalled Basheer, who was himself a Muslim. "He was still a good brother and I admired him. He had many successes on the bridge, but he was still searching. That was part of his personality. Always searching."

Sonny later said of his self-imposed exile: "I could have probably spent many more years of my life going back and forth to the bridge, practicing, and enjoying the serenity and space the bridge offered me at a time when I really needed it. I wanted to return to reality and I did."

Upon his return to "reality," he didn't especially like what he saw. He was surrounded by hustlers and drug dealers and other slicksters in the jazz clubs who wanted to sell dope to the musicians. There were the female groupies who found him attractive, as he was handsome, physically fit, and confident. He was also charming, but with a sardonic edge reminiscent of his saxophone sound.

"Spending time on the bridge gave me a better perspective about life," Sonny said. "When you are alone so much, you begin to feel and see things that are not always visible. I will always honor the time I spent on the bridge and the lessons learned. They were very important to my well-being."

Not surprisingly, Sonny named his 1962 return album, *The Bridge*. Produced by George Avakian, the sidemen featured guitarist Jim Hall, drummer Ben Riley, and bassist Bob Cranshaw. It was to become one of Sonny's best-selling records.

"I believe *The Bridge* was one of Sonny's best recordings," said Cranshaw. "It showed a different side of the man, someone who had experienced a new level of spirituality, which he had translated into his new sound. For Sonny, the power of spirituality was extremely important, and it was nothing to take for granted. His new sound was fantastic, and it was a joy playing with him each night."

Following the *Bridge* recording, Sonny continued to create albums with a noticeably different, more unusual sound. His 1962 recording called *What's New?* displayed an infusion of Latin rhythms, and on

Our Man in Jazz, recorded live at The Village Gate, he delved into the so-called "free-thing" or avant-garde movement.

Our Man in Jazz featured Cranshaw on bass, and avant-garde players such as Billy Higgins on drums and Don Cherry on cornet. Perhaps Sonny's most important recording during this period was *Sonny Meets Hawk,* one he did with his hero and greatest influence, tenor saxophonist Coleman Hawkins—one of the principal founders of bebop.

"Bean [Hawkins] showed all the cats the way," Sonny said, referring to such top-notch tenor saxophonists as Ben Webster, Chu Berry, Lester Young, Gene Ammons, Dexter Gordon, Stan Getz, and John Coltrane. "Bean was our main source and we all owe him a debt of gratitude. I felt honored being able to make the recording with him."

The album also featured Paul Bley as pianist. Sonny later made recordings with such stalwart players as pianist Herbie Hancock, himself a devout Buddhist who had helped shape the sound of Sonny's close friend, Miles Davis.

Sonny also identified with the New Age and bohemian movements, which, like him, were heavily inflected with Asian, Eastern and African music. But, it was the music and culture of India, especially the secrets of yoga, that intrigued Sonny the most.

CHAPTER 22

Wedding Bells

This was no storybook wedding. The groom rejected the customary tuxedo and sauntered into the apartment with a Mohawk haircut and a colorful Asian style silk robe. Likewise, the bride opted out of an elaborate, lacy white gown, wearing instead a simple yellow cotton dress.

No bridesmaids in fancy gowns were hovering about. In place of a ring bearer and flower girl were two enormous German Shepherds, panting and sniffing as they followed their master down the aisle.

The quirky marriage took place in 1965 in downtown Brooklyn. The groom was the eccentric and politically progressive Sonny Rollins, and the bride was Lucille Pearson, a politically conservative white woman from the Midwest. Lucille had pursued the saxophonist for eight years—finally getting her man, despite the absence of the amenities associated with traditional weddings.

They were the original odd couple: Sonny, born and bred in Harlem, and Lucille, born and bred in Kansas City. They had opposing views about race and politics. They were both strong and independent, and adamant about their respective political views.

Until the wedding, Lucille's presence in Sonny's life had been a partial one. Now and then she would return to Chicago to visit her mother, Nanette. She remained a mysterious, shadowy figure to Sonny's friends and family—it would be years before some of them were introduced to her.

The Rollins family did not meet her until 1965. "Sonny said he was going to get married in the apartment on Willoughby Walk [in Brooklyn]," Gloria said. "My father, my two children, my husband Tomlyn [Tom] Anderson, and the minister would be the only ones there."

Sonny thought having a minister was unimportant, Gloria recalled, for Sonny had already dismissed most of what passed for organized Christianity. But Lucille "wanted a minister to marry them because she wanted a religious aspect to it." Tom Anderson arranged for a minister, a young friend of the organist at their church, to perform the ceremony.

Although Lucille and Sonny had known each other for ten years and had been living together for about seven, Gloria had no recollection of ever having met her. Lucille said she had been at the Rollins apartment the day that Valborg died, but Gloria, whose mind was elsewhere at the time, did not recall seeing her.

Valborg never met Lucille, nor had Sonny's father, Walter. Gloria surmised, "You see, he may have had ambivalent feelings about marrying her. I never laid eyes on her until the wedding day.

"She was a surprise to me. I had never seen her. I only knew of her by long distance—that is, I talked to her on the phone. I met her on her wedding day. I think she spent a lot of time in Chicago. She did not want to be evaluated. I think that may have been it."

Lucille was wearing a "plain, little, yellow cotton sleeveless dress," said Gloria. "I think she had made it. The apartment looked lovely. Sonny had bought two dozen roses, and she prepared a little buffet. I told my children afterward that they never ate my meatloaf, but they ate hers."

Sonny's father Walter, a former Navy chef, baked a cake for the

Illus. 34 - Sonny Rollins, who was not known to be a conformist, introduced the Mohawk hairstyle back in the 1960s, and helped to renew the popularity of the native hairstyle.

occasion.

The wedding, said Gloria, "was hilarious! I don't think Sonny thought it was hilarious."

The wedding took place on a cold day, Gloria recalled. When the family arrived, Sonny was out walking the two dogs.

"Sonny came in from walking the dogs. He hated the cold and was bundled up in an overcoat; he had a scarf around his face like the Invisible Man, wrapped up so you could hardly see there was a person there."

Sonny went into the bedroom while the guests waited outside.

"When Sonny came out it was so startling I had to suppress a laugh," she said. "He was wearing a tall oriental fez with a tassel, and a beautiful silk gown of Chinese or Japanese style. But he had also shaved his eyebrows!" (Sonny denies ever shaving his eyebrows.)

"He looked so exotic and awful," Gloria added. "My father and I were suppressing a laugh. I knew Sonny was so sensitive that if he saw us giggling he would be so upset that he would ask us to leave."

The bewildered minister launched into a Christian ceremony. "He didn't know what he was getting into," said Gloria. "It was really funny."

Gloria's young son, Clifton Anderson, first met Lucille then too. "She was very friendly," he recalled. "I remember she used to cook real meatloaf. They had these two dogs, Major and Minor. I remember Major bit me and I was nervous around them."

The wedding took place not long after Clifton's first meeting with his famous uncle. When Sonny came to Gloria's home to visit, the boy was five or six years old.

"The first time I remember seeing him, he was wearing a Mohican, the Mohawk hairstyle," Clifton said. "I saw this person at the door, you know, this big guy with the Mohawk. I ran to hide behind my mother. I was holding onto her leg.

"'Don't be scared,' my mother said. 'Where are you going? This is your uncle.'"

Clifton remembered his mother telling Sonny that he was interested in music, that he had a musical inclination like the rest of the Rollins clan.

"Between that visit and the next time I saw him, I had decided I wanted to play trombone," he said. "That's when he bought a horn for me. I was about seven. When you're a little kid, and someone buys you something, you can relate to that. After he bought me the horn I started getting more involved, and through those years my mother would always tell me, 'You know, your uncle is a famous, great musician.'"

Both sides of the family seemed to embrace the new couple, despite differences in race, politics, and lifestyle. Clifton, Gloria, and Walter were accepting of Sonny's marriage. Even Lucille's mother, Nanette—who wasn't in attendance at the wedding—got along well with her new son-in-law.

Interestingly, Sonny's marriage to a white woman was not unusual, even in the 1960s. Most of the top jazz stars, like Charlie Parker and Percy Heath, were married to white women, many of whom also helped guide their careers.

For Sonny, no-nonsense, intelligent Lucille was a grounding force. She was pragmatic, loyal, and down-to-earth. She could provide Sonny with the stability he had been seeking for so many years. Lucille was also straight-laced, shunning drugs and drinking only socially.

Perhaps more important, Sonny knew he wouldn't have the same sort of problems with Lucille that he'd had with Dawn. Men did not ogle Lucille, whereas they had salivated over his fashion model ex-wife. He no longer experienced the excruciating jealousy and (perhaps irrational) fear of infidelity that had torn apart his first marriage.

But within a few years, Sonny once again found himself embroiled in marital strife. Just a year or two after marrying Lucille, around 1966 or 1967, he fell in love with a white Danish woman.

Sonny met the woman through the jazz tenor saxophonist Yusef Lateef, a mutual friend, while playing a gig in Denmark. Like Lateef, a member of the Ahmadiyya Muslim Community, the Danish woman was also a practicing Muslim. "She was really into it," Sonny recalled.

While Sonny never converted to Islam or took on an Arabic name like Lateef and other black jazz musicians of his era, he understood why they were motivated to do so.

"A lot of these people felt alienated from so-called white Christian religion, [and] they wanted to do something else, so that's why they did it. That's the motivation a lot of times. You have to respect that …" he said. "You don't see too many cats with Arabic names [these days]. I think it was a way of showing alienation and of showing protest from the hardships of living as a minority in a white Christian society. I think a lot of it was protesting."

While praying in his Copenhagen hotel room following a concert, Sonny had a profound, mystical experience.

"One day I was in my hotel room in Denmark, and I was gonna pray," Sonny recalled. "And you know how when you pray, you get down on the floor and you bend over and you pray to Allah, you know. So, I was doing that, and it was just like a force that came and sort of held me down in that position, sort of like a hand, while I was praying.

"It was just, you know, a force to let me know that this was something real. The power of the religion itself sort of spoke to me in that way while I was praying.

"[It was] very profound. I'll never forget it. Soon after that, I realized the strength of Islam as a religion and it being real. It's not something to jive around about, nothing to play with."

At one point during his relationship with the Danish woman, Sonny seriously considered leaving Lucille. However, his older sister insisted he return to his wife back in New York.

While Sonny didn't leave Lucille for another woman, the two separated around 1968. Lucille returned to the Midwest, where she got a job working for the University of Chicago. "We were apart for about two years," she recalled.

Meanwhile, Sonny was not only grappling with his romantic life, but also with his spirituality. Around the same time of his separation from Lucille, Sonny decided to take another sabbatical.

This time, instead of seeking refuge on the Williamsburg Bridge, Sonny would venture to the birthplace of so many spiritual traditions he embraced—India.

"That was the year all the stuff was going on in the sixties. I think he was in India during the time Robert Kennedy and Martin Luther King, Jr. were killed," she said. "Sonny's sister used to call me periodically.

She saw stuff on the news which looked like the whole city of Chicago was burning. She would call and say, 'Are you okay?' Gloria is a great sister-in-law. She's a very sensible type person, and a good person."

However, Sonny never called Lucille from India—and there was only the occasional letter. "I was pretty unhappy. I was working for a physicist at the University of Chicago, and we did these things with cosmic rays," she recalled.

"I would go down in the basement and develop these cosmic ray films in big baths, completely in the dark, and I'd be weeping. Nobody was around, and developing these stupid cosmic ray films I'd be weeping down there and nobody knew," she admitted.

But Sonny was developing his own cosmic rays half a world away, in a tradition thousands of years older than the science that Lucille knew in Chicago.

As we grow in our consciousness, there will be more compassion and more love, and then the barriers between people, between religions, between nations will begin to fall. Yes, we have to beat down the separateness."

— RAM DASS[6]

CHAPTER 23

Coming of the New Age

The cats on stage blowing out their hearts and souls were decidedly black. Though, in the audience, there was a near-absence of black faces; the ebullient fans clapping and belting out the loud chants of approval were decidedly white.

This was a typical portrait of the state of jazz, once an affordable music found in black clubs in the so-called "chitlin' district" of the South or the speakeasies in the North, the latter of which made their money from gambling, prostitution and the like. Jazz was simply an afterthought.

The absence of African Americans could mean that it was an economic thing. After all, jazz was an elite music that attracted the well-educated and well-heeled—making it difficult for most blacks to indulge in a music they had created themselves. The cost for an evening of jazz at one of New York's top clubs was always very high, making it nearly impossible for most economically-challenged blacks.

The jazz buffs in these audiences were mostly New Agers,

intellectuals, bohemians, and artists who had changed the very fabric of a music that was once steeped in the soulful, funky tradition of the Southern black Baptist church. While the 12-bar soulful blues foundation was still intact, the music had drifted dramatically more towards the East rather than the West.

The dominant reason for the music's shift was the abandonment of Christianity by Sonny Rollins and scores of other jazz musicians, who opted for the ancient forms of yoga, Hinduism, and other Eastern and African religions and cultures. Perhaps more than any other jazz innovators, Sonny and John Coltrane are responsible for the move from the West to the East.

Jazz composer and pianist Randy Weston, a strong supporter of both musicians, who has himself spent decades living in Africa and abroad, blamed the black Christian Church for the music's virtual disappearance of Christian influences.

"Sonny and many of the cats rejected Christianity a long time ago because the black church rejected them. The churches did not support us," he explained. "They have unfortunately associated us with sin and decadence, rather than seeing the great spiritual value of our music.

"Our music is and has always been spiritual, and it is this spirituality that has been the driving force of jazz since its inception," he added, noting that he would welcome a return by the black Christian church. "They would make a big difference in how the cats play the music."

On the other hand, many New Agers tend to be more spiritual than religious, meaning that a large percentage of them are either agnostic or atheistic, or both. Like many jazz musicians, when asked if they are religious, their popular refrain is: "I'm spiritual, but not religious." People who claim they are spiritual often do believe in a higher intelligence or deity, but do not want to belong to any organized religion, because they feel these old-fashioned institutions are restrictive in demanding conformity to established patterns of behavior.

The lion's share of Sonny Rollins' audiences in the late 1940s were African Americans. There would be only a small sprinkling of bohemian whites and Asians who had come to hear the fledgling tenor saxophonist grapple with bebop—the hot new jazz trend of the postwar period.

Of course, Sonny appreciated anyone who would come to hear him blow his horn, but considering the small numbers of non-black fans in those early days, it was tempting for him to view them as merely an afterthought. Yet, being the diplomat that he was, he acknowledged and treated them politely.

"I've always appreciated and respected my fans, no matter who they are," Sonny said. "I only care if they respect the music I am playing because that's what really counts. It's their love for the music that matters to me.

"At the same time, it would be nice if the brothers would show up at the concerts and clubs to offer their support," he said. "After all, jazz is our music. We created it, and the way things are going, we will have lost it if we are not careful."

Fast-forward to the year 2010, and Sonny's audience at nightclubs and concert halls is completely different. According to an informal survey of musicians and others, the breakdown was 60 percent white, 20 percent Asian, and 20 percent black, representing a substantial drop in black fans—about one-third of what it had been in decades past.

"It was amazing to see so few African Americans sitting in the audience and to see how each year the numbers would further decline," explained Clifton Anderson, the trombonist who worked as a sideman with Sonny for more than three decades. "It was a surprise to me, and I'm sure it was for Sonny, too."

The term "New Age" is itself a loose, amorphous term to describe various spiritual movements—some serious and others driven by commercialism or even charlatanism—that coalesced in the West during the last two decades of the twentieth century. It gained a foothold in the popular imagination as the millennium year of 2001 approached.

The New Age was nothing new. At the end of the nineteenth century, Helena Blavatsky, who founded the Theosophical Society, became known as the Godmother of the New Age. It was then believed by many that the dawning twentieth century would introduce a new age. Just as the current New Age movement is turning its attention to various spiritual practices introduced to the West from the East, the Theosophical Society studied Eastern religions and brought their influence from India to New York more than a century ago.

In the twentieth century, the term "New Age" gained currency among the Woodstock generation weaned on songs like "Age of Aquarius" (from the 1967 American Tribal Love-Rock Musical *Hair*) and "Let It Be" by the Beatles, and even movies like Stanley Kubrick's sci-fi film *2001: A Space Odyssey*. These songs and films were embraced by many in the counterculture who would later adopt New Age spirituality as they found themselves aging into their thirties. (It should be noted that Woodstock itself was actually advertised as "An Aquarian Exposition: 3 Days of Peace & Music.")

The New Age movement had many sources, not the least of which was America's ongoing love-hate affair with Asian cultures. Millions of Americans got their first taste of Asia as fallout from the wars with Japan in the 1940s, Korea in the 1950s, and Vietnam in the 1960s and '70s.

Though these interactions were contentious, enough philosophy seeped through to convince a significant subset of the U.S. population— especially its intellectual and artistic communities—that there might be something worthy of notice in the ancient practices that had sustained Asian cultures for many millennia.

In 1965, a major shift in U.S. immigration policy allowed large numbers of people from Asian nations to enter the country as permanent residents. As a result, many communities from coast to coast witnessed ashrams, mosques, lamaseries, and zendos (Japanese meditation halls) added to the religious landscape, where churches or synagogues had previously been the norm.

The 1960s in America also saw the rise of the Human Potential movement, as personified by the Esalen Institute in Big Sur, California in 1962. The establishment of the San Francisco Zen Center and various Transcendental Meditation locales—popularized by the Beatles during their pilgrimages to India—helped in the mainstreaming of "exotic" New Age practices in America, as did the work of poets like Alan Ginsberg, Kenneth Rexroth, and Lawrence Ferlinghetti.

Steven J. Sutcliffe, a scholar of the New Age movement, is a senior lecturer in the study of religion at the University of Edinburgh in Scotland. In his 2004 monograph, *Children of the New Age*, he wrote that New Age thinking "has an almost entirely white, middle-class demography largely made up of professional, managerial, arts, and entrepreneurial occupations."

Perceived as somewhat of a weirdo fringe movement in the 1950s and 1960s, "New Age" was embraced by baby boomers in the 1970s and 1980s, adding a degree of respectability to things countercultural. Though beatniks and jazz artists made their mark in the 1950s, the decade is still stereotyped as the bland, conforming Eisenhower era, one that viewed dissent as suspect, even unpatriotic. By the 1970s, the counterculture had at least an air of respectability about it.

This may help explain the shift in Sonny Rollins' audience, and that of audiences for jazz in general. During the 1960s and thereafter, the focus of subversive music shifted from jazz to rock, rock 'n' roll, and the sounds of the Beatles (in the group's guru-driven Transcendental Meditation phase).

The Transcendental Meditation movement originated with Maharishi Mahesh Yogi, when he began teaching his meditation technique to the public—first in India and then to the West in a series of world tours. Since then, thousands of students have joined the movement, including celebrities and scientists who have validated the benefits of meditation for a person's health and well-being.

Jazz musicians, with their urban, drug-tinged aura, were eclipsed by groovy New Age avatars with "let it be" as their words of wisdom. The trend continued as baby boomers aged. It's possible few in the 1980s or 1990s believed in the "Age of Aquarius" any more, with its tie-dye Summer of Love connotations, but many became devotees of such figures as Shirley MacLaine and Werner Erhard, who incorporated a variety of esoteric practices into their systems, which fall under the New Age umbrella in some form or another.

However, the shift to Aquarius is very real to astrologers who believe each of the twelve astrological ages is influenced by a different star sign. The Age of Aquarius heralds the changeover from Pisces to the age of the water carrier, which is supposed to bring with it significant energetic shifts in human consciousness.

The music of Sonny Rollins, too, underwent a shift during this transitional era. Major and minor changes here, there, and everywhere, until some purists felt it just didn't sound like the "real thing" anymore. It is no exaggeration to say Sonny incorporated more "world music" motifs into his approach, both to jazz and to his overall mindset. He believes that God and the yoga practices of Hindu culture have been responsible for his music, as well as for his quality of life and longevity—he turned 87 in September of 2017.

Sonny did not wear ancient traditional Indian music on his sleeve, however. Its influences are extremely subtle in his music, and he fuses it sparingly and with humility, which reflects both his change as a person and as a musician. Through decades of intense study and involvement, he understands that the focus of Indian music is far more than mere entertainment, but that it helps musicians and listeners alike experience spiritual power.

Western styles of music tend to have three components: melody, rhythm, and harmony. Indian music, by contrast, is a deeply contemplative music that focuses heavily on melodic development, where its rhythm provides the music with direction, texture, and a degree of sensuality.

Harmony, on the other hand, gives the music resonance via the use of instruments like the tanpura or swarmandal, as well as the santoor and the harmonium. The tabla adds another dimension because of its semi-melodic quality. These instruments can help the listeners reach deeper levels of spirituality, which, after all, is the goal of the music.

Dramatic changes are not new to Sonny. When he embarked on a jazz career in 1947, he was surrounded by Thelonious Monk, Charlie Parker, Miles Davis, and scores of others who were intent on constantly changing jazz and creating new modes of expression through the medium that became known as bebop.

During this time as the young Turk, Sonny was prone to experimentation. He was known for discharging harsh, sardonic honks from his horn, skipping traditional melodies and harmonies for substitute chords and performing songs at wild, breakneck tempos that prevented audiences from even tapping their feet to the music.

Then, as now, Sonny's tenor saxophone playing was consistent in that it was employing the same awesome technical facility and deft artistic improvisations that first distinguished him on such albums as *Saxophone Colossus* and *Tenor Madness*, both of which became instant jazz classics when they were released in 1956.

But, as Sonny delved more deeply into the study and practices of ancient Egyptian and Asian religions at the expense of traditional Western influences and practices, his music shifted into a new, more exotic Eastern sound, though it was not easily discernible at first.

It was Sonny Rollins, along with John Coltrane, Yusef Lateef, and other jazz musicians who may have been the first to introduce these spiritual forms into jazz as far back as the 1950s. A decade later, the Beatles and other rock artists also fused these Asian and Eastern elements, such as Indian ragas, into their music, greatly expanding the reach of ragas and Eastern music in general.

Ragas can be described as analogous to European scales or melodic modes, and they differ depending on the region of the country. For instance, North Indian ragas have different ascend and descend forms that create certain melodic armatures for either vocal or instrumental improvisation. Moreover, they are often said to have divine origins and represent a specific season or time of the day.

Which begs the question, will Indian ragas or American blues be the driving force behind jazz in the future?

> *Some realize the Self within them through the practice of meditation, some by the path of wisdom, and others by selfless service. Others may not know these paths; but hearing and following the instructions of an illumined teacher, they too go beyond death."*

—THE BHAGAVAD-GITA 13: 24-25[7]

CHAPTER 24

Meditating on a Riff

By the mid-1960s, Sonny Rollins projected the hallowed image of a humble saint because of achieving deep levels of spirituality. But there was another, disquieting side of the man: he was secretive (his family had ties to the Masons, but did not talk about it), musically merciless, and wanted to win at all costs.

For him, life was one big balancing act. As a devout believer, how could he remain faithful to God and morality, while at the same time staying on top of the heap as the number-one jazz tenor saxophonist in the world—a man who dethroned such masters as Coleman Hawkins, Don Byas, Ben Webster, Chu Berry, Dexter Gordon, and Gene Ammons?

At this existential moment, Sonny had to make some tough decisions about his spiritual and psychic direction. In such circumstances, some people might seek professional psychological help, while others might go to their clergy for redemption. Still others might fall back on the old, decadent lifestyle that initially sparked their fears.

By 1967, when Coltrane died at the peak of his popularity, it was clear that Sonny was trapped in a thick labyrinth and was desperate to find answers. To whom would he turn? An introvert, he was not the type of person who would ask for help from just anyone. A product of the streets, he was cynical and hard as nails, but this stance didn't seem to offer him the relief he desperately needed.

Sonny's problems were monumental at this juncture. They included a loss of fans because of the spiritual and technical ascendancy of Coltrane, a possible divorce from Lucille, as well as the familiar problems of exploitation by record companies and nightclubs. Combined with the political climate of the 1960s, with its racism, violence, and bigotry, it was clear by 1967 that Sonny had some tough decisions to make.

"Life was tough for me [in the] 1960s following my sabbatical," Sonny said. "For a while, I thought I had conquered most of my fears. It was just the opposite. At times, things seemed to be getting worse, and I needed solutions to my mounting problems."

What was Sonny to do? For two years, the reclusive man had virtually lived on the Williamsburg Bridge, studying yoga and other Eastern traditions in the hope of finding enlightenment and direction. Some of the tools he embraced, such as Kriya yoga, were so far out that devotees claimed they could perform miracles—even bringing people back from the dead and speaking directly to God.

After years and years of attempting to meditate, Sonny failed to achieve this level of God-realization. Such a letdown was devastating to a man who had the worldwide reputation of being "Mr. Spirituality." Sonny had to ask himself whether he was, after all, a big phony.

Meditation is considered by practitioners as natural as breathing. Though Sonny had desired this kind of spiritual enlightenment since childhood, he seemed powerless to achieve it in his adult life.

Still, Sonny knew that if he did the same-old things to get his life on track, he would have fallen back into the same dark pit he occupied before his cure from drug abuse in 1955. Life had been a living hell for him, and he didn't want to fight those demons again with the hovering fear that he could not triumph over them as he once did.

At the age of 37, it would have been weird for the eccentric middle-aged man to hang out again on a New York City bridge—tooting his horn over the waters below, seeking higher spiritual ground for answers. If Sonny was to seek a geographical cure this time, it had to be farther, much farther, than the Williamsburg Bridge.

Typical of Sonny's independent mindset, he decided to travel thousands of miles to India, where he hoped to find the solutions he so urgently needed. He believed he could discover in India the kind of mysticism he could not find in the busy, hectic pace of New York and other American cities.

An intellectual and avid reader, Sonny was partially inspired to make the long trek after reading countless books, most notably *Autobiography of a Yogi.*

While Sonny was attracted to Kriya yoga, he preferred the path of Advaita Vedanta for solutions to his problems. Sonny believed that yoga itself would play an important role in helping him to cope with the new challenges he was facing. After all, it was Kriya yoga and other forms of Indian mysticism that had helped Coltrane fight his own problems, such as heroin addiction.

And so it was that Sonny packed a couple of bags and his tenor saxophone and boarded a flight from JFK airport to Bombay. To him, India beckoned as an intriguing land of wondrous mysticism.

While on the plane, he spoke to a man who suggested he go to an ashram in Bombay's Powaii neighborhood. An ashram—which comes from the Sanskrit root *śram*, meaning, "to toil"—is a monastery or secluded spiritual hermitage, often used for religious retreats and instruction.

Sonny agreed that an ashram would be the ideal place to work with a master in studying hatha yoga and on his life and purpose. The seclusion of an ashram would not be challenging to him, because he had always lived a somewhat reclusive life. He had a reputation among some friends and fans of being basically a hermit.

The ashram Sonny journeyed to was operated by Swami Chinmayananda Saraswati, a famous spiritual leader and teacher who sought to spread the ancient practice called Advaita Vedanta.

He was a prolific writer who made many commentaries on both the *Upanishads,* an ancient body of teachings, and the *Bhagavad Gita,* another important Hindu text. Mostly, Sonny studied these old teachings with the swami, plus the yoga sutras. More emphasis was placed on the lessons and less on the actual postures of hatha yoga.

Sonny was not the only Westerner at the ashram; there were other students, some from Europe, who were also there. They shared conversations and meals, "endlessly discussing things among ourselves." While Sonny did perform for his fellow students and occasionally made trips downtown, he didn't do so anywhere else in Bombay during his time at the ashram.

His main purpose, after all, was not to show off or refine his musical talents but to achieve a deeper sense of God-realization. He wanted to learn how to meditate properly, which he believed he needed to do to reach this sacred level.

Even as he sought greater spiritual grounding in India, Sonny was not unaware of the currents swirling about him in the jazz world. Sonny knew he needed to

Illus. 35 - Sonny Rollins, who had studied Hinduism, yoga, and other Asian religions and cultures by reading countless books in America, finally got a firsthand view of India, where he lived in an ashram for four months in 1967.

keep his fan base and attract new and younger audiences in the face of Coltrane's popularity.

Coltrane had himself embarked on a spiritual journey through Eastern mysticism before his death in 1965. Trane recorded an album in 1965 called *Om*, which he described as "the first syllable, the primal word, the word of power."

Indeed, in Hinduism "om" is a sacred syllable, one that symbolizes the entire universe in Hindu thought. It is a holy spiritual incantation used in public *puja* (ceremonial worship), as well as in private prayers and meditation.

Coltrane's *Om* album included chants from the *Bhagavad Gita* and the *Tibetan Book of the Dead*, a Buddhist sacred book. Coltrane's exploration of Eastern religions had captured the attention of the Beatles and other rock 'n' roll musicians, along with their young fans. Though college students and other younger listeners who had once been jazz fans were now gravitating toward rock music, they made an exception for John Coltrane. While Sonny and other jazz musicians were grappling with a declining jazz market, Coltrane's career was flourishing.

The spiritual journeys of both Sonny and Trane paralleled that of others in the West who were seeking to drink at the wellsprings of traditions outside of their own. In the liner notes to his 1965 album *A Love Supreme*, Coltrane wrote, "I experienced, by the grace of God, a spiritual awakening which was to lead me to a richer, fuller, more productive life. At that time, in gratitude, I humbly asked to be given the means and privilege to make others happy through music."

As for Sonny, he became visibly frustrated with his inability to meditate during his stay at the ashram. The Advaita Vedanta tradition in which he immersed himself is based on the principle that one's soul, or Ātman, is identical to the deepest cosmological reality known as Brahman. Devotees of the Advaita school try to achieve enlightenment by seeking knowledge about these realities, using meditation as the primary tool.

Toward the end of his time at the ashram, Sonny approached his teacher with his concerns. He told his swami that he had trouble sitting still and meditating quietly. His mind still wandered, and nothing particularly spiritual seemed to happen when he sat in attempted stillness.

His swami told Sonny not to worry about traditional meditation: "When you're playing your saxophone, you're meditating," he said.

Sonny hadn't realized it, but when he played his horn, he was present in a way that many people can only achieve through meditation. That revelation was a relief for Sonny. He realized he no longer had to sit in a lotus position for hours; he had a spiritual practice all his own, one that was as natural to him as breathing and, in fact, relied on the great mastery of his breath.

CHAPTER 25

Transformation

Did Sonny Rollins really glow in the dark? Did he really levitate? Was his spiritual evolution so intense he began to display uncanny powers that were baffling to both fans and friends alike?

When Sonny returned from India, Sonny's wife, Lucille, and his sister, Gloria, witnessed seeing his "body light up like a Christmas tree" while passing and looking into his bedroom. "I don't think he knew that we saw what had happened. It was startling and a little scary," said Gloria.

Sonny, who is secretive and rarely discusses his inner most beliefs about otherworldly matters, however, admitted to being able to levitate. "It's something I like to do," he said, declining to discuss the ancient practice of rising from the floor to the ceiling.

Sonny believes in astral travel and has practiced levitation. Levitation or transvection is the rising of a human body or other objects into the air by mystical means. It defies the laws of gravity, and has baffled the scientific community for centuries. However, it has been proven levitation becomes a real possibility if the pull of gravity is counterbalanced by a strong magnetic field. Perhaps, Sonny was able to create such a field within his aura.

Friends and family recall that Sonny has always displayed a strong spiritual side, but "Sonny seemed to have transformed into a different person after he had spent several months living in an ashram in India," recalled Gloria. "He walked with the air of a yogi, although he downplayed it since he has always been modest."

It was this modesty that helped Sonny expand his following of jazz fans to new agers and other bohemian types who dramatically changed both his music and persona. He was beginning to attract fans of the Beatles, John McLaughlin and other pop, rock, and jazz bands who had incorporated *ragas* (Indian scales) and spirituality itself into their music.

Sonny Rollins' trip to India in the late 1960s—the ancient, mysterious land of mysticism and meditation—helped to transform him from a former troubled youth into a commanding sage possessing deep morality and spirituality.

Much to his surprise, India possessed a strong jazz environment that competed with major European cities, like London, Paris, Rome, Stockholm, Munich, and Copenhagen.

In the 1920s, while New York, New Orleans, and the aforementioned cities were buzzing with the relatively new sounds of jazz, the music was well and alive in Mumbai (formerly known as Bombay) and in Kolkata (formerly known as Calcutta). These cities served as an escape for African American jazz musicians.

Between the 1930s and 1950s, India witnessed its "golden age of jazz." The players included jazz artists Leon Abbey, Crickett Smith, Creighton Thompson, Ken Mac, Roy Butler, Teddy Weatherford, who had become famous for playing with Louis Armstrong. He and the others had fled America for its massive racism and lack of support of jazz.

But, it was also the spirituality that enamored Sonny of India. Mysticism and spirituality have historically attracted visitors from all over the globe. Yoga and Ayurveda, as well as different religions, have played integral roles in the development and existence of spirituality for centuries.

Sonny first headed to India in 1967. Upon his return several months later, he appeared to possess a sense of ESP and other hidden powers that baffled his relatives, colleagues, friends, and others all the more.

"Sonny was always a little far-out," said Bob Cranshaw, his bassist and band member who had accompanied him for decades. "He was always a little secretive and rarely shared his personal information with us. India definitely had an impact that changed his views and outlook on life."

Regardless of the explanation, the strange and the supernatural seem to follow Sonny wherever he goes. Sonny's nephew, Clifton Anderson used other-worldly terms to describe Sonny's arrival at Tokyo's Narita International Airport, on one particular trip to Japan.

Tall and imposing, Sonny easily towered over the other passengers swarming through the busy terminal. Then, out of nowhere, a group of Buddhist monks suddenly arrived, with trademark shaved heads and richly dyed orange robes. Without a word, they quickly surrounded Sonny like a band of angels in a baroque painting.

For a few moments, they encircled the jazz legend, gushing over him as a kindred spirit. In a flash, Sonny and the monks vanished from the airport, leaving members of his band baffled.

Was the group of monks nothing more than a mirage? Did they literally "spirit" him away on some astral fast lane? Clifton wasn't sure exactly what happened that day at the Tokyo airport, but it was par for the course as a member of Sonny's inner circle.

"Weird things were always happening with Sonny," declared Clifton, who is a realist and not prone to exaggeration. "He would constantly blow away the musicians in the band—not just because of his incredible genius as a musician. He constantly kept them guessing about his different acts and odd behavior."

A case in point—one more down-to-earth than supernatural: Clifton often found himself wearing the same color shirt as Sonny, even though they always dressed independently. If Clifton came onstage wearing a red shirt, Sonny would suddenly appear in a shirt of the same color. If Clifton chose a green shirt for the next concert, Sonny would also show up in green.

At first, he brushed it off as a fluke. After weeks of such "coincidences," Clifton began to wonder if his uncle had a sixth sense. It turned into a lighthearted game for the two: Clifton purposefully chose an unusual color for a shirt, like yellow, and lo and behold, Sonny would show up for the concert wearing bright yellow.

This is a phenomenon that has been observed among people who are on the same frequency. It is said when two (or more) people spend time together, they exchange energy and can pick up each other's vibrations, even at a distance. Thus, there are reports of couples who know about each other's well-being, even when they are separated. For example, a person might just "know" their partner has had an accident or an experience involving powerful emotions.

It can be said Sonny can have a direct hypnotic effect on his fans, a kind of magnetic charisma unconnected to supernatural phenomena. On one occasion, when Sonny walked into a live concert at New York's Lincoln Center in the 1980s to hear a jazz group perform, several hundred fans in the audience turned their heads for a few minutes from the stage to stare at him in silence until he sat down.

On another occasion at New York's Village Vanguard, Sonny became annoyed that photographer Ray Ross was distracting his performance by taking too many pictures. Without notice, Sonny walked off the stage; he continued to play with his left hand, and picked up Ross and deposited him outside the club with his right. After this superhuman feat, he sauntered back in, continuing with the music and not missing a beat.

"Sonny can be a mystery to me and his many fans around the world," admitted Clifton, who is perhaps one of a handful of relatives, friends, and musicians who have intimate knowledge of the saxophonist. "He's a great human being, but I must admit that he keeps a lot of us in the dark."

Sonny did not merely dabble in these practices because they appeared novel and exotic; he took them quite seriously as an adept. What is it, then, about Sonny that makes even the most devoted of intellectuals listen with an open mind? Whatever the reason, an aura of mystery, magic, and seriousness surrounds Sonny. He has the demeanor of a mystic and a sage, and his fans certainly treat him with the reverence usually reserved for holy men.

Sonny's explorations of Eastern forms of meditation and spirituality coincided with a major shift in American cultural landscape from "religion" to "spirituality," during the mid- and late-twentieth century. The phenomenon is described by some as "the empty pew," whereby many younger members of various congregations left the churches, synagogues, and temples to embrace and practice spirituality in its various forms.

Sonny Rollins directly, and indirectly, helped to spur this larger worldwide cultural change from West to East, one that transformed his own life.

As a person puts on new garments, giving up old ones, the soul similarly accepts new material bodies, giving up the old and useless ones."

— THE BHAGAVAD-GITA 2:22[8]

CHAPTER 26

The Fashionista and the Pharaoh

Synchronicity. Destiny. Fate. Whatever you call it, the night in 1958 that Jackie Lewis first saw Sonny Rollins was no coincidence.

For 18-year-old Jackie, it seemed like any other night out in San Francisco. A music lover, she and her good friend Jean Williams liked to check out concerts after their classes at San Francisco State College. They would line up to see the hottest acts from the East Coast perform, including a young Sonny Rollins, who was performing at the Jazz Workshop club.

Born in New Orleans to African American parents, both with Cherokee blood, Jackie's family relocated to Salt Lake City when she was four years old. Since childhood, she had been immersed in music, having been a soloist with the Salt Lake Symphonic Choir and an a capella choir at South High School.

As Jackie left the club that night, she stumbled across a musician who would one day be much more than just a musical idol. Sonny was standing on the sidewalk in the moonlight, a nearly mystical aura surrounding him as he took puffs of his cigarette. He had an undeniable presence, which came through both on and offstage.

Jackie turned to Jean, whispering in her ear, "Oh, *that's* the kind of man I'd like."

It was clear, though, that Sonny was already taken. His new wife, Dawn, was on his arm as he smoked on the street corner. Jackie's interest in the musician was seemingly no more than a passing fancy. She soon returned to college, nearly forgetting about the intriguing young saxophonist.

Little did she know, this was only the beginning.

~

Bored with her courses, Jackie left college to pursue a greater dream—a career in the world of high fashion. She moved to New York City in 1960 and was quickly hired as a hostess at the Village Gate, the famed jazz club in Greenwich Village. There, Jackie would once again come across Sonny Rollins—but this time, it would be much more than a passing glance.

Sonny, back from his woodshedding hiatus on the Williamsburg Bridge, had been performing throughout New York City, including the Village Gate. When she saw Sonny again, Jackie had a flashback to the night she had seen him in San Francisco. He still had the same spiritual, almost regal air. It was so intimidating, in fact, that Jackie said she was "scared to death of him."

"He walked in and, you know, you felt his presence," she said. "It was just much more than I had ever experienced. I had never seen anybody like that before."

"He used to come in all the time during the day, when I was in the office, and talk to me," Jackie remembered.

While Sonny later told Jackie that he would come to the club just to see her, she couldn't fathom why he wanted to spend so much time talking to her. Although she was always stylish, Jackie was a bit insecure about her looks. "I've never thought of myself as beautiful because I grew up in a home where my sisters were very beautiful, and

I was the ugly duckling."

Jackie said she never felt that there was a profound connection between the two of them, at least not at that time: "He was always very polite and very respectful, and I would just answer the questions he would ask, and we might say something, we'd laugh at something, and then I'd go on and continue working. We never had any kind of rapport with each other."

The two soon fell out of touch. Jackie left her job at the Gate and moved to Paris to pursue her dream of working in high fashion. Sonny, on the other hand, had a thriving career, and he was also soon to marry his second wife, Lucille.

But, they say the third time's the charm, and for Sonny and Jackie, their third meeting was unforgettable.

The year was 1968. Jackie had just returned from Paris, where she had opened a boutique. She hoped to make a similar splash in the New York fashion scene.

One evening after work, Jackie was riding her bicycle home when she felt an odd presence. "I was on 8th street between 6th and 5th Avenues, and I was talking to someone out on the street, and I felt something," she recalled. It was a feeling she had not experienced in seven years, since her last meeting with Sonny.

"I turned and looked over [my shoulder], and there he was, standing on the sidewalk. He was looking with his back to me, watching me in the reflection of the glass. And when he saw me turn and look, he turned around and smiled. And you know, I got that smile, oh God!" She laughed with girlish delight, remembering the exuberance of the moment.

"So he walked over to me and we started talking. He said he was going to be performing. I think he was just coming in at the [Village] Vanguard, and it was his first time performing in a while. He said he had been watching me in the window, and he said, 'Yeah, I've always admired you, ever since you worked at the Gate.' And I said, 'You did?' He invited me to see his show that night, to which I went."

Handsome, tall, and charismatic, Sonny had never been short of romantic admirers. He loved women as much as they did him,

Illus. 36 - Former fashion model and designer Jackie Lewis, Sonny Rollins' longtime love interest, is now teaching yoga and spirituality at the retreat she owns in Negril, Jamaica.

and several of his past girlfriends and lovers in the 1950s had been disappointed to discover they weren't the only woman in his life. Even when he was married, Sonny still maintained several paramours.

Though Sonny was married to Lucille until her death in the 2000s, their relationship was rocky at times. Some of his acquaintances speculated the tension was because they were an interracial couple in the 1960s. As a white woman in the largely black jazz scene, it wasn't always smooth sailing. Although he has never confirmed this, his sister Gloria wondered if Sonny was ambivalent about marrying Lucille. After all, many hardly knew she existed, since she was rarely seen around clubs and did not spend much time with jazz musicians.

The 1960s weren't just a tumultuous time in Sonny's personal life. Racial, social, and political tensions in the United States were at an all-time high, as the Civil Rights Movement gained steam.

Sonny was profoundly disturbed to hear of the violence perpetrated against his brothers and others in the movement: four little girls blown to pieces by a bomb in a church basement in Birmingham, Alabama, the Mississippi murders of Chaney, Goodman and Schwerner, the murder of Medgar Evers, the racial unrest in Watts and Detroit.

Under Sonny's nose, riots ripped Brooklyn, the Bronx, and Newark, as well as his home turf of Harlem, and, of course, there was the assassination in April 1968, of Rev. Dr. Martin Luther King.

And there were other things on Sonny's mind. The jazz world was also struggling, battered by the hyper-popular music of the British Invasion. The Beatles and the Rolling Stones crashed onto the music scene and quickly dominated album sales, putting many jazz musicians out of work.

Trying to catch the will-o'-the-wispy taste of music fans had always been a challenge. Swing had given way to bebop in the 1940s, and bebop transformed into hard bop at the end of the decade. By the mid-1950s, rock 'n' roll rode over them all on the twanging guitars of Elvis Presley and Bill Haley and the Comets.

These changing styles meant bread and butter to jazz musicians. You changed and went with the flow, or you slipped into obscurity unless you were distinctive enough—somebody like Frank Sinatra—to ride out all variations. In the 1950s, several new styles of jazz developed, including "modal jazz," and "cool jazz."

At the time, it had been enough to keep selling records and packing clubs. Among the intellectual jazz crowd, the rock 'n' rollers were considered merely "white trash," and there was no competition when deciding which style of music was superior.

But, the British Invasion was something else.

Unlike Elvis and country-tinged rock 'n' roll, the music by the Beatles and the Rolling Stones was as intellectual and complex as jazz. While it was grounded in European classical music, the new rock 'n' roll was infectious enough to convert a wide audience. It was Brit Rock, and it took America by storm.

As a jazz musician, Sonny felt the pressure of this new wave coming over the Atlantic. Combined with the tumultuous state of the country and his personal need for spiritual wisdom, Sonny once again felt the need to go looking for answers.

This time, his search would not be accompanied by Lucille. The couple separated, and Sonny disappeared again—at least from her. "We were apart for about two years," Lucille later recalled.

Sonny became a spiritual pilgrim, traveling all over the world to search for answers. In Denmark, he felt the hand of Allah on him while he was praying with Sufi masters. He continued on to India, where he lived in an ashram, studying yoga and Hinduism. In Japan, he became an apprentice to a Zen Buddhist master.

Meanwhile, Lucille went back home and worked at the University of Chicago. While she was there, Sonny found a partner who was on his level, someone on the same journey of self-discovery. She felt his presence and was open to the full spectrum of Sonny's far-out spirituality. It was not simply an affair—it was a meeting of minds.

"He would talk to me," Jackie remembered. "We would have conversations on the phone, and they were not—it was not necessarily a highly sexual relationship. It was more of a mental and spiritual connection. We would just talk, and I was fascinated by his mind."

In particular, she was impressed by Sonny's ability to pick up on things from the other side of the globe. "He would call me sometimes, and say, 'I know you have a red dress on, and I'm not through traveling, I just got back from Australia.' You know, I said, 'Oh my God, this man's crazy!' You know, he was just so unique and different."

In the five years that Jackie and Sonny saw each other, he would introduce her to a whole new world, the realm of spirituality and mysticism that he had discovered during his sojourn on the Williamsburg Bridge.

"Sonny was my mentor," Jackie stated. When she first became involved with him, she was a spiritual novice. "I knew nothing about metaphysics, I knew nothing about meditation. And, I must say, he inspired me to look into yoga and meditation."

For Jackie, being with Sonny was an encounter with the supernatural; it was as though a deity had been brought to earth in the form of this imposing jazzman. "I was always overwhelmed by him, his presence, you know. He was very godly or kingly. And even when we'd just sit and talk, it would be like I was sitting and talking to a higher being. That's all I can say at this point in my life, looking back on it, because at that point I didn't know what it was."

But their relationship was not simply centered around awe—there was also a very real personal connection, the type Jackie had not anticipated during her days as a hostess. "Each conversation was just amazing because we would, he would talk about everything, you know. And it would always be from how he felt about life, how he looked at life, his day. One of the things he would always say to me was that he was very jealous because I had my life very organized."

The god-man was human, too.

Sonny did not merely introduce Jackie to meditation and yoga; he also brought her into the secretive world of the Rosicrucians. Sonny had joined the Rosicrucians after he left the public eye in 1959, and he had become more and more versed in their esoteric mysticism and philosophy ever since.

The Rosicrucians are "a high order of metaphysics," Jackie explained. "It's a teaching, and the Rosicrucians go back to Egypt. They're from the ancient Egyptian teachings, such as of the pharaohs and the priests. They operated from a metaphysical perspective, just like all your Kings and Queens have a seer around, who is the metaphysical person, probably an alchemist, or who is able to tell them what to do from a spiritual perspective, and how life just is, and keeping that person on track."

But the Rosicrucians are also an organized society: "The Rosicrucians are [a lot like] the Masons." In fact, several high levels of Masons take the Rosy Cross—the Rosicrucian symbol—as their emblem.

Rosicrucianism is considered to be an esoteric organization, similar to the Golden Dawn and Theosophical Societies founded at the end of the 19th century, as well as the Ordo Templi Orientis, which eventually came under the leadership of the notorious occultist Aleister Crowley. Rosicrucianism is commonly associated with the study of magic and, in particular, alchemy.

However, the actual organization and history of Rosicrucianism is more complicated. The Rosicrucian society to which Sonny and Jackie belonged—which traces the roots of its teaching back to Egypt—is the Ancient Mystical Order Rosae Crucis, or AMORC. This is a society of esoteric study, offering education to willing members on such topics as metaphysics, mysticism, psychology, and parapsychology. It offers increases in psychic ability, aura projection, and knowledge of ancient philosophy, all geared towards the improvement of the lives of its members.

According to AMORC's official history, Leonardo da Vinci, René Descartes, Isaac Newton, Benjamin Franklin, and Thomas Jefferson have all been members of the Rosicrucian Society. AMORC itself was not founded until 1915, by H. Spencer Lewis.

Throughout its history, Rosicrucianism has been viewed with distrust. While it was founded as an ostensibly Christian movement, it was frequently denounced as false alchemy or black magic by clergy and other concerned citizens. It also faced particular opposition from the Jesuits. More recently, Rosicrucianism has been accused of being either a conspiracy or a brainwashing cult.

To Sonny and Jackie, much of Rosicrucianism's history was secondary to its power as a tool for personal growth. "You're working from metaphysics, teaching principles of, you know, one God, one man, you know, divine. Just like Buddhism, it's the same," Jackie said. "All of those teachings are the same; they just have different names."

In other words, Rosicrucianism is just another form of spiritual pursuit. In many of its forms, Rosicrucian spirituality focused on alchemy. Alchemy is often thought of as a completely material pursuit—alchemists are rumored to have searched for a means to turn lead and other worthless metals into gold.

However, alchemy was just as much a hermetic, inward-looking pursuit, focused on the inner workings of the spirit rather than the physical world. As McIntosh explained, "there is an inner alchemy concerned with perfection of the soul and an outer, complementary alchemy concerned with perfection of matter and the body."

Such a search for perfection was perfectly suited to Sonny's own quest for jazz supremacy. Just as the alchemist sought to remove any and all impurities from his soul, Sonny constantly practiced in the hope of further refining his musical style. To understand the processes of the alchemists is to understand a great deal of the jazzman's endless attempts to reach perfection.

Another Rosicrucian teaching, this one specific to the AMORC, is that of reincarnation. While reincarnation is commonly associated with Indian philosophies like Hinduism, and Buddhism, Jackie said that such a belief is found all over the globe: "It's Egyptian, it's Rosicrucian, it's old metaphysical teaching." She also noted its close ties to Cherokee and other Native American traditions, as well as those from Africa.

To be more specific, Jackie pointed to an instance concerning the spirit that enters the body of a newborn child: "In Africa, they have the shaman come in to tell the parents and the grandparents who the spirit is that is coming in, so they are better able to educate that child."

Sonny's mystical journey took him back into the past, giving him a glimpse of a time long before that of jazz cats and nightclubs, showing him a desert kingdom hugging a fertile river.

"He had mentioned that in another life he was Akhenaten," Jackie said. Sonny first told Jackie the story of his past life in jest. "He was

Illus. 37 - Pharaoh Akhenaten … or Sonny Rollins?

kind of testing me." But Jackie's mind opened, and she believed.

Akhenaten had been a significant figure in Egyptian history. "He was one of the greatest pharaohs, and he changed Egypt: they had many gods and he attempted to change the system to be under one god."

Akhenaten sought to center Egyptian worship upon Aten, the disc of the sun, which had previously been considered an aspect of Ra, the sun god. Akhenaten, previously known as Amenhotep IV, changed his name in order to honor the solar deity.

Akhenaten has also been linked with other religious figures. "The story of Akhenaten is the same story [as] of Moses," Jackie said. "In fact, there is a question whether Moses and Akhenaten were not the same. The two stories of Moses and Akhenaten correlate exactly. They both were found in a basket, they both disappeared, and Akhenaten had, I think, a reign of 17 years and then he went away; they've not been able to find his tomb."

The sudden disappearance of the pharaoh could explain the sudden emergence of a new religious leader among the Jews: "They've never found his place of burial, and Moses appeared, maybe three years later," she noted.

Was it this ancient king, a proud monotheist, who gave Sonny his incredible presence and royal air? Did the spiritual force that permeated Sonny's life draw its power from the mystical rites of ancestral Egypt? Was Sonny reincarnated to bring harmony to the world once again?

Jackie certainly thinks so. "We were together in Egypt," she attested. But she is quick to point out that she was not Akhenaten's wife, Nefertiti, but rather the pharaoh's mother. Somewhat eerily, the two reincarnated Egyptians would later see an exhibit at the Brooklyn Museum on the topic of Akhenaten himself.

Jackie was thoroughly captivated by Sonny's mystical presence. Even now, she sees him as a supernatural being, incarnated on Earth to help bring about greater peace and understanding.

Upon hearing the story of the bells that rang at Sonny's birth, she was not in the least surprised. "He is a very special being that was coming back. That sounds very right. When certain beings come back to the planet, they come in for many reasons. And when they come in, there is, of course, there is the ushering in of that soul."

Jackie also doubts that heroin could have ever killed Sonny because his spirit was too important to die before it had completed his mission: "The other side of it is that he is a divine spirit, he's come in here to do some very special work, so if it's not his time to go, he wouldn't go. He's come in to make an impact upon the planet, which he has done, but I don't think his work is finished. I think there's so much. I think there's something else."

Were those two bells that resounded over Harlem at the moment Sonny entered the world a sign of a deity taking a physical form? Did they welcome a sage whose sermons would be told through a saxophone? Is Sonny Rollins a divine being who will live on until he has completed his mission on Earth?

If so, this being did not limit himself to the tenets of Rosicrucianism. "I would say he's probably closer to Buddhism," Jackie noted. "He also was a Buddhist; he had a guru he was very devoted to."

But, ultimately, it was not Buddhism or Rosicrucianism that was of supreme importance. Spiritual truth lives beyond the differing religious and esoteric traditions but is common to all of them. Real spirituality is not confined anywhere, and as Jackie said, "He lives it, and it's not either-or."

"He's so immersed within his spirituality, 'cause I'm saying he lives it; most people talk it. He saw the bigger picture, not the small picture. You know, most people just see the dot on the paper; he would see the whole area around the dot and the paper."

But, ultimately, Sonny and Jackie's run would come to an end in 1973. Sonny would venture back into the world of music again, and he needed Lucille.

"He got in touch and eventually came back to Chicago a couple times," Lucille recalled. "I don't know how it happened; we just got back together." Ever the conservative, she said nothing else on the subject. But soon their marriage had re-formed, and they were back together at Willoughby Walk.

Lucille's mother Nanette was living alone in Chicago at the time—her husband had died many years earlier. She moved to Willoughby

Walk with the reunited couple.

"We got her an apartment, and she lived with us," Lucille said. "She and Sonny became very close." Later, when they moved to upstate New York, Nanette went along with them—she would live there for the rest of her life.

Jackie sees Sonny's return to Lucille as a result of his need for order. "He needed someone to protect him," Jackie said. Lucille was the perfect person for the job. She would help him negotiate with record companies, assist him in recordings, and give him the organizational skills that he so envied.

Jackie was unwilling to play that role. "I had my own business," she said, "And I was not interested in living his life for him. I could not live in his shadow. I had my own life." To devote herself completely to him was not an option. "I had my clothing store. I didn't have time."

However, Sonny and Jackie's breakup served to spur her further on her own spiritual journey. While she was with Sonny, she had mostly marveled at his spiritual exploits. However, after they stopped seeing each other, things changed. "For me," Jackie recalled, "it was after we broke up that I began to search because I was so pained."

Sonny's influence ultimately would direct Jackie to a journey that utilized multiple paths towards enlightenment. Nowadays, she said, "I go to American Indian sweat lodges and peyote churches; I go to Buddhist meditations for three days, weekend sit. I do it all because I don't believe that there is just one way."

Perhaps it was Sonny's influence that has led Jackie to her current work: running a New Age spa in Negril, Jamaica. "We're a spiritual spa, so when people come, they're seeking knowledge; they're looking to figure out how to better deal with their lives. I teach yoga and meditation."

Jackie had once learned yoga and meditation from the reincarnated spirit of Akhenaten—and now she teaches others "how to look at life from a different perspective. You know, to possibly think maybe that you had another life, to look at your life, that maybe life is not what you see, maybe there is something else."

If Sonny's appearance on Earth has been for the purpose of

enlightening others, the effects of his contact with Jackie can certainly be seen radiating throughout a community of spiritual seekers. The affair had come and gone, taking place at the same time as Sonny's second retreat from his normal schedule of touring and recording. He had introduced another into the spiritual fold, but he still had his own future to think about—and the competition he faced not from other jazzmen, but from other styles of music. And the beat goes on.

CHAPTER 27

Nippon Soul

The relentless news media hovered all over the place, their cameras clicking non-stop as scores of highly-charged and excited visitors descended on Narita International Airport in Tokyo. They were gazing at the just-landed jet with curiosity.

Did it mean some VIP was about to step out of the airplane? Was this person a head of state arriving for talks about a political crisis in Japan? Was he or she a Hollywood movie star coming to the country to promote a new film?

Who was in the giant airplane that caused so much commotion for the Japanese—a people who are usually calm and collected?

"I didn't know what was going on," declared Sonny Rollins, who was on his first visit to Tokyo in 1963, two years after returning from his two-year sabbatical from the jazz scene. "The cat on the plane must be important if he can cause that kind of excitement among so many different people."

Surprise! The cat was none other than Sonny himself. After

embarking from the jet, he was quickly surrounded by frantic well-wishers seeking to get his autograph—or to simply touch him.

The Japanese, who tend to value different art forms as almost sacred, are especially drawn to jazz. Using heavy African American influences, they went on to create their own unique style of jazz, one of only a few derivatives that have earned the respect of hard-nosed puritanical black musicians. They believe many Japanese musicians have a sensitivity like theirs.

Of the thousands of American jazz musicians who have performed in the country, there is a prevailing consensus that Sonny is the all-time favorite. One reason is he has embraced the low-key temperament of the Japanese and firmly honors their formal traditions. He is also one of the jazz pioneers who believe the Japanese have captured the essence of jazz, as well as blues.

As a result, Sonny is idolized and is as popular as American pop icon Michael Jackson. In the United States, he enjoys a similar degree of fame, but not to the extent of it as in Japan. His fanbase in Japan also includes devotees of other styles, such as rhythm and blues, rock 'n' roll, and New Age.

Sonny is revered as a Buddha of sorts in Japan. He may not be regarded as a holy man, but many Japanese in the Buddha and spirituality worlds certainly see him as a wise man—someone who has been awakened from a long and deep sleep of ignorance stemming from his devoted involvement with the practice of Buddhism. They maintain he is a man who has discovered an understanding of both worldly and otherworldly matters.

However, even after more than half a century of study and involvement in Buddhism, Sonny sees himself simply as a "humble student" of the ancient religion. It is this self-effacement and humility that many Japanese people like about Sonny.

The media and hordes of fans in the airport wanted to see Sonny not just because of his prowess as the top jazz tenor saxophonist, but also because of his reputation as a man of deep spirituality and devotion to Buddhism. He still wears his Harlem street armor, but also walks and talks with the modesty of a Buddhist monk.

Illus. 38 - Sonny Rollins, who was responsible for helping to create more jazz fans in Japan than anywhere in the world, had a little help from one of his sidemen and friends, Yoshiaki Masuo. Their association began in 1973 and has continued through today.

Though the dominant native religion in Japan is Shinto, Buddhism claims an estimated 35 percent of Japan's total population of 128 million, including many jazz musicians and artists. The religion can be traced back to its arrival to Japan during the 6th century, a transplant from the kingdom of Baekje in Korea.

Other forms of Buddhism came to Japan in the 12th century, with the establishment of the shogunate and the move of the administrative capital to Kamakura. The most popular of these forms was Zen, with several branches of its own.

Although Sonny developed an interest and appreciation for many other non-Western faiths and religions, it was yoga and Zen Buddhism that struck his fancy the most.

"Buddhism has aspects of more of the metaphysical than a lot of other major religions, so I think that people look for self-improvement and other means or approaches to really improve themselves through something spiritually, [which leads] them to that sort of thing," explained nephew and trombonist Clifton Anderson. "Buddhism tends to speak to that a little bit more.

"I don't know the extent of Buddhism's popularity among jazz musicians," he added. "But there was a time, many years ago in New York City, when it was almost like a fad, a trend, for everyone to get involved in the Buddhism movement. Some of the major jazz musicians practicing Buddhism are Herbie Hancock and Buster Williams, and I think, Steve Turre.

"I can't say that Sonny is just a strict Buddhist, I don't know that he practices Buddhism solely or exclusively. He practices yoga, but he's also pulled different things from different other religions, so I don't know that he would say that he's only a Buddhist or a Christian or any one of those religions.

"He told me that the first time he went to Japan he was very comfortable when he got there, with the people, and that they reminded him of black people. He said they had a kind of feeling that was like ours, so he was very comfortable when he first went there," Clifton explained.

Sonny started his love affair with Japan in 1963, and passionately defends their unusual approach to grasping jazz. Some critics argue its jazz musicians are merely clones of black Americans. "That's not true. Japanese musicians tend to be very precise. They copy us first in order to master our music, then proceed to develop their own original styles," Clifton noted.

The love fest between Sonny and the Japanese is reciprocal: many jazz aficionados in Japan agree he is arguably the greatest living jazz musician—a master craftsman who acquired his skills partly because of the deft concentration he learned, in part, through the practice of Buddhism.

"The concentration has given me the focus that I've needed not only as a musician, but in my personal and spiritual life, which was once unstable and chaotic," recalled Sonny. "Japan has been extremely important. The country has been helpful because of the magnitude and culture of its people."

Illus. 39 - The prodigious trombonist Clifton Anderson said Sonny Rollins believed the Japanese people possess "a kind of soulfulness and beauty" that resembles that of African Americans.

Sonny recollected: "When I first arrived in Japan in 1963 for a cultural arts group, I was already well-known. *Saxophone Colossus*, you may know, is the best-selling jazz instrumental of all-time in Japan, so I arrived there with a reputation of being sort of a god.

"But outside of that," he continued, laughing sarcastically as he was prone to do, "when I stepped off the plane in Tokyo, I breathed a huge sigh of relief. I think much of it was being in a non-white country for the first time, but also, I had been into Asian and Eastern religions and philosophy and here I was in a [largely] Buddhist country."

Sonny immediately related to the people, the customs, and the cultural traditions, visiting many temples, shrines, and monasteries, and feeling an immense sense of peace and tranquility. He was introduced to a Zen master named Masahiro Oki by a Japanese fan, and they kept in touch after Sonny returned to New York.

Five years later, Sonny would further explore Zen during his second trip to Japan. He would reconnect with Oki in Mishima, a town in the foothills of Mount Fuji, where the spiritual master had established his own school for "Oki Yoga" or "Zen Yoga," his unique blend of Zen, yoga, martial arts, and other disciplines.

"It was a great learning experience for me to be exposed to Buddhism," recalled Sonny. "The Japanese take Buddhism very seriously. It helped me to center my life after being exposed to the fast lane in the Big Apple. I needed the balance that Buddhism gave me."

Sonny needed not only the support of Buddhism in Japan, he needed their support as jazz fans. At the time, rock 'n' roll was beginning to overtake jazz in the United States and Europe. Sonny, who was a product of the post-bop jazz tradition, was being confronted with major changes in jazz, such as the avant-garde "freeform" and "modal" styles.

In Japan, he was faced with a major dilemma. His older fans demanded he play the music of the masters, such as Coleman Hawkins, Charlie Parker, and others of the bebop and post-bop periods. The Japanese went wild and demanded he perform classics, such as tracks from the albums *Saxophone Colossus* and *Tenor Madness*.

The Japanese love affair with jazz is one of the modern world's most curious phenomena. How is it that an island nation that values conformity and identity—often looking at foreigners with hesitancy—came to embrace an art form that originated in black America? How is it that the Japanese, whose musical forms are often governed by norms created over several millennia, are such fans of the experimental, improvisational medium that is jazz?

It has been documented that many Japanese were exposed to jazz (and other American musical forms) during the six-year occupation period following World War II. Not long after the Japanese surrender in 1945, occupying servicemen could be seen dancing with kimono-clad Japanese women at jazz clubs like Oasis of the Ginza in Tokyo.

That said, it is also true that prewar Japan was a sophisticated and cosmopolitan society that embraced many cultural artifacts from the West, ranging from architecture to literature and music. As early as 1929, Japanese were hearing the word "jazz" in a film called "Tokyo March."

Sometimes called "J-Jazz," Japanese jazz represents a fusion of different styles of American jazz with various styles of Japanese music. Jazz came to Japan through American jazz bands touring the country, as well as Filipino bands, who had in turn been introduced to jazz through Americans occupying the Philippines.

By the early 1920s, jazz scenes began to emerge in cities like Osaka and Kobe. Within a few years, jazz was flourishing in Japan; by 1924, there were 20 dance halls in Osaka alone. Japan's first international jazz star also emerged in the 1930s, a young trumpeter by the name of Fumio Nanri.

However, some of the more conservative and elite members of Japanese society regarded jazz as too American, and in 1927, the city of Osaka shut down its dance halls. The jazz scene then moved to Tokyo, the nation's capital.

To appease some of the criticism toward jazz, composers Ryoichi Hattori and Koichi Sugii began to create their brand of Japanese jazz. They blended American jazz with older Japanese folk songs and theatrical tunes, and penned new jazz songs with traditional Japanese melodies.

In 1933, the first *jazu kissa*—a jazz café—opened in Osaka. Called Chigusa, it represented the first of many jazz coffee houses, which have been a fixture of Japan's jazz culture.

Though jazz was labeled as "enemy music" and banned during World War II, there was no stopping the music's meteoric rise. By then, the genre had become too popular for a complete ban to be successful. Jazz-like songs, often presented as patriotic music, continued to be performed.

During the post-World War II Allied Occupation—from 1945–1952—American soldiers stationed in Japan were a perfect market for Japanese jazz, stimulating the development of Japan's jazz scene. Pianist Toshiko Akiyoshi came to Tokyo in 1948, intent on becoming a professional jazz musician.

She put together the Cozy Quartet, which came to the attention of Hampton Hawes, then stationed in Yokohama. In turn, Hawes alerted Oscar Peterson about Akiyoshi, who later trained at Boston's Berklee School of Music.

By the late 1950s, Japanese jazz was back. Creativity abounded, and avant-garde and free jazz developed and flourished. Among the top names were Yosuke Yamashita, Sadao Watanabe (who had been part of the Cozy Quartet), Masahiko Satoh, Ryo Kawasaki, Toru Okoshi, and Makoto Ozone. Most of the Japanese jazz musicians had a strong connection to the United States, and many had trained there.

In the United States after World War II, some of the biggest jazz fans were to be found among the young Nisei (second-generation Japanese) who had been held in internment camps during the war, mostly in the American West, though a major facility was also located in Arkansas. Perhaps it was their sense of having been exiled that made them feel camaraderie with the black jazz musicians who were also feeling a sense of exile in America.

One Japanese American who embraced jazz in a big way is Nobuko "Cobi" Narita, founder of the Universal Jazz Coalition in 1976 New York, which showcased many prominent artists over a 40-year period. She also started the New York Women's Jazz Festival, now known as International Women in Jazz.

As a fifteen-year-old in 1941, Cobi and her family were forcibly removed from their home in California and interned in the Gila River Detention Center in Arizona. Now in her late 80s, Narita reflected on her love for jazz in an interview published in *JazzTimes*: "I have always listened to the music we call jazz. It just fit me," she said, "and I fit it."

Likewise, Japan seemed to "fit" Sonny. "Japan is a wonderful country," he said. "It's free of many of the distractions found in a lot of other places, especially in New York City. I always felt a sense of ease and joy when I spent time in Japan."

Clifton echoed Sonny's views. "One of the things about the Japanese that I liked culturally was that the people take a lot of pride in what they're doing, in their artisanship, and of course for their jazz musicians. They're very well educated in jazz music and jazz musicians, much more so than Americans, so that's another aspect that was very impressive about the Japanese.

"Also, their courtesy towards one another—there are a lot of little things that you find there. They're very appreciative of the music. The first times that I went there I had to get used to the fact that the audience was very, very polite so that they didn't want to applaud or clap or yell or anything during the concert, so they were very quiet and at first you'd think well maybe they're not digging the music, but it's that level of courtesy and respect that they show for the musicians and the music.

"And they're generally energetic; they have an energy that's very different from Europe or America. It's like a more soulful thing, I guess that's the way I can put it, like it's just kind of reminiscent of our own black soulfulness. They seem to have a clear understanding and feeling of black people's music," he said.

Clifton strongly disagrees with the criticism that the Japanese have cloned American jazz and other music styles. "I have heard a lot of incredible Japanese cats who have been successful in creating original and outstanding jazz," he said, pointing to Japanese trumpeter Terumasa Hino, who he calls "a fantastic player who has proven his mastery on his horn."

Some critics have asserted the Japanese failed to capture the true essence of jazz, which is African American blues. But, according to Clifton, "Japanese people are very soulful, and they seem to have a natural affinity for the blues and our black culture. Japanese musicians are terrific players and they understand the music better than most other countries."

One reason for their expertise is their close relationship and collaboration with American trailblazers. Many of these prodigious Japanese jazz musicians include Hino, Sadao Watanabe, Toshiko Akiyoshi and Yoshiaki Masuo.

Masuo, the famed Japanese jazz guitarist, stands out. He appears to understand the distinctive style of Sonny's approach to bebop and other jazz styles better than many others. The main reason is his years of personal tutelage by Sonny, as a sideman.

"Sonny has real depth, which is why so many Japanese people love the man and his music," explained Masuo, who played with Sonny intermittently from 1973 through 1986. During this time, he travelled all over the world with Sonny, including Japan.

Growing up in Tokyo, the guitarist was also influenced by his father Hiroshi Masuo, a jazz pianist. "My father was one of the pioneers in Japan who started to play jazz before World War II," he said. "My father was influenced by Teddy Wilson, Nat King Cole, George Shearing, and Bud Powell, but he was more into Nat King Cole and Teddy Wilson."

Masuo arrived in the United States in 1971 to hear and meet firsthand some of the pioneers of jazz, not realizing he would one day play with one of his idols, Sonny Rollins, a star beyond reach for most musicians, both American and foreign.

"I was going to stay just one year in America, but I ended up living there. I still live here now," he said. "Before I went to America, I was playing with Sadao Watanabe. He still is the number one popular jazz musician here [in Japan]. He's 85 years old now. He was my first boss. He picked me up when I was 20 years old, so I learned a lot from him.

"I met Sonny in 1973 and then he picked me up, and when I started with Sonny, his teaching was on a totally different level. The music is very hard to explain with words. It's a whole new experience for me; he opened up new things for me, I didn't know that kind of world existed.

To me, the whole wide world was in front of me when I played with him," he added.

Although he is neither a Buddhist nor a member of any religion, Masuo has respect and admiration for all of them, including Christianity. "I am spiritual, not in a religious sense. I am connected to the whole thing [all religions and faiths]," he said.

During his tenure with Sonny, did he see visible signs of his mysticism and spirituality? "To me, he is really a human being, a close friend, and a beautiful human being," said Masuo, who is now 71. "I've read books on Buddhism, yoga and the Bible, and I've learned from all of them."

According to Masuo, Japanese jazz fans love Sonny, but they love lots of other musicians, too. They can appreciate the depth of his music because Sonny has so many different sides to him, which can't be explained in one word.

When asked about the musical differences between Sonny and Coltrane's spirituality, Masuo replied "He's so, so different from Coltrane. You can't compare them."

"I think [spirituality in jazz] is a good thing," he continued. "To me, it's part of the same spring, something comes up from there. Music comes from there, so all the music to me is spiritual."

The first album Masuo played on with Sonny was *Horn Culture*, followed by *The Cutting Edge*, and also the live album, *Live in Japan*, and a live album in Montreal. The two also performed together on *Reel Life*.

Perhaps most important is that the exchange between Sonny and the Japanese is mutual. Sonny gave them the guidance of jazz, whereas they gave him the direction of Zen Buddhism—one of the two most important spiritual forces in his life. Zen Buddhism, along with yoga, help keep Sonny grounded and balanced.

In Japan, a star was reborn.

There is that inner spiritual journey that I think all great musicians have to go through. You have to find out who you are, you have to decide what you want to present to the world in a positive way to make the world a better place, and however you get to that, everybody has their different ways."

— BILL O'CONNELL, PIANIST

CHAPTER 28

Bop to Pop

Sonny Rollins' diehard fans swerved and swayed in ecstasy while listening to the pulsating rhythms of the whimsical Caribbean song, "St. Thomas." He melded it with the complexities of modern bebop. But, there was a different reaction from veteran fans when he tried to fuse disco, rock, Latin, and other pop music styles into bebop.

Among the reasons they accepted "St. Thomas" was Sonny's family's island origins, and that he had been performing it for decades. On the other hand, the rigid fans thought that those pop music styles were somewhat crass and that it was beneath his dignity to play "superficial" fusion songs.

Still, a younger generation of jazz fans, beginning in the late 1970s, jumped for joy when Sonny switched from bop to pop, attracting devotees of Donna Summer, the Rolling Stones, Dave Valentin, David Bowie, and other pop performers. The old-timers acted as if their hero had committed a heinous crime.

"St. Thomas" is a major part of the repertoire of Sonny's stage performances and recordings. He recorded it back in 1956 on his album *Saxophone Colossus*, which had originally been recorded under the name of "Fire Down There" by composer and pianist Randy Weston. Sonny renamed it to pay homage to his family's ancestry of St. Thomas in the Virgin Islands.

"A lot of people thought Sonny had sold out," said bebop drummer Art Taylor, his childhood friend and former teenage band-member. "Miles [Davis], Herbie [Hancock], and a lot of other cats were doing the fusion thing too with a lot of success, so I guess Sonny wanted to join them."

Around this time, Sonny hired Bill O'Connell, a talented pianist who had played with fusion star Dave Valentin and others to help him with the authenticity of the Latin and rock sounds. "However, Sonny never said 'play this way or that way' while performing tunes, like Stevie Wonder's 'Isn't She Lovely,'" said O'Connell.

"I was always into the Latin jazz thing, and that even appealed to him in terms of my playing, I think. He didn't tell me how to play, you got a feeling of how to work your thing into Sonny's thing. I wanted to jump into the stratosphere with Sonny. Sometimes that was great, and it was some of the best music we played together.

"Something Sonny wanted was for the rhythm section to hold down the fort (which means to play softly and accompany him as the soloist, rather than having several instruments performing at the same time) while he explored the outer universe, as opposed to going with him on that journey. I can't say he discouraged me from that; it was just a feeling. Sonny was not big on pianists."

"Sometimes you'd almost feel like you're getting in the way. I felt like some of the greatest stuff I ever heard him play on the bandstand was when he would play a ten minute *cadenza* (solo). He'd finish a tune and then he'd take a cadenza that would just blow everybody away.

"The thing about Sonny is that he not only plays over the changes, the harmonic scheme, he also plays over the melody. The melody is a big part of his playing, you have Sonny repeating the melody in the solo and always comes back. That was illuminating to me, to hear how important the melody was to him," O'Connell added.

Illus. 40 - Sonny hired pianist Bill O'Connell during his musical foray into fusion.

During these cadenzas, Sonny would play the melody, but he would also inject a humorous nursery rhyme. He was always sarcastic and sardonic. "The crowd would go nuts," O'Connell remembered.

"I remember one time in an airport where someone came up to him and asked for his autograph, and he looked at me and went, 'Oh, the price of fame!'

"I remember one rehearsal, in particular, Sonny didn't give me any sheet music, he would teach it to me. I'd sit at the piano and try to work out the changes to it and that way, once I had a song, I learned it. There was no going from music to memorization, almost getting fed it intravenously, it was part of your DNA. From what I've heard, it was kind of what Monk did. People would go over to Monk's house and he would teach them the tunes. Sonny did a little bit of that too. It was refreshing to come to it from a different angle."

O'Connell agreed that Coltrane made musicians more spiritual. "There is that inner spiritual journey that I think all great musicians have to go through. You have to find out who you are, you have to decide what you want to present to the world in a positive way to make the world a better place, and however you get to that, everybody has their different ways. I would say the search for meaning, the search for generally adding something positive to the world, is in my music. If that's a spiritual journey, so be it.

"But again, I don't know if you need to be part of a church or religious thought to necessarily be spiritual. You talked about Trane. Trane to me, it was just that inner journey to discover what means something to you that you can share with the world. To me, that's the important thing," O'Connell said, adding:

"I got along great with him. It wasn't like 'the great Sonny Rollins.' Once you got to know him, he was like everybody else…On a musical level, I was aware that I was playing with someone who was very enlightened. I sensed that enlightenment."

The rhythms shifted from disco to rock and Latin. The listeners took to the dance floor and boogied the night away while listening to fusion recordings by Sonny Rollins, whether it was live or on recordings.

The rhythms emanating from Sonny's band were a far cry from

the rhythms of hard bop jazz, which Sonny had helped to popularize during the 1950s and 60s. During this time, hoofers found it virtually impossible to dance to the music on such albums as *Tenor Madness, Saxophone Colossus,* and other jazz classics that propelled him to win international jazz polls as the top new tenor saxophonist.

While Sonny's new music had a commercial tinge, the melodies and harmonies were still intact. It was distracting to many die-hard purists, but Sonny could still improvise with the same gusto and majesty that distinguished his early career.

Bebop, it should be remembered, discouraged the use of dance rhythms to distinguish it from the dance rhythms of the big bands of the 1930s. It was a dramatic departure for Sonny, who had been an ardent supporter of listening to music with a serious ear, rather than dancing to it.

By the time Sonny returned from his second hiatus, the jazz world was changing, still reeling from the blow dealt to it by the sudden and overwhelming popularity of rock 'n' roll. The British Invasion had coincided with jazz at its most experimental moment—the so-called "free jazz" that did not accord with traditional systems of key and rhythm.

The audience for such a style was increasingly rarified and academic: jazz was falling out of favor with the masses. Rock was a perfect substitute, accessible and catchy, and it out-competed jazz at every turn. The jazzmen thus found themselves between a rock and a hard place.

Hoping to regain some popularity on the back of the new genre, many jazzmen—among them Sonny Rollins—turned to "fusion," a combination of jazz and rock styles. Fusion fueled an explosion of static in the jazz world, and critics quickly branded the records as subpar, a cop-out to popular tastes. Jazz purists were indignant, branding fusion the death knell of bebop. What was fusion but slow tempos played over and over again, with no challenging passages, no improvisation, none of the originality that had created a new art form?

Musicians who couldn't handle bebop played fusion. And those who could play bebop, like Sonny, Miles Davis, Percy and Jimmy

Heath, Herbie Hancock, and Freddie Webster among others, were diluting their talents by playing fusion.

Starting with 1972's *Next Album*—his first album since 1966's *East Broadway Run Down*—Sonny began dabbling in the new, hybrid genre.

"I don't think he went full-force into any one kind of style in particular," recalled nephew Clifton Anderson. "He was experimenting when he made records. What he did that turned off some of the jazz purists was, he started using electronic instruments. He started using the electronic piano and the electric bass."

Throughout the 1970s, Sonny would incorporate elements of funk, R&B, and, of course, disco into his music. In 1976, he released the album *The Way I Feel*, which featured the track "Shout it Out."

Anderson remembered that "'Shout it Out' was a Patrice Rushen song. It was a funky song...[Sonny] wrote a tune called 'Disco Monk,' and then he had another tune—which I personally really dug—called 'Harlem Boys.' It had a disco beat." Sonny also played a lot of jazz/calypso songs at this time, which Anderson said were "second nature" to him due to his growing up in a Caribbean family.

While Sonny's new sound might have attracted new listeners with commercial tastes, critics and more traditional fans were far from thrilled. "A lot of them wanted the old Sonny," remembered pianist Mark Soskin, who began playing with Sonny in the late 1970s.

The critics in New York, he recalled, were particularly brutal, and Sonny was always prepared to take them head-on. "It was a different kind of feeling when we played New York. He was going out there to do battle," Soskin said. "It wasn't the audience, because all the audiences who came loved Sonny. It was the critics."

Sonny's critics were quick to point fingers—he wouldn't be playing this stuff out of his own volition, they reasoned, and there were plenty of targets for blame. There were three entities that may have driven Sonny into the commercial idiom: Miles Davis; his record company, Milestone Records; and his wife, Lucille.

Beginning with *Next Album*, Sonny released a string of albums on Milestone Records, a record company founded by Orrin Keepnews and Dick Katz. "I remember somebody blamed Orrin Keepnews for making Sonny do these sort of things because he was producing," Lucille said. "Sonny never did fusion-fusion. I mean, it was very mild. It was ludicrous, too, because nobody's ever told Sonny what to do."

Lucille herself would also face accusations of leading Sonny into fusion—even if he did not go as far into the style as Miles or Herbie. She would be branded as a whitewasher, turning the jazz giant away from true jazz towards a more commercial sound.

By this time, Lucille—a self-confessed "efficiency freak" and "neat nerd"—was managing Sonny's career. "There was nobody else to do it," she explained matter-of-factly. "Sonny never liked to deal with people," she said. She loved the managerial aspects of her new position, but she was less than thrilled with booking the gigs.

"I always hated that," she said, "When I first started doing that, I used the phony name Janice Jestahe, but I hated it." Eventually, the couple would work with professional booking agents, but the reins of management remained in Lucille's hands.

Lucille plunged headlong into the task of bringing order to Sonny's professional life. Together they were a demanding business team— his sidemen were expected to always be on time at airports, at gigs, or at studios, and they were expected to pick up rapidly what Sonny wanted from them. He was as demanding of his musicians as he was of himself—they had to be talented, compatible, and humble.

Lucille handled travel details, arranging limousines and buses in the States, Europe, and Japan. Sonny was playing concerts in large arenas now—in Europe and Japan, he filled every venue.

"We go on concert tours," she said. "We go for the big places. The Omni Rae Shin Bin in Tokyo was the last thing I booked directly. We play places where you don't have to worry about anything, like the Ravinia in Chicago, the Monterey Festival."

They played clubs from time to time, but the money and the treatment had to be right. If Sonny and Lucille didn't know the owner, they demanded a deposit up front. "We played The House of Blues in New Orleans," said Lucille. "The House of Blues in Hollywood."

There would still be a few club dates, here and there, but they were carefully selected, and there was seldom more than one a year in New

York. Sonny and Lucille were after bigger venues, looking to pack theaters and arenas. Sonny wanted to elevate the music, to find a larger audience to appreciate his work.

While Lucille might have been managing his career, she vehemently denied pushing Sonny toward a more commercial sound. "I never told Sonny what to play. Nobody could," she said. "I never made him play anything. When we went into studios to record, I didn't even know what he was going to record."

Sonny was, as always, an independent soul, and he would not let public opinion sway the direction he was taking his music. Once, Lucille recalled, in Hollywood, an older musician criticized Sonny at a show. "You shouldn't be playing that song," he said.

Lucille said Sonny didn't respond. "He'd never say anything." But if she had been there, she said, she would have told the guy off. "It was stupid, trying to tell him what to play. When we go in to record, I don't even know what he's going to play. I haven't even heard anything he's going to record until he comes in that day. The other day when we walked in, I said be sure to give us a list of the songs so we can write them down." That anyone would blame her, or anyone else, for leading Sonny into fusion is, she said indignantly, "a joke."

But, she noted, some of the criticisms aimed at Sonny were valid. There were "some bad records made in the 70s. There are some I didn't particularly like. But that was only because Sonny liked to try new things. He gets tired of people talking only about the old bebop. Playing the old bebop, that's fine, and he still plays it. But he plays what he wants to."

Even if she did not guide him into fusion, Lucille would exert her influence on Sonny's records in other ways. At first, she said, she was not into the production side of the music. However, during one recording session in California, she began to make her opinions heard. "We went down to Los Angeles to do one of those albums in the 70s, and Orrin Keepnews was producing," she said.

"I wasn't involved in it. Some guy had done some arrangements. The studio guys came in, and they put these arrangements behind the stuff that had already been recorded, or they put them down first and then Sonny recorded. I can't remember which. But I really hated it, and I started to cry.

"We were in the middle of a studio in the middle of Hollywood someplace, and I had to leave in disgrace because I was crying. I left and went back to the hotel because I was making a fool of myself. And I wasn't involved at that point."

Later, she talked to Sonny about the studio arrangement. "I told him I just didn't like it. I just told him, well, I hated it!" It was changed—and soon Lucille's concerns became more extensive. She didn't like some of the arrangements others produced. She didn't like the way the tracks were mixed. She didn't always like the sound.

Gradually, Lucille began to take over the mixing and production side of recordings. Sonny had little patience with such details, and he allowed Lucille to take the reins.

"He trusts my ear pretty much," she said. "He trusts my taste." But, there are still elements of the recording decided by Sonny, and only Sonny. "He's the one who chooses the guys."

Clifton said his uncle is "not so hands-on in the production sense of records. He gets into a certain degree of the production, and then he's had enough. He leaves it to Lucille." Clifton noted the problems with such an arrangement. "Well, Lucille's production skills are very limited."

In later years, Sonny and Lucille moved to Fantasy Records because they did not interfere with production, Clifton said. Sonny didn't want to bother with it—he was more concerned with live shows and practice than he was with recording—and Lucille wanted total control. "If they went with another label, I think they would be really pressuring them for production assistance," said Clifton. "Lucille doesn't want any part of that."

Under Lucille's management and Sonny's constant drive for improvement, the band became more and more disciplined. It was a whole different world from the beginning of Sonny's life, when musicians showed up to sessions late and strung out.

"Sonny definitely did not like lateness," Mark Soskin recalled. "I remember somebody coming into the lobby late. Sonny was always extremely on time."

On the rare occasions that happened, Sonny would let the tardy musician know he was not pleased without saying a word. It was more his manner that let them know, and they got the message. "Sometimes, he might tease them a little," said Lucille.

Sonny's crossover efforts didn't end there. He recorded a big hit with the Rolling Stones called "Waiting on a Friend" on the album, *Tattoo You.* Sonny reportedly asked Mick Jagger, the Stones' lead singer and co-composer of the song, to dance to the song in the studio so he could get the feeling for it. It worked. The album became a number one hit on several music charts.

The critics could say whatever they wanted to about fusion. He would play however he wanted to. In 1981, he would contribute a blazing saxophone solo to "Waiting for a Friend," a cut off the Rolling Stones' album *Tattoo You.* Sonny was a force of nature, and nothing would stand in his way.

CHAPTER 29

Town Hall Collapse

Doctors at New York's Bellevue Hospital were dumbfounded when they examined the body of a man brought into the emergency room because he keeled over during a jazz concert at Town Hall. His heart, lungs, muscles, and other vital signs were strong, and they estimated his age to be that of an 18-year-old.

But they soon discovered that the man was, in fact, age 52—despite nearly a decade of shooting heroin into his veins, boozing excessively, and living the high life of a jazz musician. He rarely slept at night and got only minimal amounts of sleep during the day, because he practiced his horn several hours a day.

The patient was Sonny Rollins, the jazz great. His exceptional healthiness was yet another reason fans around the world regarded him as a superior creature—a man who had not only risen to the level of being the number-one jazz tenor saxophonist, but someone who may have mastered some of the secrets of aging and other enigmas of the universe.

Sonny had keeled over during one of his typical, hard-blowing performances. It happened on April 24, 1983, on the same bill with jazz trumpeter Wynton Marsalis as a guest soloist. Although Marsalis was only 23—and considered to be the new top jazz trumpeter—Sonny had challenged his stamina repeatedly during the performance.

Sonny's reputation was always to outplay other musicians on stage, and he had achieved his goal before collapsing. The rhythmic tempos were played at super-human speed, which may be one of the reasons for his attack. He later told doctors he believed he fell because of his excessive intake of vitamins.

After some tests and against medical advice, Sonny signed out shortly after arriving, said Steve Matura, a spokesman for the hospital, preventing them from learning why the middle-aged man had the body of a teenager.

"The medical staff couldn't believe it when they examined Mr. Rollins," said Emily Iker, a physician at Cabrini and St. Vincent Medical Centers in New York City who attended the concert and also examined the patient. "Former heroin addicts are not usually that healthy, and they certainly don't look as vibrant as he did."

A case in point. Sonny's idol, alto saxophonist Charlie Parker, died at the age of 34 due in part to his many years of being addicted to heroin, which led to many other bodily complications. In fact, thousands of jazz musicians across the globe also died young as a result of heroin addiction—thinking that they could improve their quality of playing the way Parker did.

"It didn't matter how great Sonny was, he would not have survived if he had continued to use heroin and other dangerous substances," explained Dr. Iker.

"Still, it was amazing for me to see and hear a 52-year-old man play so brilliantly, with his level of stamina, for such long periods of time, but we wanted to know more about his secrets. Obviously, he had been doing something special, which is why he was in such good medical condition. We were not able to determine the cause of his collapse because he left the hospital too soon for us to know," she added.

Lucille Rollins' account of why he collapsed may have been linked to his high blood pressure. "I remember, on the morning of his fall, that he hadn't eaten. I made it a point to always make him eat something first thing in the morning. 'Don't ever not eat, don't try to go a whole day and night without eating,' I said to him.

"When he fell, it was one of the scariest things I had ever seen in my life," she added. "I feared the worst, but I hoped for the best. I felt wonderful after seeing that he was okay after the fall. Following the event, we both started to get frequent medical tests to check the status of our health conditions."

Sonny attributed his recovery, in part, due to a healthy lifestyle that developed during his years after Lexington and during his two-year Williamsburg Bridge sabbatical in 1959. "I learned a lot during this time," he said. "I studied yoga, Buddhism, and Ancient Egyptian religions and cultures," which gave him a different perspective on health habits, as well as life itself.

Observed Sonny: "Well, as far as the body is concerned, I wouldn't really know. I guess it's in the genes, but I am certainly not an expert. I'll leave that up to the doctors to decide why I seem younger to them. Maybe it stems from the fact that after I got strung out, in the 1950s, I got into a health kick and I guess it kicked in during the 1980s."

Sonny started lifting weights, eating organic foods, and began a strict regimen of taking vitamins "so that I could boost my stamina, which was important to me because I needed that high level of energy to play the kind of difficult tunes I heard in my head and that I wanted to play. Playing our music is not a toy."

Illus. 41 - Sonny Rollins: Blowing his tenor saxophone with all his might.

CHAPTER 30

Daughter Dearest

"Let me in! I want to see Daddy!*"* Even behind closed dressing-room doors, Sonny Rollins' musicians could hear the ear-splitting shrieks of the woman outside. They listened as a few muffled, gruff, male voices began to speak, only to be interrupted by more desperate shouting from the woman.

What the hell is causing all that ruckus? The musicians wondered, glancing at each other quizzically.

Neither the musicians nor the concertgoers at the Los Angeles theater had been prepared for such a volatile scene. Security certainly hadn't anticipated having to restrain such a boisterous, demanding woman at a Sonny Rollins concert.

The jazz titan certainly had legions of devoted fans, many of whom would stand outside his dressing room door asking to see him, but none were quite as demanding and boisterous as this woman.

The incident occurred during the mid-1990s. By that time, Sonny—in the vein of a rock star—was one of a handful of jazz musicians whose music generated such a mesmerizing effect on fans that they would exhibit wild enthusiasm and excitement.

Usually, jazz, bohemian, and New Age listeners—who represent Sonny's fan-base—are deliberately cool and laid back. They rarely express the sort of zealous admiration of musical stars that rock 'n' roll fans do—even though they feel equally exhilarated.

During the concert, the security guards found themselves with what they felt was a potentially dangerous groupie demanding to see the star player. They knocked on the dressing room door, which opened to reveal a handful of perplexed musicians.

"There's a woman outside who says she's Sonny Rollins' daughter," a guard said. "She is demanding to see him."

"Sonny doesn't have a daughter," one of the musicians said. "I've known Sonny for decades, and he's never mentioned having any children, especially a daughter, so I don't know if she's telling the truth or not."

But the woman continued to scream from the lobby. "He's my father! I want to see him now. Why won't you let me see my father? Let me in! I demand to see him immediately!" she shouted.

Confused, the guards went to Sonny and Lucille to ask what they should do with the troublesome woman. They decided to let her in, having a gut feeling about the woman in question. When she entered the dressing room, their suspicions were confirmed.

"Daddy!" the woman shouted. "It's me, Suzanne!" (While the name Suzanne is fictitious, the person is real; her name has been changed for privacy.)

Sonny, smiling, but sweating profusely from an intense, long and grueling performance, gave the woman a bear hug as she entered his dressing room. "How you doing? It's good to see you; it's been a long time since I last saw you," he said. "I'm sorry that you had to fight your way past the security guards in order to see me."

Suzanne gave him a big grin, squeezed him back and declared: "It's fine, Daddy. I can see that everybody here wants to meet you and get your autograph. They really dig you. I love you, too, and I dig your music. I understand why so many people want just to get a piece of you. I'm just so proud to be your daughter."

After chatting for a while, Sonny told her he had to leave the room because he had to change his wet clothes and get ready for the second set. At his request, Lucille then gave her two tickets and asked her to attend the next set. The father and "daughter" hugged again, and she left the dressing room and walked outside the theater, looking proud and victorious that Sonny had given her so much attention.

Outside there were two lines—one for fans who already had tickets for the show and the other for adoring fans desperately trying to purchase tickets. Unfortunately, they were told that the concert had been sold out.

Meanwhile, Suzanne, looking at the disappointed fans, started to hawk the tickets Sonny had just given her. She began to try to sell the tickets, going from one person to the next to find anyone who would be willing to pay cash for the tickets.

The police, always on the lookout for scalpers, quickly descended on Suzanne. "But Sonny just gave me those tickets! He's my father!" She cried as the cops handcuffed her and shoved her in the backseat of the patrol car.

Fans standing in both lines appeared to be shocked that cops had taken away a woman who claimed to be Sonny Rollins' daughter. There were constant stares and expressions of concern that she would be locked up simply for trying to sell tickets she claimed her father had given her.

But who was this woman, really? Was Suzanne actually the daughter of Sonny Rollins, or was she just a con artist?

For decades, Suzanne had been a recurring character in the soap opera that was Sonny's life. She had been in and out of the lives of the Rollins family since the 1950s, when Sonny first met Suzanne's mother, Holly.

Like many of Sonny's lovers, Holly (whose name is also fictitious) had been a beautiful woman. "She was very attractive, always kind of flirtatious," recalled his sister, Gloria Anderson.

Holly had been involved in a love affair with Sonny at the height of his heroin addiction. She began to use drugs, and he wondered whether he was responsible for getting her hooked.

"But I don't know if that's necessarily true, because she might have been going down that road on her own, long before she met Sonny," Gloria pointed out. "I was suspicious from the moment I met her."

Even so, Holly soon became a full-fledged junkie and turned to prostitution for drug money. "I don't know if she was prostituting at the time that Sonny was going around with her, but, by the time their relationship ended, she was prostituting."

Sometime after the relationship ended, Holly revealed to Sonny that she was pregnant. Months later, she gave birth to a baby girl—but as far as Gloria and the rest of the Rollins family was concerned, the baby was not Sonny's.

"When we saw her, she was light complexioned and looked almost white. Our family looked at her and said, 'Oh, you know that's not Sonny's child. There's no way that could be Sonny's child because both he and Holly were brown-skinned," Gloria said.

Gloria remembered that Holly had been sleeping with a German man around the same time she was seeing Sonny. Given Suzanne's very light complexion, she suspected this man was the true father.

Gloria observed, "Holly was definitely prostituting by that point. I don't think she knew who the father was, but Sonny isn't listed as the father of Suzanne on the birth certificate."

As Suzanne grew up, Holly's drug addiction worsened. "When Holly was strung out, she could not take care of Suzanne," Gloria said. Even though she wasn't his biological daughter, Sonny "asked everyone to look after her because he felt responsible for her mother getting strung out. Sonny felt obligated."

At the time, Gloria was living with her family at her brother Val's office on 163rd Street in Harlem. "My grandmother, my father's mother, was very dark-skinned. She had a real color complex. She saw Suzanne, being as light as she was, and wanted us to take her in," she said.

"Suzanne came to live with us for a year or two. She even went to school with my children," Gloria recalled. "Then, Suzanne moved back with her mother, but her mother was just a mess. Her mother started seeing this guy who was a limousine driver, and they moved out to

California."

Some years later, Suzanne's life took an even more tragic and bizarre turn: her mother was found murdered in a hotel.

"After Holly died, Suzanne started going around with this chauffeur, the limo driver Holly was seeing. He had an affair with Suzanne, and then they ended up getting married and having kids together," Gloria said.

"She's out in California now, and when she comes to New York, Sonny talks to her every once in a while," Gloria said. "He'll give her a little money. He feels as though he has an obligation to Suzanne because of her mother."

Suzanne continued to insist Sonny was her biological father, much to Gloria's chagrin. "She kept calling Sonny 'Dad.' For a little while, I would just let it go because she didn't know who her real father was and she didn't have any family other than us.

"Sonny didn't really resent her calling him 'Dad,' but the thing is, she started trying to capitalize on him. She became like her momma, kind of like a schemer, so she would hit him up for money all the time," Gloria said.

Ultimately, Suzanne's failure to acknowledge her true parentage caused a rift between her and Gloria. "We had a big falling out, years ago. She came to New York to ask me for a copy of her birth certificate. I told her I didn't know if I had it, even though I did.

"I said, 'Suzanne, he is not your father, and you need to stop calling him that. You need to stop acting like he's your father. He was nice enough to take care of you because your mom was unable to look after you, but that's as far as it went.

"'He's not your blood father, and if he was your blood father, his name would have been on your birth certificate as your father. There's someone else's name on it,'" Gloria said. "'The easiest thing to do would be to take a DNA test, but Suzanne never wanted to do that."

Gloria speculated Suzanne refused to take a DNA test because she knew deep down she wasn't Sonny's daughter. If the test showed her father was someone else, Suzanne would likely feel as though she couldn't ask Sonny for money any longer.

Gloria was not alone in believing that Suzanne was not Sonny's daughter. There was a consensus among family and friends that Suzanne called him her father because he was a famous musician who was loved by millions around the world.

Whether she is his daughter or not, Sonny refuses to acknowledge her in conversations or news interviews.

CHAPTER 31

Lucille: A Love Lost

They were not the kind of couple you'd see walking in the park, holding hands and hugging, but to the surprise of many family and friends, their relationship was far more romantic than many thought.

It was not a marriage made in heaven, but when Lucille Pearson Rollins died in 2004 from complications of a stroke at the couple's remote Germantown, NY farm, it represented one of the most devastating periods in Sonny Rollins' life. She was 76, and they had been married for 39 years.

"After she died," a close friend recalled, "Sonny went into a deep funk. He wouldn't talk to people, and he wouldn't answer his phone. He stopped practicing and playing gigs. She was apparently more important to him than most of us ever imagined."

Love aside, it was not a smooth marriage. Sonny never discussed it publicly, but he was bothered by the massive criticism leveled by friends and fellow musicians against Lucille for the poor quality and commercial bent of the more than dozen recordings she co-producer and engineered. Jazz critics, musicians, and older fans said the recordings she worked on, beginning in the 1970s, fell short of his prodigious talents.

Lucille first met Sonny in the late 1950s in Chicago, when she and her girlfriend went to see one of his performances at a local club. She was smitten and eventually followed her new love interest all the way to New York City.

"I didn't especially like Lucille's politics from the very beginning," said Sonny. "What I did like about her was her devotion to both me and jazz, which was very important to me. I needed a woman who understood the eccentricities of both my lifestyle and jazz itself."

A decade later, Sonny and Lucille decided to make their romance "legal" when they decided on wedlock. It was an unusual marriage. In fact, the attendees were quite aghast when Sonny married Lucille—not just because she was a white country girl from Kansas City, a political right winger and the quintessential "plain jane" type—but because Sonny was dressed in a robe like a monk and was acting weirder than usual.

Sonny was always an odd fellow, but by 1965, at his wedding, he had become a different person. Yet, while he displayed this eccentric behavior and humor, he seemed to have become more gracious and intellectual.

"Sonny had a different aura," said sister Gloria Anderson. "I liked the new Sonny because he reminded me of the young boy rather than the person who had spent time behind bars. His new spiritual persona was extremely appealing, for one thing, because he had moved away from some of the old friends who, I believe, had helped to corrupt him."

In 1959, Sonny had shocked the jazz world when he abruptly stopped playing his horn at a time when he was earning $2,000 per night—nearly ten times as much as other players.

In 1961, before his marriage and upon his return from the Bridge, girlfriend Lucille Pearson had witnessed this transformation. Despite her personal history of conservatism, she too accepted the new Sonny. During this time, he was able to not only improve his playing but had

Illus. 42 - Lucille Rollins and husband Sonny share a happy moment. Their marriage was rocky at times because of his affairs with other women.

apparently learned some of the spiritual secrets of ancient Egypt, India, and Asia.

On one occasion, Lucille witnessed what she thought was a bizarre event that completely "startled" her, said Gloria. "Lucille told me once, that when they were living in Brooklyn, Sonny's entire body started to glow and light up while he was doing pull-ups on a bar. She had never seen anything like it before. That was not the first time, there were other strange events, too."

Friends say Lucille's acceptance of Sonny's peculiar behavior was one of the reasons he chose to marry her—a marriage that lasted for 39 years. She didn't like many of his liberal political views, especially concerning black activism, but she remained silent because of her love for him.

There was yet another reason Sonny married Lucille—her deft business acumen. As a white woman, she could negotiate business deals better with white club owners and record companies, many of whom were blatantly racist and who routinely paid black performers less money. Some even compensated musicians with dope since they knew many musicians were strung out on heroin.

"Lucille was an excellent manager," said Clifton Anderson, who declined to talk about her work as a co-producer of his recordings. "What I can say is that the music business is hard and racist. These white business people respected her more because she was white. I believe that she was, in turn, able to get better deals and more money than maybe a lot of us (blacks)."

Lucille took charge of Sonny's business career in 1971 and resumed after another one of his many unannounced sabbaticals. She then served as his co-producer and made his recordings more commercial, as well as enabling him to become the second most financially successful black jazz musician ever, after Miles Davis.

Business may not have been the only attraction to Lucille. What about love and romance? Sonny was a master balladeer who played pretty, romantic love songs on his recordings. He was also known as "a lady's man," someone who was flirtatious and appreciative of the opposite sex. Moreover, he had a reputation for having hidden relationships with other women.

Whether he did or did not, one thing became clear, which was finally revealed after Lucille died in 2004. Sonny was deeply in love with her after all. The love affair between Sonny and Lucille, who was two years older than Sonny, shocked relatives and friends.

Hollie West, a respected music critic for both the *Washington Post* and the *New York Daily News*, declined to criticize Lucille outright for her work as his co-producer and engineer. "Let's just say his older recordings were phenomenal, which established him as one of the greatest tenor saxophonists ever. The records produced by Lucille were somewhat lacking, compared to the older stuff."

Even many of Sonny's longtime fans did not like the dozen-plus recordings she produced, starting with "Love at First Sight" in 1980 on the Milestone label. The recordings completely changed Sonny's sound and style.

"I won't say that the recordings produced by Lucille were bad, but they certainly were not up to his high level of performance," said West. "I much prefer his recordings dating back to the 1950s when he emerged as one of the top tenor saxophonist on the scene."

One of the biggest complaints against Lucille came anonymously from Sonny's band members, most of whom, like Sonny himself, tended to be politically progressive and pro-black. They expressed disdain for the way she often dismissed the civil rights movement and its direction. During one incident when Sonny and his band members were on a bus trip headed to Boston in the 1990s, Lucille shocked them when she made the following comment. "Wow, I forgot to send in my political contribution to the Rudolph Giuliani campaign for mayor of New York City."

Band members were visibly shaken by her comments. They stared at Lucille with anger and disbelief. They didn't believe she could support a candidate most blacks asserted was racist and who, along with Police Commissioner William Bratton, was mostly responsible for the heavily criticized stop-and-frisk policies and police brutality cases against blacks in New York City.

Sonny didn't utter a word or show any visible response to her comments and the facial reactions of the musicians. "Sonny simply turned his entire body toward the window and looked out for several minutes," said one of the musicians. "He was definitely embarrassed and didn't want to deal with the situation."

Furthermore, Lucille didn't have the hip artsy attitude that hipsters consider essential. A professional secretary, she came from the Midwest, and she did not hide her upbringing. She was friendly, skillful, and diplomatic. But when it came to business negotiations, she was at the top of her game. Despite her political bent and squareness, Sonny was impressed by Lucille's business savvy, but he was the one to make the final decisions.

CHAPTER 32

The Veil

It was a steamy summer day in August 2012 when Sonny Rollins arrived in Marciac, France for the final show of a European concert tour. The morning before he was supposed to play before thousands of adoring fans, he became frantic after discovering that he had lost one of his partials (false teeth).

While anyone would have been frustrated in that situation, it was particularly disturbing to a man whose career rested on his ability to blow a saxophone. "I couldn't find the bottom partial. I needed the partial in order to play this evening, plus I had to record a video that night," he said.

Although Sonny is usually calm and collected—as one would expect of a yogi—he couldn't help but grow tense. He hysterically searched through his hotel room, unzipping, and rifling through his bags, stripping off the bedsheets, and looking under the bed—but to no avail.

"I was up the creek, man. I was concerned about the gig; everything was on me," he said, referring to the fact that he had to pay the musicians and the hotel. He was also concerned about his fans, who had been eagerly awaiting this concert for months.

Sonny was in France to perform at the Marciac Jazz Festival, which takes place annually between the end of July and the middle of August. An estimated 250,000 jazz lovers and tourists congregate in this walled village, which was founded in the 13th century. Located in the famously chic South of France, Marciac is near the border of Spain.

"I didn't know what to do. In fact, I called [the hotel staff] downstairs and said, 'Look, I think I lost my partial. I might have thrown it out by mistake. Is there any way you guys could look through the garbage to see if you can find it?'

"They were nice people; they said, 'Yes, we'll look.' Since we were out in the country, I knew they weren't getting the garbage picked up every day, so the partial might still be there," he reasoned.

Sonny hung up the phone and sat down on his hotel bed, discontented, and brimming with anxiety. Then suddenly, everything changed.

"I happened to look up, and I saw what looked like a veil. I looked up in the sky. I was in my hotel room, but it was like looking up in the sky. There was something else behind this veil. It was the most indescribably beautiful thing I've ever seen. I can't describe it; it was like another world," Sonny remembered.

He explained: "The veil was covering this world. But what happened was, that veil parted just a little bit, the veil just came apart a little bit, and behind it I saw this [vision], which was like a different world—some people would say heaven, or whatever."

Even after decades of yoga, meditation, astral travel, and levitation, Sonny had never experienced anything quite like this. It was a transcendent experience, one in which Sonny caught a glimpse of reality as it truly was.

"I don't know how long it lasted. It was just a little bit, just enough for me to see this fantastic reality of infinity, or whatever else it is. 'Man,' I said, 'wow, I feel better.' Nothing happened. I didn't find my partials, but I just felt that everything would be all right. Whatever happened, it would be all right."

Had Sonny made a brief sojourn to heaven and back?

Religious theorists might answer "yes," but Sonny, ever the skeptic, declined to reveal his innermost thoughts, not just about his miraculous experience, but about many other things.

In many cultures and religions, heaven represents a cosmological or other-worldly place. It is home to God (or gods), angels, jinn, saints, and revered descendants who have ended up there after death. Some scholars theorize that heavenly beings can "incarnate" or descend to Earth and that earthly beings can travel to heaven in the afterlife.

This belief is found in many religious traditions, from the Abrahamic religions to Eastern philosophies. Heaven is a place many religious people, including Christians, aspire to enter after the death of the physical body.

In some instances, they believe humans can even go to heaven alive, which may have been what happened to Sonny in that French hotel room. He had been a practitioner mainly of yoga (from the Hindu tradition), but he also accepts some aspects of other systems, such as Buddhism.

Christianity views heaven as a metaphorical locale where God's glory can be experienced as a beatific vision by angels and by those saints who have achieved heavenly bliss after overcoming the trials of human existence. But to other Christians, heaven is a physical place "up in the sky" to which, for example, the Virgin Mary was taken after her death. The Catholic dogma of the Assumption of the Virgin Mary, which is celebrated by a holy day on August 15, holds that she was assumed into heaven "body and soul."

According to Scripture, Enoch and Elijah were also assumed into heaven, body and soul (Genesis 5:24, 2 Kings 2:11, Sirach 44:16, Sirach 49:15, Hebrews 11:5).

Thousands of people report they have had what are called near-death experiences (NDEs), or out of body experiences (OBEs)—being clinically dead and experiencing floating out of one's body, and being able to see physical reality from an elevated position. Some of these people recall having met deceased family members and traveling

Illus. 43 - Sonny Rollins played one of his best performances ever at a concert in Marciac, France after he caught a glimpse of Heaven or some otherworldly destination. Marciac, which has one of the largest jazz festivals in the world, is located approximately 50 miles of Lourdes, where St. Bernadette famously saw apparitions of the Virgin Mary.

through a tunnel toward a light, then being welcomed by an entity corresponding to their belief system: Jesus, a saint, or a deity.

Reflecting further on his experience in the hotel room in Marciac that afternoon Sonny affirmed that "it was one of the most extraordinary experiences in my life." As he sat there in awe, the veil eventually closed, and Sonny returned to his usual state of consciousness.

Was it reminiscent of the "out-of-body" incident reported in Paul's second letter to the Corinthians, about the man who was "caught up into the third heaven"? For the toothless Sonny, this was no time for philosophical speculation. He got up and began to look under the chair where he had placed one of his bags. On the floor, a small container had suddenly appeared. Shocked, he opened it to find his bottom partial, at last.

Relieved at his find, Sonny began to laugh, amazed that he had found exactly what he had been looking for—perhaps through divine intervention. Perhaps it was an example of an "apport," an object that manifests itself as a gift from the spirit world. Regardless of the explanation, Sonny was relieved that he would be able to play that night and that the show would go on.

But what exactly was this veil that Sonny saw? What and where was this spiritual world that lay beyond it?

Although Marciac is a rather small town (or commune), with a population of just over 1200, its love for jazz is enormous. Jazz is taught as a regular subject in local schools, and the town has acquired worldwide notoriety for its annual "Jazz in Marciac" festival. Some of the biggest names on the contemporary jazz scene perform at the festival, which has been held every August since 1978.

At a time when jazz festivals in America are in major decline, jazz is alive and kicking in France and many other European countries, like Denmark, Finland, Sweden, Italy, Germany, England, and Spain. It is massively popular in Japan and Korea.

In addition, these countries provide constant gigs for American jazz musicians, especially black ones, while America ignores them. It is ironic that these countries are so active when the birthplace of jazz, America, supports other music styles.

Illus. 44 - Marciac, which is situated in the south of France, is so enamored of jazz that it has the above statue of Wynton Marsalis blowing his trumpet. The town also hosts almost a quarter of a million jazz lovers from all over the world during its annual summer jazz festival in August.

France stands out for several reasons. One of them is that during the early 20th century, the French allowed band leader James Reese Europe and countless other African American bands to perform in fancy concert halls while in America, they were only allowed to play in brothels and other houses of ill-repute.

Interestingly, while France is considered one of the most secular countries in the world, it is there that Sonny experienced the mystery of the veil. According to the Eurobarometer Poll conducted in 2010, 27 percent of French citizens said they believe in God; 27 percent responded that they believe in a spirit or life force, and 40 percent said they didn't believe in anything. Yet, the best-known apparition (supernatural) sites are in Lourdes, France and Fatima in Portugal. Lourdes created its first medical bureau in 1883 to check the validity of reported cures.

In 2012, the same year Sonny reportedly witnessed the veil, one study concluded that some of the cures "were currently beyond our ken, but still impressive, incredibly effective and awaiting a scientific explanation."

Significantly, Marciac is located some 50 miles north of Lourdes, the market town also known worldwide for its Marian apparitions. An estimated six million people visit Lourdes each year to witness the site where, in 1858, Bernadette Soubirous claimed to have glimpsed the Virgin Mary, who showed her an underground spring reputed to have healing powers.

Also in the south of France stories abound about Mary Magdalene, who, after the death of Jesus Christ, supposedly arrived on the coast of Provence in a rudderless boat, where she preached and taught the message of transforming love. It is said that she converted the royal family and the entire local population to Christianity. She then spent the last 30 years of her life in prayer and meditation in a mountain cave.

This cave in the south of France, where Mary Magdalene was supposed to have lived and preached, exists to this day as a shrine dedicated to her memory.

Perhaps there is something in the water in southwestern France, or perhaps it is what New Age aficionados might call "high vibrations"—a place with strong spiritual energy. No matter what the explanation, it was the site of a seminal moment in Sonny's spiritual life.

The vision of what lay behind the veil "was something that shocked me back into reality, the reality of what the real world is," Sonny said. "The real world isn't what we're living in now. Living on Earth is a test that we've got to go through. That's all this is; it's not the real thing. I saw a glimpse of the real thing, just a little bit. The veil just opened a little bit."

What Sonny may have been referring to is the Hindu concept of maya, which means "illusion." Maya has sometimes been described as the veil that clouds our understanding of true reality. In the Advaita Vedanta school of philosophy, which Sonny studied intensely at the ashram in India, maya creates the illusion that the world around us is what's real.

But for Advaita Vedantists—and possibly for Sonny—Brahman is the Ultimate Reality, true and unchanging. In everyday life, people identify with their egos, their individual selves. Our true, divine self is called the Ātman, which is, in essence, the same as Brahman. In other words, teaches Advaita Vedanta, we are just blind to the fact that our true selves are the same as the Ultimate Reality, which exists "behind the veil" of ordinary experience.

For a moment in that hotel room in Marciac, that veil lifted for Sonny. Even as life went on as usual, something inside him had changed. As was the case with many mystics past and present, Sonny's glimpse of the divine left him with an unbelievable sense of joy. "After that, for months I was just bursting out and couldn't contain myself," he remembered.

The incident begs the question: did Sonny Rollins leave earth and achieve the ultimate destination in life or afterlife? Was this an out-of-body experience that transfigured him, like Christ upon the Tabor mountaintop? All he wanted was his bottom partial, and he got an upper room.

CHAPTER 33

Closing Out

Sonny Rollins is not called the "Saxophone Colossus" without good reason. Most jazz saxophone players typically perform solos that range between three to ten minutes. For Sonny, however, his phenomenal nonstop solo time could extend to a breathtaking 15, 20, or 30 minutes without pause.

His extreme playing time was bound to catch up to him, however. In 2012, Sonny was forced into retirement because of what doctors diagnosed as "idiopathic pulmonary fibrosis," a rare, serious lung disease in which the tissue becomes thickened, stiff, and scarred. It's known in medical circles as "fibrosis." While there is no known cure for IPF, doctors work with patients to find ways to treat the problem.

Compounding matters, he suffers from prostatitis, which is a nagging inflammation of the prostate gland. It brings about swelling and pain under the bladder and in front of the rectum in men. Prostate problems will affect as many as half of all men at some point in their lives.

Illus. 45 - Sonny Rollins, who retired in 2012, can no longer play his tenor saxophone. Instead, he plays the piano, and according to friends, he sounds like Thelonious Monk, his mentor.

Despite his medical problems, Sonny, who turned aged 88 in 2018, continues to prove he is no ordinary man. He successfully fought heroin addiction at age 25 while literally thousands of other addicts died. Sonny has aided his recovery by consuming turmeric, wild salmon, and daily consumption of vitamins and other green nutrients.

"Despite his age and health, Sonny continues to be amazing," explained Clifton Anderson, his nephew and former trombonist, who is one of only a few relatives still alive. (His brother, Dr. Val Rollins, 90, resides in an assisted living arrangement in New Rochelle, NY.) "[Sonny's] mind is as sharp as ever, and he is still composing—this time at the piano rather than with his tenor saxophone."

Sonny continues to practice yoga, both mentally and physically, and also took up Pilates for some time. He said it "has made a major difference in his life. It has helped me to stand up straighter and given me greater posture." Pilates has not been shown to be an effective overall medical treatment, but many practitioners, including Sonny, believe regular Pilates sessions can aid muscle conditioning in healthy adults, as compared to those who don't exercise.

Proper breathing has been called one of the hallmarks of the Pilates method. Experts report that effective breathing cleans the body and improves circulation. Although Sonny has known the value of breathing since he first started playing the saxophone at age 13, he learned a different technique through his study of yoga. He perfected it during his two-year sabbatical in 1959 when he heightened his practices of yoga, Buddhism, and other Eastern religions and lifestyles.

"I believe in breathing through my nose," he said. "Most people breathe through their mouths. That's cool for them, but I have found breathing through the nose to be far more effective and useful. It has given me greater control in improving my overall health, especially when I played my ax (horn)."

Doctors have not revealed the possible origins of his pulmonary problems, but they could be linked to the 9/11 World Trade Center bombing, which has been connected to hundreds of other cases near the site.

"On September 11, 2001, I was in my rehearsal studio six blocks away from the World Trade Center when the explosions occurred," said Sonny, who lived on nearby Greenwich Avenue at the time. He was then in his early seventies, and a limp had begun to impair his mobility.

Nevertheless, he walked down forty flights of stairs and onto Chambers Street, finally making his way to safety. His New York City apartment was ruined—he would abandon it soon after—but the far greater catastrophe was the loss of life for so many people: "The whole area was evacuated. I left my studio with my horn under my arm," Sonny recalled.

The terrorist attack gave Sonny a glimpse of "the horrors of war. I can't image being in a war seeing people who kill other people. It is one of the most horrendous things on this planet. I don't understand this level of inhumanity—man against man."

Four days later, the atmosphere still somber, Sonny played a concert in Boston—it was released as a live album in 2005 titled *Without a Song (The 9/11 Concert)*.

During these days of retirement and living alone, Sonny thinks increasingly about his legacy. "I hope I have made a difference in the lives of people, through not only my music but through my acts."

Although Sonny has always been somewhat reclusive, he continues to see old friends and colleagues on occasion. In 2016, his former guitarist Yoshiaki Masuo spent the afternoon with Sonny at his Woodstock home. "We had a great time," Masuo recalled.

Masuo said that Bob Cranshaw, Sonny's longtime bassist, had recently passed away, "and I really felt I have to see Sonny now, because you never know what's going to happen. I needed to see Sonny for a while. He looked good, he was happy, and he was in peace. He told me he was reading Buddhism and yoga books, and I felt he was really peaceful.

"When I saw him, Sonny said he didn't miss playing. There's a standard song called 'The Heather on the Hill,' [from the musical *Brigadoon]* and there was a guitar at Sonny's house and I started playing it. It's an old standard tune, but that's one of the things I love about Sonny, when he's playing those standard tunes. He can sing those tunes.

"When I went to see Sonny, one thing I really wanted to ask him was why he picked me up [as a musician in 1973]. He said I got 'a feel' for jazz. We connected; it was so easy to play with him.

"I don't know if it's spiritual or not, but we were connected. That's the magic of the music, that's what makes music one of the great things. You're just connected or not; when you're connected, you don't need to talk about anything, you just go with the music."

In the end, it's all about legacy—from the lows of addiction and imprisonment—to the immense highs of being a yogi of universal depth and spirituality.

Sonny gave his memorabilia in 2017 to the Schomburg Center for Research in Black Culture, located in his old Harlem neighborhood. The Schomburg Center is a research library of the New York Public Library, providing an archival repository for information related to people of African descent worldwide.

During the fall of 2017, Sonny also made a generous donation to Oberlin College, to establish the Oberlin Conservatory of Music Sonny Rollins Jazz Ensemble Fund. Sonny's gift to Oberlin grew out of his friendship with author and musician James McBride, a 1979 graduate. It was made in recognition of Oberlin's longstanding advocacy of social justice.

In the nineteenth century, Oberlin was the first American college to admit students of color and the first to confer degrees on women. One of its early alumni was Will Marion Cook, a black violinist and composer (class of 1888) who went on to become a teacher and mentor to Duke Ellington.

"That the legendary Sonny Rollins—an artist of truly extraordinary accomplishment, soulfulness, and character—would entrust Oberlin to steward his legacy is the highest honor, and deeply humbling," said Dean of the Conservatory Andrea Kalyn in accepting his gift, adding:

"We are so very grateful to James McBride—whose own life and work stands in testament to Oberlin's values—for shepherding this gift, which has a singular power to demonstrate for our students the full dimension of their obligation as musicians in this world, to inspire them to fulfill that obligation far beyond their years as students, and so to advance Oberlin's own legacy of impact."

As a result of Sonny's gift, Oberlin jazz studies majors may now audition for the Oberlin Sonny Rollins Jazz Ensemble—"The Sonny Ensemble." Students may be accepted into the ensemble through annual auditions at any time during their Oberlin Conservatory education. Four criteria will be used in evaluating students: an audition for Oberlin's jazz faculty, evidence of academic achievement, thoughtful response to a question about the place of jazz in the world, and service to humanity.

The Sonny Ensemble will perform in flexible configurations, in both formal settings and outreach programs, in venues across Ohio and various parts of the world. Called "Sonny Scholars," members must dedicate at least two semesters to performing in the ensemble.

A release from Oberlin at the time of the bequest quoted Sonny, who described his motivation in these words:

"The humanity element has to be a big presence in everything young players do," said Sonny. "People are hungry for a reason to live and to be happy. We're asking these young musicians to look at the big picture, to tap into the universal power of a higher spirit, so they can give people what they need.

"Giving back to others teaches inner peace and inner spirituality. Everything is going to be open for them, if they devote themselves in this way."

Equally significant is the movement, that picked up steam in 2017, to rename the Williamsburg Bridge the "Sonny Rollins Bridge," which would remind New Yorkers traveling between Manhattan and Brooklyn of the legacy of Sonny Rollins, his woodshedding years there, and what he means not only to the Big Apple but to the jazz world at large.

One day, the legendary Sonny Rollins, who is regarded as the "greatest living jazz musician" by much of the jazz world, will be honored with similar legacies. There is no way to predict the future of this jazz yogi, who has profoundly influenced the musical styles of numerous saxophonists—and jazz itself—worldwide.

When the icon dies, many of his Christian fans might say he went to heaven to blow his horn with Gabriel before God. Others in the world of spirituality, including Sonny himself, might argue he will be reincarnated. Given his history of strength and survival, he may live to be 100 years or older.

Sonny will be remembered for many things. They include his sharp intellect, his creative genius, and his philosophy that there is only "one truth," referring to his view that all belief systems should be respected and held in high esteem.

I believe in karma, so I'm trying not to do too much harm in this lifetime...Karma is when you believe in reincarnation that you live many lives. You have one soul reincarnated into many bodies until you get to the point where you are more perfect, more godlike."

— Sonny Rollins

Standing Ovation

Sonny Rollins' musical contributions cannot be overstated. The accolades he has received over the past seven decades reveal just how legendary a figure he is in jazz. He may have received more prestigious awards than any other jazz musician in the history of the genre.

One of his most famous fans, President Barack Obama, agrees. In 2010, Obama presented Sonny Rollins with the National Medal of Arts, the most prestigious award given to artists and patrons of the arts by the United States.

In making the presentation, Obama, who recalled that he had once owned Sonny's albums on vinyl, said of the jazz titan: "Widely recognized as one of the most important and influential jazz musicians of the post-bebop era, Mr. Rollins' melodic sensibilities, playing style, and solos have delighted audiences and influenced generations of musicians for over 50 years."

In addition to the National Medal of Arts, Sonny has received

Illus. 46 - Sonny Rollins was awarded the National Medal of Arts by former President Barack Obama, a self-proclaimed fan, in 2010.

countless awards over the span of half a century. These include several Grammy Awards: Best Jazz Instrumental Album for 2002's *This Is What I Do,* a Lifetime Achievement Award in 2004, Best Improvised Jazz Solo for 2006's *Why Was I Born?* and a 2015 Hall of Fame Award for his classic 1962 album *The Bridge.*

He was also given the 2007 Polar Music Prize for being "for over 50 years one of the most powerful and personal voices in jazz," the Miles Davis Award at the 2010 Montreal Jazz Festival, and the 2009 Australian Cross of Honour for Science and Art, 1st Class.

Sonny has been elected to the Down Beat Jazz Hall of Fame (1973) and the American Academy of Arts and Sciences (2010). He was also honored by the Kennedy Center on his 81st birthday (September 7, 2011), and by the city of Minneapolis, Minnesota.

Sonny has also received honorary Doctor of Music degrees from Wesleyan University, Long Island University, Duke University, New England Conservatory of Music, Colby College, Rutgers University, The Juilliard School, University of Hartford, and Berklee College of Music, as well as an Honorary Doctor of Arts from Bard College.

The Gift of Meditation

Even God may be challenged when it comes to straightening out the nasty, often tedious disputes found among various competing religious and spiritual forces in the world.

In fact, divine intervention is usually the only solution to the different raging battles among these hardcore devotees—each of which insists that God has personally blessed their particular faith over the others.

Yet, when it comes to the practice of meditation, virtually all sides become like-minded. The practitioners of meditation often believe only those who achieve deep levels of concentration can learn the secrets of the universe—including the discovery of God and unlocking the closely guarded spiritual truths that liberate practitioners from the shackles of everyday life.

Today, meditation is the driving force behind the continuing rise in the worldwide movement known as spirituality—or what many once called the New Age movement—which represents an alternative approach to traditional Western religion. The focus of the New Age is on spirituality, mysticism, holism, and environmentalism.

Nowadays, when traditional believers ask spirituality proponents, "Are you religious?" the reply is often, "No, I am spiritual."

Right or wrong, a growing number of Christians, Jews, Muslims, and others—who are often at odds with each other—agree that meditation is the ultimate solution to the nagging problems often found in organized religions. However, some groups tend to prefer transplanted foreign faiths, such as yoga, Hinduism, Buddhism, Jainism, Taoism, Baha'i, and Ahmadiyya and other forms of Islam.

Many Westerners tend to be more attracted to Asian and Eastern religions and cultures, but a closer look at European and American Christianity, Judaism, and Native American religions reveals that each has its own powerful form of spirituality, which are often ignored even by many devotees of their own faith. All are equally valid and stress the importance of meditation.

The Keetoowahs, a religious order of the Tsalagi (Cherokee Indians), prevail as one of the most powerful and sacred when it comes to spirituality among different native peoples. Their belief system is largely unknown because the U.S. government banned all native religions for hundreds of years as illegal until 1978. But for them, their unique practice of meditation represents the highest form of spirituality. They engage in acts of purification, fasting, sweating, and dancing all night while reciting mysterious and hallowed chants.

Meditation is strongly acknowledged in Hindu literature, in the *Upanishads* and in the *Mahabharata*, the latter of which includes the *Bhagavad Gita*. According to religious scholar Gavin Flood, the earlier *Brihadaranyaka Upanishad* is referring to meditation when it states that "having become calm and concentrated, one perceives the self (*ātman*) within oneself."

However, the practice of meditation is not a slam dunk for many people. It takes days, months, and years for people to fully achieve this high level of concentration. People in deep meditation can appear to be dead, and the appearance of it can be frightening.

When a possum is "playing dead," his body becomes curled and stiff. It can even be prodded, picked up and carried away without any response. Following a silent period—ranging from a few minutes to several hours—the animal usually regains consciousness when a slight twitching of the ears is noticed.

In 1970, a soft-spoken and humble Indian-American man started acting like a possum when he entered a laboratory full of American scientists who were skeptical about his claim of being dead while being alive at the same time. He also modestly told them of his other secret powers learned from growing up in caves in the Himalayas.

His name was Swami Rama. During his presentation, he repeatedly stunned the scientists by his ability to hold his breath for hours on end and stop his brain waves and heartbeat. He would appear dead—yet he remained conscious. He could also create scary-looking tumors on his arms and make them vanish within a matter of hours.

For most disbelievers, this is the stuff of wild superstition and fairy tales. However, for two credible and respected Western-trained physicians—Rudolph Ballentine, MD, and Alan Hymes, MD— these two aforementioned tall tales are true, despite the doubts and suspicions harbored by Western science.

As authors of the book, *Science of Breath*, they confirmed Rama had proven his amazing abilities when he appeared in a laboratory filled with Western scientists. Some of them remained skeptical, but others were convinced Rama was legitimate.

While Rama did not reveal his secrets, he and the physicians believe, through proper breathing and meditation, people can consciously achieve both voluntary and involuntary control of respiration. They asserted that breath is the key to the control over the autonomic nervous system.

In fact, some believe a person can live on breath alone. According to practitioners of Inedia (Latin for fasting) or breatharianism, humans can exist without food or water. They believe people can live entirely on prana, which means "life force" in the Hindu tradition. Since sunlight is a primary source of prana, some breatharians claim it is all one needs to survive.

Although doctors and scientists consider breatharianism extremely dangerous (indeed, lethal), they do recognize the incredible power of breathing. Indeed, the doctors who witnessed Swami Rama's ability to regulate his breath in the lab were astounded by what they saw.

"By learning to manipulate their breathing patterns, yogi gained conscious control over their brain function to an extent scarcely anyone in the West would have imagined possible—until Swami Rama walked into the lab," the doctors stated in their book.

During their studies, they said they "uncovered and explored an area of consciousness beyond thought, a non-conceptional level of heightened and broadened awareness that could only be approached by stepping outside the arena of our everyday thinking. The technique of inward attention, which allows one to explore this level of consciousness, is called meditation."

The problem is, informal studies show true meditation is difficult, if not impossible, to achieve. In fact, meditation can represent the height of utter boredom, especially for artists, musicians, intellectuals, and would-be spiritualists who fail to benefit from its demanding practice of sitting still and silent for hours and hours in a dimly-lit room, humming odd-sounding, foreign phrases like *om* ad nauseam. For them, creativity equals activity, and Eastern postures are foreign to their habitual way of behaving.

However, there are many kinds of meditation. Many Western adherents of the practice claim that it is not necessary to sit in a lotus position to achieve peace of mind and a level of concentration that allows a person to connect to such energetic qualities as serenity, gratitude, or hope.

At the same time, meditation can be exciting and stimulating for its luckier adherents, who proclaim its benefits to the heavens: it helps get them in touch with God, heal their sicknesses, increase their abilities to focus and concentrate, and can even fill the spiritual void left from their abandonment of organized religion.

For Western devotees of Eastern practices, there have been few books as influential as Paramahansa Yogananda's *Autobiography of a Yogi.* First published in 1946, the book introduced millions of Americans and Europeans to meditation and yoga—in particular,

Kriya yoga.

Kriya practitioners say that it is an ancient practice that was revitalized by Mahavatar Babaji through his disciple Lahiri Mahasaya in the 1860s. Largely unknown to the public at large, Kriya is extremely complex; it is mystical and difficult for Westerners and Easterners alike to understand.

Hatha yoga has the most appeal because followers can exercise, lose weight, and improve their overall health. However, Kriya is not the sort of yoga practiced in gyms and fitness studios across America— its purpose is not to give the practitioner washboard abs or muscular arms. According to Kriya Yoga International, Kriya is "a meditation technique to help spiritual seekers attain Self-realization, which means to be in constant communion with God.

"Through this technique, the seeker or student can perceive the presence of God within, as well as in all of creation. To attain this state requires regular and sincere Kriya meditation and living a life of love and service."

Through *pranayama* (breathing), *mantras* (a repeated word or sound), and *mudras* (hand gestures), the practitioner hopes to enter into a state of deep tranquility and communion with God.

Traditionally, Kriya was transmitted from a guru to a disciple, and it was essentially an esoteric, secretive practice. Of course, with the publication of *Autobiography of a Yogi*, some of these secrets were revealed to and became practiced by the world at large.

Bebop jazz musicians were among the first to embrace Kriya yoga and other forms of meditation back in the 1940s, but it took British rock musicians and Hollywood actors in the 1960s to popularize it further. For example, notables like Dennis Weaver, Andrew Weil, Linda Evans, and George Harrison of the Beatles loudly proclaimed the merits of this mysterious form of spirituality that originated thousands of years ago in India.

Steve Jobs, the founder of Apple and arguably the most influential person in modern technology, was able to attract scores of new followers when he disclosed that he had embraced the teachings of Yogananda. Many of Apple's original customers in the 1980s were also intellectuals and artists drawn to the creative features of the Mac computer and its unique software.

However, not everyone has embraced Kriya yoga with open arms. Srinivas Aravamuda, the late Indian-born American scholar, dean, and professor of English Literature and Romance Studies at Duke University, criticized the contents of Yogananda's book as "miracle-invested territory whose single most memorable feature ... is a repetitive insistence on collocating the miraculous and the quotidian. The autobiography is an eclectic insistence of sorts that might be dubbed a hitchhiker's guide to the paranormal galaxy."

These comments by Aravamuda and other critics have been largely ignored because of the massive appeal of Yogananda's teachings of Kriya and different types of meditation. Buddhist approaches to meditation have also been enormously popular in recent years, and its advocates have declared it a virtual panacea to life's problems.

In recent years the actor Richard Gere invited the 14th Dalai Lama—the head of Tibetan Buddhism, who now resides in exile in northern India—to appear before packed audiences at venues like Radio City Music Hall in New York. In one of his talks there, the Dalai Lama introduced ancient scripts and extolled the value of meditation. "It is better to meditate for five minutes and get up from your mat happy than meditate for three hours and get up from your mat miserable," he said.

According to the Triratna Buddhist Community, meditation "is the only real antidote to our own personal sorrows, and to the anxieties, fears, hatreds, and general confusions that beset the human condition. Meditation is a means of transforming the mind."

For many centuries, meditation has been used by clergy of different faiths as a tool to help people become more attuned to their belief systems and make them stronger adherents to those faiths. Medical personnel have used it to reduce great levels of stress, anxiety, and depression, and even as a pain killer for many patients when medications don't work.

"I've seen the power of meditation and how it's helped many of my patients cope with pain and other problems," said Jess Geevarghese, an Indian-American yoga teacher who has worked at many major medical institutions, such as the prestigious Memorial Sloan Kettering Cancer Center in New York City. "Meditation has become an important adjunct to traditional therapy."

However, Geevarghese, who has studied in top universities in America as well as at an ashram in India, also pointed out "meditation is not a slam-dunk for all patients who wish to achieve a deep level from it." She emphasized that meditation is one of life's "greatest challenges," and something so important that it should not be viewed too simplistically.

"True meditation requires many months and maybe years for some people to be able to achieve an effective state of concentration," she added. "Once it happens, their lives change for the better, and they begin to achieve many of the things they have long sought, but rarely found. Unfortunately, some people become impatient and give up. Meditation requires great patience in order to receive its many rewards.

"People should not try to meditate at first for long hours. It's difficult. They should start out with only five or 10 minutes at first and gradually extend their time. I've seen the benefits of gradual, rather than lengthy, times of meditation."

In the West, Christian meditation is equally valid as an access point to deeper spiritual realities. However, over the centuries, it became the province of an elite group of priests and nuns who thought that ordinary laypeople could not practice its methods or achieve its effects. It typically focuses on specific thoughts involving Jesus and the Virgin Mary, and reflections on the love of God. To many in the West, Christian meditation lacks the appeal of more "exotic" forms of meditation.

However, meditation is also currently practiced by congregations in some Christian churches, where it is a means to reflect upon passages from the Bible or other sacred writings and deepen one's personal relationship with God.

Some of the oldest references to meditation are found in the Hindu *Vedas*, a collection of sacred texts dating from around 1500 years before the birth of Christ. By the fifth and sixth century BCE, Buddhists and

Jains on the Indian subcontinent, and Taoists and Confucianists in China, were also developing their own forms of meditation.

Meditation—especially as it was practiced in India—was relatively unknown to many Americans in the early twentieth century, at a time when the vast majority of Americans were practicing Christians. Meanwhile, Hindu meditation began to be secularized by Westerners as a way of fostering self-growth and reducing stress.

In the 1930s, scientists and other researchers started studying both secular and non-secular meditation. Since then, there have been over a thousand studies on meditation published in English. By the 1970s and 1980s, there were large numbers of scientific studies dedicated to the subject, such as the one referenced at the beginning of this preface.

In 1971 the American-born author, Richard Alpert, later known as Ram Das, who had studied with a guru in India, published his enormously popular book, *Be Here Now*, which tells his story and recommends techniques for meditation, yoga and *pranayama* (breathing).

"Now, though I am a beginner on the path," he wrote, "I have returned to the West for a time to work out karma or unfulfilled commitment. Part of this commitment is to share what I have learned with those who are on a similar journey."

Two years later, in 1973, George Harrison composed his song "Be Here Now," which was in part inspired by the book by Ram Das. Stephen Holden of the *New York Times* described the track in the magazine *Rolling Stone* as a "meltingly lovely meditation-prayer."

Today, there is a new focus on what is called "New Age" meditations, which are heavily influenced by Eastern philosophy, Hinduism, and Buddhism. New Age meditation, which is a melding of Eastern philosophy and Western beliefs, represents yet another incarnation of the practice of meditation. It continues to evolve as more New Agers and others pursue their interests in Eastern religions and cultures.

Meditation is receiving widespread support even in Washington, DC. The Food and Drug Administration, which is in the business of studying and approving new drugs, has issued reports indicating meditation has played an important role in helping patients who suffer from stress and other psychological problems.

Although there are many valid schools of meditation, those emanating from Hinduism appear to be the most popular. This is due largely to the endorsements by many American jazz and rock 'n' roll performers, like Sonny Rollins, John Coltrane, and the Beatles— musical trailblazers who have put these exotic religions, and meditation itself, on the map for a larger worldwide audience.

Many devout adherents of meditation have become divinely spiritual, but many others have made a sham of it through pretense and grandstanding, preventing meditation from being widely considered as one of the most powerful weapons in the human arsenal to achieve peace and prosperity.

Our usual understanding of life is dualistic: you and I, this and that, good and bad. But actually these discriminations are themselves the awareness of the universal existence. 'You' means to be aware of the universe in the form of you, and 'I' means to be aware of it in the form of I. You and I are just swinging doors. This kind of understanding is necessary. This should not even be called understanding; it is actually the true experience of life through Zen practice."

— SHUNRYU SUZUKI[9]

Discography

STUDIO ALBUMS

Year	Album	Label
1953	*Sonny Rollins with the Modern Jazz Quartet*	Prestige
1954	*Moving Out*	Prestige
1955	*Work Time*	Prestige
1956	*Sonny Rollins Plus 4*	Prestige
	Tenor Madness	Prestige
	Saxophone Colossus	Prestige
	Rollins Plays for Bird	Prestige
	Tour de Force	Prestige
	Sonny Boy	Prestige
1957	*Sonny Rollins, Vol. 1*	Blue Note
	Way Out West	Contemporary
	Sonny Rollins, Vol. 2	Blue Note
	The Sound of Sonny	Riverside
	Newk's Time	Blue Note
	Sonny Rollins Plays (split album with Thad Jones)	Period
1958	*Freedom Suite*	Riverside
	Sonny Rollins and the Big Brass	MetroJazz

Year	Album	Label
1958	*Sonny Rollins and the Contemporary Leaders*	Contemporary
1962	*The Bridge*	RCA Victor
	What's New?	RCA Victor
1963	*Sonny Meets Hawk!*	RCA Victor
1964	*Now's the Time*	RCA Victor
	The Standard Sonny Rollins	RCA Victor
1965	*Sonny Rollins on Impulse!*	Impulse!
1966	*Alfie*	Impulse!
	East Broadway Run Down	Impulse!
1972	*Next Album*	Milestone
1973	*Horn Culture*	Milestone
1975	*Nucleus*	Milestone
1976	*The Way I Feel*	Milestone
1977	*Easy Living*	Milestone
1979	*Don't Ask*	Milestone
1980	*Love at First Sight*	Milestone
1981	*No Problem*	Milestone
1982	*Reel Life*	Milestone
1984	*Sunny Days, Starry Nights*	Milestone
1985	*The Solo Album*	Milestone
1987	*Dancing in the Dark*	Milestone
1989	*Falling in Love with Jazz*	Milestone
1991	*Here's to the People*	Milestone
1993	*Old Flames*	Milestone
1996	*Silver City*	Milestone
	Sonny Rollins + 3	Milestone
1998	*Global Warming*	Milestone
2000	*This Is What I Do*	Milestone

Year	Album	Label
2006	*Sonny, Please*	EmArcy

LIVE ALBUMS

Year	Album	Label
1957	*A Night at the Village Vanguard*	Blue Note
1959	*Sonny Rollins at Music Inn*	MetroJazz
	Oleo 1959	Old Style
1962	*Our Man in Jazz*	RCA Victor
1965	*There Will Never Be Another You*	Impulse!
1973	*Sonny Rollins in Japan*	Victor (Japan)
1974	*The Cutting Edge*	Milestone
1978	*Don't Stop the Carnival*	Milestone
1987	*G-Man*	Milestone
2001	*Without a Song: The 9/11 Concert*	Milestone
2008	*Road Shows, Vol. 1*	Doxy
2011	*Road Shows, Vol. 2*	Doxy
2014	*Road Shows, Vol. 3*	Doxy
2016	*Road Shows, Vol. 4: Holding the Stage*	Doxy

GUEST APPEARANCES

Year	Artist	Album	Label
1949	Babs Gonzales	*Weird Lullaby*	Bluenote
	J.J. Johnson	*Mad Be-Bop*	Savoy
	J.J. Johnson	*J. J. Johnson's Jazz Quintets*	Savoy
	J.J. Johnson, Kai Winding, Benny Green	*Trombone By Three*	Prestige

Year	Artist	Album	Label
1949	Fats Navarro	*The Fabulous Fats Navarro*	Blue Note
	Bud Powell	*The Amazing Bud Powell, Vol. 1*	Blue Note
1951	Miles Davis	*Miles Davis and Horns*	Prestige
	Miles Davis	*Down*	Jazz & Jazz
	Miles Davis	*Dig*	Prestige
1953	Miles Davis	*Collectors' Items*	Prestige
	Thelonious Monk	*Thelonious Monk and Sonny Rollins*	Prestige
1954	Miles Davis	*Bags' Groove*	Prestige
	Art Farmer	*Early Art*	New Jazz
	Thelonious Monk	*Monk*	Prestige
1956	Ernie Henry	*Last Chorus*	Riverside
	Max Roach (with Clifford Brown)	*Clifford Brown and Max Roach at Basin Street*	EmArcy
	Max Roach	*Max Roach + 4*	EmArcy
1956-57	Max Roach	*Jazz in ¾ Time*	EmArcy
1957	Kenny Dorham	*Jazz Contrasts*	Riverside
	Dizzy Gillespie	*Duets*	Verve
	Dizzy Gillespie (with Sonny Stitt)	*Sonny Side Up*	Verve
	Abbey Lincoln	*That's Him!*	Riverside
	Thelonious Monk	*Brilliant Corners*	Riverside
1958	Modern Jazz Quartet	*The Modern Jazz Quartet at Music Inn Volume 2*	Atlantic
1978	McCoy Tyner, Ron Carter, and Al Foster	*Milestone Jazzstars in Concert*	Milestone
1981	The Rolling Stones	*Tattoo You*	Rolling Stones

Photo Credits

Illus. 1 *Gandhara Buddha, 1st-2nd century CE,* 2004, Tokyo National Museum. Photographer: World Imaging. From: Wikimedia Commons.

Illus. 2 *Abyssinian Baptist Church, Harlem,* 2006. From: Wikimedia Commons.

Illus. 3 *Mother AME Zion Church,* 2014. From: Wikimedia Commons.

Illus. 4 *Washington, D.C. Paul Robeson, baritone,* 1942. Photographer: Gordon Parks. From: Library of Congress.

Illus. 5 *Marcus Garvey, 1887-1940,* 1924. From: Library of Congress.

Illus. 6 *Map of 377 Edgecombe Avenue, New York, NY,* 2010s. From: Google Maps.

Illus. 7 *Photograph of Walter William Rollins and Clifton Anderson,* date unknown. From: Clifton Anderson's personal collection.

Illus. 8 *Studio portrait of Ginger Rogers,* 1937. From: Wikimedia Commons.

Illus. 9 *Photograph of Sonny Rollins playing saxophone as a child,* date unknown. From: Sonny Rollins/Facebook.

Illus. 10 *Portrait of Charlie Parker, Tommy Potter, Miles Davis, Duke Jordan, and Max Roach, Three Deuces, New York, N.Y., ca. Aug. United States,* 1947. Photographer: William P. Gottlieb. From: Library of Congress.

Illus. 11 *Photograph of Robert Bandy,* 1943. From: *New York Daily News.*

Illus. 12 *Jazz drummer and band leader Art Blakey at radio interview, KJAZ, Alameda CA,* 1982. Photographer: Brian McMillen. From: Wikimedia Commons.

Illus. 13 *Portrait of Thelonious Monk, Minton's Playhouse, New York, N.Y., ca. Sept. United States,* 1947. Photographer: William P. Gottlieb. From: Library of Congress.

Illus. 14 *Photograph of young Sonny Rollins playing saxophone,* date unknown. From: Sonny Rollins/Facebook.

Illus. 15 *Portrait of Babs Gonzales, New York, N.Y., Between 1946 and 1948. United States,* 1946. Photographer: William P. Gottlieb. From: Library of Congress.

Illus. 16 *Percy Heath performing at the Heath Brothers concert, Rockefeller Center, NYC, June, 1977.* Photographer: Tom Marcello. From: Wikimedia

Commons.

Illus. 17 *Photograph of Horace Silver and Sonny Rollins,* date unknown. Unknown photographer. From: Sonny Rollins/Facebook.

Illus. 18 *Photograph of the Federal Medical Center, Lexington (FMC Lexington),* date unknown. From: *Lexington Herald-Leader*

Illus. 19 *Wabash Avenue YMCA, Chicago IL., 2010.* Photographer: Andrew Jameson. From: Wikimedia Commons.

Illus. 20 *Photograph of Sonny Rollins, Clifford Brown, Richie Powell, and Max Roach,* date unknown. Unknown photographer. From: Sonny Rollins/Facebook.

Illus. 21 *Associated Booking Corporation promotional photo of Clifford Brown,* 1956. From: Wikimedia Commons.

Illus. 22 *Dawn Finney is Exercising at the Seaside - Jet Magazine, May 19, 1955.* From: *Jet Magazine.*

Illus. 23 *Mahavatar Babaji.* Illustration from *Autobiography of a Yogi.* From: Wikimedia Commons.

Illus. 24 *John Coltrane,* 1963. From: Wikimedia Commons.

Illus. 25 *Photograph of Clifton Anderson, Gloria Anderson and Sonny Rollins,* date unknown. From: Clifton Anderson's personal collection.

Illus. 26 *Photograph of Hugh Wyatt, Larry Ridley, and Sonny Rollins,* date unknown. Unknown photographer. From: Hugh Wyatt's personal collection.

Illus. 27 *Photograph of Sonny Rollins and Dr. Valdemar Rollins,* date unknown. From: Clifton Anderson's personal collection.

Illus 28 *Photograph of Sonny Rollins and Amanda Wyatt,* c. 1990. Unknown photographer. From: Hugh Wyatt's personal collection.

Illus. 29 *Photograph of Ruby Dee and Sonny Rollins,* date unknown. Unknown photographer. From: Hugh Wyatt's personal collection.

Illus. 30 *Album covers of Freedom Suite (Riverside Records, 1958) and We Insist! (Candid Records, 1960).* From: Wikimedia Commons.

Illus. 31 *Photograph of Sonny Rollins and Max Roach,* date unknown. Unknown photographer. From: Past Daily.

Illus. 32 *Photograph of Valborg and Walter William Rollins,* date unknown From: Clifton Anderson's personal collection.

Illus. 33 *Williamsburg Bridge, New York,* 2017. Photographer: Acroterion. From: Wikimedia Commons.

Illus. 34 *Photograph of Sonny Rollins,* date unknown. Unknown photographer/ source.

Illus. 35 *Cropped photograph of Sonny Rollins in India,* 1967. From: *Taj Mahal Foxtrot* by Naresh Fernandes.

Illus. 36 *Photograph of Jackie Lewis,* date unknown. Photographer: Brennan Cavanaugh.

Illus. 37 *A Bust of Amenhotep IV/Akhenaten in the Luxor Museum, Egypt,* 2007. Photographer: Paul Mannix. From: Wikimedia Commons.

Illus. 38 *Photograph of Sonny Rollins and Yoshiaki Masuo,* date unknown. From: *Swing Journal.*

Illus. 39 *Photograph of Clifton Anderson,* date unknown. From: Clifton Anderson's personal collection.

Illus. 40 *Photograph of Bill O'Connell,* unknown date. Photographer: Phil Maturano. Courtesy Bill O'Connell.

Illus. 41 *Sonny Rollins at the San Francisco Opera House,* 1982. Photographer: Brian McMillen. From: Wikimedia Commons.

Illus. 42 *Photograph of Sonny Rollins and Lucille Rollins,* unknown photographer. From: Hello Jazzlady.

Illus. 43 *Photograph of Sonny Rollins performing in Marciac,* 2012. Photographer: Patrick Guillemin.

Illus. 44 *Photograph of entrance to Jazz in Marciac festival,* date unknown. Unknown photographer/source.

Illus. 45 *Sonny Rollins at Newport,* 2008. Photographer: RI-Jim. From: Wikimedia Commons.

Illus. 46 *Sonny Rollins in Concert, 2007.* Photographer: Hans Reitzema. From: Wikimedia Commons / *Barack Obama,* 2011. From: Pixabay.

Endnotes

1   Paramhansa Yogananda, *The Essence of Self-Realization: The Wisdom of Paramhansa Yogananda*, ed. Swami Kriyananda (Nevada City, CA: Crystal Clarity Publishers, 2009), 191

2   Charles Egan, *Clouds Thick, Whereabouts Unknown: Poems by Zen Monks of China* (New York: Colum-bia University Press, 2010), 25.

3   "The Oneness of Existence," Vedanta Society of Southern California, 2016, https://vedanta.org/what-is-vedanta/the-oneness-of-existence/.

4   Richard Brent Turner, *Islam in the African-American Experience*, 2nd Ed. (Bloomington, IN: Indiana University Press, 2003), 133.

5   Rabbi Dusty Klass, "Why is Buddhism so attractive to Jews?" Lecture at Congregation Shir Hadash, Los Gatos, CA, August 15, 2014.https://www.shirhadash.org/content/why-buddhism-so-attractive-jews.

6   Marianne Schnall, "Exclusive Interview With Ram Dass," *Huffington Post*, August 21, 2013. https://www.huffingtonpost.com/mari-anne-schnall/exclusive-interview-with-_13_b_3790005.html.

7   Eknath Easwaran, *To Love Is to Know Me: The Bhagavad Gita for Daily Living, Volume III* (Tomales, CA: Nilgri Press, 2002).

8   A. C. Bhaktivedanta Swami Prabhupada, *The Bhagavad Gita As It Is,* (Los Angeles, CA: International Society for Krishna Consciousness, 1989), 96.

9   Shunryu Suzuki, *Zen Mind, Beginner's Mind: Informal Talks on Zen Meditation and Practice* (New York, Weatherhill Publishing, 1970), 14.

Index